W9-ATH-689

WITCHES' BREW

Also in the Macmillan Midnight Library Series

CHILD'S PLOY

MACMILLAN · MIDNIGHT · LIBRARY

Horror and Supernatural
Stories by Women

WITCHES' BREW

EDITED BY

MARCIA MULLER

AND

BILL PRONZINI

MACMILLAN PUBLISHING COMPANY
New York

Macmillan Publishing Company
866 Third Avenue, New York, N.Y. 10022
Collier Macmillan Canada, Inc.

Library of Congress Cataloging in Publication Data
Main entry under title:
Witches' brew.
1. Horror tales, English—Women authors. 2. Horror tales, American—Women authors. 3. Supernatural—Fiction. 4. Short stories, English—Women authors. 5. Short stories, American—Women authors. I. Muller, Marcia, II. Pronzini, Bill.
PR1309.H6W57 1984 823'.0872'089287 84-10026
ISBN 0-02-599230-9

8 7 6 5 4 3 2 1

Printed in the United States of America

Contents

Acknowledgments

The editors gratefully acknowledge permission to reprint the following:

"The Gray Men," by Rebecca West. Copyright © 1927 by D. Appleton & Company. Reprinted by permission of A. D. Peters & Co., Ltd.

"The Lamp," by Agatha Christie. Reprinted by permission of Dodd, Mead & Company, Inc., from *The Golden Ball and Other Stories* by Agatha Christie. Copyright © 1924, 1926, 1929, 1934, 1971 by Christie Copyright Trust.

"The Cyprian Cat," by Dorothy L. Sayers. Copyright © 1940 by Dorothy L. Sayers. Reprinted by permission of Watkins/Loomis Agency, Inc.

"A Haunted House," by Virginia Woolf. From *A Haunted House and Other Stories* by Virginia Woolf. Copyright © 1944, 1972 by Harcourt Brace Jovanovich, Inc. Reprinted by permission of the publisher.

"The Idol of the Flies," by Jane Rice. Copyright © 1942 by Jane Rice. First published in *Unknown Worlds*. Reprinted by permission of the author and Robert P. Mills, Ltd., her agent.

"Judgement Day," by Flannery O'Connor. From *Everything That Rises Must Converge* by Flannery O'Connor. Copyright © 1965 by the Estate of Mary Flannery O'Connor. Reprinted by permission of Farrar, Straus and Giroux, Inc.

Witches' Brew

Introduction

THE ROOTS of the modern horror story can, of course, be found in the Gothic tales of the late eighteenth and early nineteenth centuries. And it is to these beginnings that we can also trace the influence women authors have had on the genre—an influence that is by no means inconsequential, and that has persisted in the psychological horror novels of the present day.

The most notable early practitioner of the art was Ann Radcliffe (1764–1823), whose novels of terror and suspense brought the Gothic into the vogue it has enjoyed for close to two hundred years. While employing the standard Gothic trappings of moldering castles, tormented noblemen, evil suitors, and beleaguered maidens, Mrs. Radcliffe added both a terrifying sense of the unknown and a realistic resolution that finally accounted for her stories' eerie events. Her novels, which are considered landmarks in the field, create an atmosphere of terror by the use of well-selected sinister details that have apparent supernatural causes. The shadow that suddenly falls over the shoulder of the heroine or the strange notes of music heard in the dead of night are no less frightening because they are rationally explained in the final pages. The best of these novels are probably *A Sicilian Romance* (1790), in which Radcliffe introduces the mad wife who has been locked away and forgotten in an isolated room of the castle; *The Mysteries of Udolpho: A Romance Interspersed with Some Pieces of Poetry* (1794); and *The Italian; or, The Confessional of the Black Penitents* (1797), her most accomplished work, which refines her suspenseful technique of creating dramatic emergencies that repeatedly draw the reader's attention from the central mystery of the plot.

One of the best-known disciples of the Radcliffean school of the Gothic was Charlotte Brontë (1816–1855). Her classic *Jane Eyre*, published in 1847, follows the traditional pattern but also shows a considerable grasp of psychological elements that give her heroine far more depth than the heroines of Radcliffe. Jane Eyre's struggle against the domineering males who attempt to manipulate her life carries strong undertones of early feminism; and Jane's personal growth amid the mysteries of Thornfield Hall transforms the novel from merely a frightening tale to a study of young womanhood pitted against seemingly impossible odds.

Like her sister, Emily Brontë (1818–1848) was a disciple of Radcliffe, and was also influential in the Gothic novel's development as a standard literary form. In *Wuthering Heights* (1847) the dark force at work is the unearthly spiritual tie between a strange man, Heathcliff, and the heroine, Catherine Earnshaw. Brontë uses her considerable descriptive talents to heighten the suspense by linking the couple's obsessive connection to the barren moors of Yorkshire; the theme of nature's power to oppress and destroy the human spirit pervades the novel. Brontë's distortion of ordinary psychological elements removes her work from the category of terror-on-the-moors and makes it a literary examination of man's destruction by the unknown.

In the United States, other women authors were emerging who gave the Gothic a particularly American flavor. No less a storyteller than Louisa May Alcott (1832–1888) experimented with the form; recent collections of her "unknown thrillers"—*Behind a Mask* (1975) and *Plots and Counterplots* (1976)—reveal the author of such genteel tales as *Little Women* to have had a firm grasp of Gothic conventions and an eerie—even lurid—imagination. These surprising stories abound with haunted castles, demon lovers, hysterical heroines, drug experimentation, and sinister sounds in the night.

While the Gothic form was being developed and refined, the stage was being set for the creation of genuine horror stories—and it was a woman who gave us the most memorable early work. In 1817 Mary Wollstonecraft Shelley entered into competition with her poet husband, Percy Bysshe Shelley, and friends Dr. John William Polidori and Lord Byron, to see who could create the most horrific tale. From this contest—which was the result of extreme boredom while the group was vacationing—emerged Mary Shelley's *Frankenstein; or, The Modern Prometheus.*

The story of the mad Dr. Frankenstein and his loathsome and vengeful artificial man makes certain moralistic statements on the sin of intellectual pride and mankind's cruelty to the physically deformed; however, these are overshadowed by the dreadful elements of grave-robbing, madness, and murder that capture the imagination of readers to this day. It is true that there are astonishing errors of logic in the work—why, for example, would Dr. Frankenstein rush out to take a bride after the monster had informed him, "I will be with you on your wedding night"?—but we are able to forgive them because we are otherwise caught up in the doctor's dilemma and (perhaps) in sympathy for the monster's plight. Although Shelley wrote other novels and stories, *Frankenstein* remains her greatest contribution to the literature of the macabre.

Shelley, of course, has had her imitators from the nineteenth century to the present. But as modern horror fiction developed, the trend moved away from manufactured monsters and toward the exploration of psychological phenomena. In the early twentieth century, the focus of such writers as Gertrude Atherton, Violet Hunt, Mrs. Margaret Oliphant, May Sinclair, and Mrs. J. H. Riddel was on the effect of unexplained events—largely supernatural—on realistically drawn characters. Many of these ghostly tales had ambiguous resolutions, which often made them even more terrifying; the best example is Charlotte Perkins

Gilman's masterpiece, "The Yellow Wall Paper," which appears in these pages. In addition, these authors did not always allow good to triumph over evil, and so did not temper the basic theme: that strange forces inimical to man seek to destroy the order of his world.

Realism of both setting and character also became important in the early twentieth century and often presented a marked contrast to the eerie events depicted in macabre fiction. One of Edith Wharton's many fine ghost stories, "All Souls" (1916), is a good example of this—a drama of witchcraft and possession played out against the most ordinary of backgrounds, a modern suburban home. Similar works of the period proved that a moldering castle or crumbling abbey is not necessary to promote a pervasive atmosphere of terror.

After World War II, horror fiction became even more firmly based in realism and relied even more heavily on modern psychological principles. Elizabeth Bowen's weird stories, collected in *The Demon Lover* (1945), are set against a carefully detailed background of wartime London. The stories of Cynthia Asquith in *This Mortal Coil* (1947), and of Mary Elizabeth Counselman in her frequent contributions to the great magazine of horror, *Weird Tales*, deal with a variety of realistic modern situations. Likewise reflective of the contemporary world are the macabre stories of mystery writers Agatha Christie and Dorothy L. Sayers; of the queen of the modern Gothic, Daphne du Maurier; and of mainstream writers Rebecca West, Flannery O'Connor, and Joyce Carol Oates.

Among the important shapers of horror fiction over the past thirty years is still another woman, Shirley Jackson. The title story of her 1949 collection, *The Lottery*, is one of the handful of truly terrifying (and therefore oft-imitated) works in the field. And in her superior 1959 novel, *The Haunting of Hill House*, in which she explores the sociology of a group of people engaged in the psychic investigation of a house reputed to be haunted, she manages the difficult feat of making the house itself, with its unique history, emerge as a character every bit as real and complex as her human protagonists. The macabre story has, indeed, come a long way since the days of the dwelling place as a mere Gothic prop.

The stories in this anthology span nearly two hundred years and the entire spectrum of horror and supernatural fiction, from the Gothic romance of Ann Radcliffe's "The Haunted Chamber" to the subtle, disturbing dread of Joyce Carol Oates's "The Bingo Master." We think you'll find them among the very best the genre has to offer.

Pleasant reading.

And pleasant dreams. . . .

—Marcia Muller and Bill Pronzini

San Francisco, California
December 1, 1983

The Haunted Chamber

ANN RADCLIFFE

Ann Radcliffe (1764–1823) is generally regarded as the mother of the Gothic novel. Born in London and privately educated, she published her first work, The Castles of Athlin and Dunbayne: A Highland Story, *at the age of twenty-five. It is with* The Mysteries of Udolpho *in 1794 that Mrs. Radcliffe achieved a milestone in the history of the Gothic, for the tale of a beautiful heroine persecuted by dark forces in a sinister castle ends with a believable rationale for the terrifying events that have taken place.* The Italian; or, The Confessional of the Black Penitents *(1797) broke further ground with the use of conversational explanations of otherwise inexplicable happenings. ''The Haunted Chamber'' contains the type of oppressive setting and situation Mrs. Radcliffe is noted for; and, while the story proceeds to a seemingly impossible turn of events, she provides her typically realistic solution in the postscript.*

THE COUNT gave orders for the north apartments to be opened and prepared for the reception of Ludovico; but Dorothee, remembering what she had lately witnessed there, feared to obey; and not one of the other servants daring to venture thither, the rooms remained shut up till the time when Ludovico was to retire thither for the night, an hour for which the whole household waited with the greatest impatience.

After supper, Ludovico, by the order of the count, attended him in his closet, where they remained alone for near half an hour, and on leaving which his lord delivered to him a sword.

'It has seen service in mortal quarrels,' said the count, jocosely; 'you will use it honourably no doubt in a spiritual one. Tomorrow let me hear that there is not one ghost remaining in the château.'

Ludovico received it with a respectful bow. 'You shall be obeyed, my lord,' said he; 'I will engage that no spectre shall disturb the peace of the château after this night.'

They now returned to the supper-room, where the count's guests awaited to accompany him and Ludovico to the north apartments; and Dorothee, being summoned for the keys, delivered them to Ludovico, who then led the way, followed by most of the inhabitants of the château. Having reached the back staircase, several of the servants shrunk back and refused to go further, but the rest followed him to the top of the staircase, where a broad landing-place allowed them to flock round him, while he applied the key to the door, during which they watched him with as much eager curiosity as if he had been performing some magical rite.

Ludovico, unaccustomed to the lock, could not turn it, and Dorothee, who had lingered far behind, was called forward, under whose hand the door opened slowly, and her eye glancing within the dusky chamber, she uttered a sudden shriek and retreated. At this signal of alarm the greater part of the crowd hurried down, and the count, Henri, and Ludovico were left alone to pursue the inquiry, who instantly rushed into the apartment, Ludovico with a drawn sword, which he had just time to draw from the scabbard, the count with a lamp in his hand, and Henri carrying a basket containing provision for the courageous adventurer.

Having looked hastily round the first room, where nothing appeared to justify alarm, they passed on to the second; and here too all being quiet, they proceeded to a third in a more tempered step. The count had now leisure to smile at the discomposure into which he had been surprised, and to ask Ludovico in which room he designed to pass the night.

'There are several chambers beyond these, your excellenza,' said Ludovico, pointing to a door, 'and in one of them is a bed, they say. I will pass the night there; and when I am weary of watching, I can lie down.'

'Good,' said the count; 'let us go on. You see, these rooms show nothing but damp walls and decaying furniture. I have been so much occupied since I came to the château, that I have not looked into them till now. Remember, Ludovico, to tell the housekeeper tomorrow to throw open these windows. The damask hangings are dropping to pieces; I will have them taken down, and this antique furniture removed.'

'Dear sir,' said Henri, 'here is an armchair so massy with gilding, that it resembles one of the state chairs in the Louvre more than anything else.'

'Yes,' said the count, stopping a moment to survey it, 'there is a history belonging to that chair, but I have not time to tell it; let us pass on. This suite runs to a greater extent than I imagined; it is many years since I was in them. But where is the bedroom you speak of, Ludovico? These are only ante-chambers to the great drawing-room. I remember them in their splendour.'

'The bed, my lord,' replied Ludovico, 'they told me was in a room that opens beyond the saloon and terminates the suite.'

'O, here is the saloon,' said the count, as they entered the spacious apartment in which Emily and Dorothee had rested. He here stood for a moment, surveying the reliques of faded grandeur which it exhibited, the sumptuous tapestry, the long and low sofas of velvet with frames heavily carved and gilded, the floor inlaid with small squares of fine marble, and covered in the centre with a piece of rich tapestry work, the casements of painted glass, and the large Venetian mirrors of a size and quality such as that period France could not make, which reflected on every side the spacious apartment. These had also formerly reflected a gay and brilliant scene, for this had been the state room of the château, and here the marchioness had held the assemblies that made part of the festivities of her nuptials. If the wand of a magician could have recalled the vanished groups—many of them vanished even from the earth!—that once had passed over these polished mirrors, what a varied and contrasted picture would they have exhibited with the present! Now, instead of a blaze of lights, and a splendid and busy crowd, they reflected only the rays of the one glimmering lamp which the count held up, and which scarcely served to show the three forlorn figures that stood surveying the room, and the spacious and dusky walls around them.

'Ah!' said the count to Henri, awaking from his deep reverie, 'how the scene is changed since last I saw it! I was a young man then, and the marchioness was alive and in her bloom; many other persons were here too, who are now no more. There stood the orchestra, here we tripped in many a sprightly maze—the walls echoing to the dance. Now they resound only one feeble voice, and even that will, ere long, be heard no more. My son, remember that I was once as young as yourself, and that you must pass away like those who have preceded you—like those who, as they sung and danced in this most gay apartment, forgot that years are made up of moments, and that every step they took carried them nearer to their graves. But such reflections are useless—I had almost said criminal—unless they teach us to prepare for eternity, since otherwise they cloud our present happiness without guiding us to a future one. But enough of this—let us go on.'

Ludovico now opened the door of the bedroom, and the count, as he entered, was struck with the funeral appearance which the dark arras gave to it. He approached the bed with an emotion of solemnity, and, perceiving it to be covered with a pall of black velvet, paused. 'What can this mean?' said he, as he gazed upon it.

'I have heard, my lord,' said Ludovico, as he stood at the feet, looking within the canopied curtains, 'that the Lady Marchioness de Villeroi died in this chamber, and remained here till she was removed to be buried; and this perhaps, signor, may account for the pall.'

The count made no reply, but stood for a few moments engaged in thought, and evidently much affected. Then, turning to Ludovico, he asked him with a serious air, whether he thought his courage would support him through the night. 'If you doubt this,' added the count, 'do not be ashamed to own it; I will release you from your engagement without exposing you to the triumphs of your fellow-servants.' Ludovico paused; pride and something very like fear seemed struggling in his breast: pride, however, was victorious;—he blushed, and his hesitation ceased.

'No, my lord,' said he, 'I will go through with what I have begun; and I am grateful for your consideration. On that hearth I will make a fire; and with the good cheer in this basket, I doubt not I shall do well.'

'Be it so,' said the count: 'but how will you beguile the tediousness of the night, if you do not sleep?'

'When I am weary, my lord,' replied Ludovico, 'I shall not fear to sleep; in the meanwhile, I have a book that will entertain me.'

'Well,' said the count, 'I hope nothing will disturb you; but if you should be seriously alarmed in the night, come to my apartment. I have too much confidence in your good sense and courage to believe you will be alarmed on slight grounds, or suffer the gloom of this chamber, or its remote situation, to overcome you with ideal terrors. Tomorrow I shall have to thank you for an important service; these rooms shall then be thrown open, and my people will then be convinced of their error. Good night, Ludovico; let me see you early in the morning, and remember what I lately said to you.'

'I will, my lord. Good night to your excellenza—let me attend you with the light.'

He lighted the count and Henri through the chambers to the outer door. On the landing-place stood a lamp, which one of the affrighted servants had left; and Henri, as he took it up, again bade Ludovico 'good night,' who, having respectfully returned the wish, closed the door upon them and fastened it. Then, as he retired to the bedchamber, he examined the rooms through which he passed with more minuteness than he had done before; for he apprehended that some person might have concealed himself in them for the purpose of frightening him. No one, however, but himself was in these chambers; and leaving open the doors through which he passed, he came again to the great drawing-room, whose spaciousness and silent gloom somewhat startled him. For a moment he stood looking back through the long suite of rooms he had just quitted; and as he turned, perceiving a light and his own figure reflected in one of the large mirrors, he started. Other objects, too, were seen obscurely on its dark surface, but he paused not to examine them, and returned hastily into the bedroom, as he surveyed which, he observed the door of the Oriel, and opened it. All within was still. On looking round, his eye was caught by the portrait of the deceased marchioness, upon which he gazed for a considerable time with great attention and some surprise; and then, having examined the closet, he returned into the bedroom, where he kindled a wood fire, the bright blaze of which revived his spirit which had begun to yield to the gloom and silence of the place; for gusts of wind alone broke at intervals this silence. He now drew a small table and a chair near the fire, took a bottle of wine and some cold provision out of his basket, and regaled himself. When he had finished his repast he laid his sword upon the table, and not feeling disposed to sleep, drew from his pocket the book he had spoken of. It was a volume of old Provençal tales. Having stirred the fire into a brighter blaze, trimmed his lamp, and drawn his chair upon the hearth, he began to read; and his attention was soon wholly occupied by the scenes which the page disclosed.

The count, meanwhile, had returned to the supper-room, whither those of the party who had attended him to the north apartment had retreated upon hearing Dorothee's scream, and who were now earnest in their inquiries concerning those chambers. The count rallied his guests on their precipitate retreat, and on the superstitious inclinations which had occasioned it; and this led to the question, whether the spirit, after it has quitted the body, is ever permitted to revisit the earth; and if it is, whether it was possible for spirits to become visible to the sense? The baron was of opinion, that the first was probable, and the last was possible; and he endeavoured to justify this opinion by respectable authorities, both ancient and modern, which he quoted. The count, however, was decidedly against him; and a long conversation ensued, in which the usual arguments on these subjects were on both sides brought forward with skill and discussed with candour, but without converting either party to the opinion of his opponent. The effect of their conversation on their auditors was various. Though the count had much the superiority of the baron in point of argument, he had fewer adherents; for that love, so natural to the human mind, of whatever is able to distend its faculties with wonder and astonishment, attached the majority of the company to the side of the baron; and though many of the count's propositions were unanswerable, his opponents were inclined to believe this the consequence of their own want of knowledge on so abstracted a subject, rather than that arguments did not exist which were forcible enough to conquer him.

Blanche was pale with attention, till the ridicule in her father's glance called a blush upon her countenance, and she then endeavoured to forget the superstitious tales she had been told in the convent. Meanwhile, Emily had been listening with deep attention to the discussion of what was to her a very interesting question; and remembering the appearance she had seen in the apartment of the late marchioness, she was frequently chilled with awe. Several times she was on the point of mentioning what she had seen, but the fear of giving pain to the count, and the dread of his ridicule, restrained her; and awaiting in anxious expectation the event of Ludovico's intrepidity, she determined that her future silence should depend upon it.

When the party had separated for the night, and the count retired to his dressing-room, the remembrance of the desolate scenes he had so lately witnessed in his own mansion deeply affected him, but at length he was aroused from his reverie and his silence. 'What music is that I hear?' said he suddenly to his valet. 'Who plays at this late hour?'

The man made no reply; and the count continued to listen, and then added, 'That is no common musician; he touches the instrument with a delicate hand. Who is it, Pierre?'

'My lord!' said the man, hesitatingly.

'Who plays that instrument?' repeated the count.

'Does not your lordship know, then?' said the valet.

'What mean you?' said the count, somewhat sternly.

'Nothing, my lord, I mean nothing,' rejoined the man submissively; 'only—that music—goes about the house at midnight often, and I thought your lordship might have heard it before.'

'Music goes about the house at midnight! Poor fellow! Does nobody dance to the music, too?'

'It is not in the château, I believe, my lord. The sounds come from the woods, they say, though they seem so very near; but then a spirit can do anything.'

'Ah, poor fellow!' said the count, 'I perceive you are as silly as the rest of them; tomorrow you will be convinced of your ridiculous error. But, hark! what noise is that?'

'Oh, my lord! that is the voice we often hear with music.'

'Often!' said the count; 'how often, pray? It is a very fine one.'

'Why, my lord, I myself have not heard it more than two or three times; but there are those who have lived here longer, that have heard it often enough.'

'What a swell was that!' exclaimed the count, as he still listened; 'and now, what a dying cadence! This is surely something more than mortal.'

'That is what they say, my lord,' said the valet; 'they say it is nothing mortal that utters it; and if I might say my thoughts—'

'Peace!' said the count; and he listened till the strain died away.

'This is strange,' said he, as he returned from the window. 'Close the casements, Pierre.'

Pierre obeyed, and the count soon after dismissed him, but did not so soon lose the remembrance of the music, which long vibrated in his fancy in tones of melting sweetness, while surprise and perplexity engaged his thoughts.

Ludovico, meanwhile, in his remote chamber, heard now and then the faint echo of a closing door as the family retired to rest; and then the hall-clock, at a great distance, struck twelve. 'It is midnight,' said he, and he looked suspiciously round the spacious chamber. The fire on the hearth was now nearly expiring, for his attention having been engaged by the book before him, he had forgotten everything besides; but he soon added fresh wood, not because he was cold, though the night was stormy, but because he was cheerless; and having again trimmed the lamp, he poured out a glass of wine, drew his chair nearer to the crackling blaze, tried to be deaf to the wind that howled mournfully at the casements, endeavoured to abstract his mind from the melancholy that was stealing upon him, and again took up his book. It had been lent to him by Dorothee, who had formerly picked it up in an obscure corner of the marquis's library; and who, having opened it, and perceived some of the marvels it related, had carefully preserved it for her own entertainment, its condition giving her some excuse for detaining it from its proper station. The damp corner into which it had fallen, had caused the cover to be so disfigured and mouldy, and the leaves to be so discoloured with spots, that it was not without difficulty the letters could be traced. The fictions of the Provençal writers, whether drawn from the Arabian legends brought by the Saracens into Spain, or recounting the chivalric exploits performed by crusaders whom the troubadours accompanied to the East, were generally splendid, and always marvellous both in scenery and incident; and it is not wonderful that Dorothee and Ludovico should be fascinated by inventions which had captivated the careless imagination in every rank of society in a former age. Some of the tales, however, in the book now before Ludovico were of simple structure, and exhibited nothing of the magnificent machinery and heroic manners which usually characterized the fables of the twelfth century, and of this description was the one he now happened to open; which in its original style was of great length, but may be thus shortly related. The reader will perceive it is strongly tinctured with the superstition of the times.

THE PROVENÇAL TALE

There lived, in the province of Bretagne, a noble baron, famous for his magnificence and courtly hospitalities. His castle was graced with ladies of exquisite beauty, and thronged with illustrious knights; for the honour he paid to feats of chivalry invited the brave of distant countries to enter his lists, and his court was more splendid than those of many princes. Eight minstrels were retained in his service, who used to sing to their harps romantic fictions taken from the Arabians, or adventures of chivalry that befell knights during the crusades, or the martial deeds of the baron, their lord; while he, surrounded by his knights and ladies, banqueted in the great hall of the castle, where the costly tapestry that adorned the walls with pictured exploits of his ancestors, the casements of painted glass enriched with armorial bearings, the gorgeous banners that waved along the roof, the sumptuous canopies, the profusion of gold and silver that glittered on the sideboards, the numerous dishes that covered the tables, the number and gay liveries of the attendants, with the chivalric and splendid attire of the guests, united to form a scene of magnificence such as we may not hope to see in these degenerate days.

Of the baron the following adventure is related:—One night, having retired late from the banquet to his chamber, and dismissed his attendants, he was surprised by the appearance of a stranger of a noble air, but of a sorrowful and dejected countenance. Believing that this person had been secreted in the apartment, since it appeared impossible he could have lately passed the ante-room unobserved by the pages in waiting, who would have prevented this intrusion on their lord, the baron, calling loudly for his people, drew his sword, which he had not yet taken from his side, and stood upon his defence. The stranger, slowly advancing, told him that there was nothing to fear; that he came with no hostile intent, but to communicate to him a terrible secret, which it was necessary for him to know.

The baron, appeased by the courteous manner of the stranger, after surveying him for some time in silence, returned his sword into the scabbard, and desired him to explain the means by which he had obtained access to the chamber, and the purpose of this extraordinary visit.

Without answering either of these inquiries, the stranger said that he could not then explain himself, but that, if the baron would follow him to the edge of the forest, at a short distance from the castle walls, he would there convince him that he had something of importance to disclose.

This proposal again alarmed the baron, who would scarcely believe that the stranger meant to draw him to so solitary a spot at this hour of the night without harbouring a design against his life, and he refused to go; observing at the same time, that if the stranger's purpose was an honourable one, he would not persist in refusing to reveal the occasion of his visit in the apartment where they stood.

While he spoke this, he viewed the stranger still more attentively than before, but observed no change in his countenance, nor any symptom that might intimate a consciousness of evil design. He was habited like a knight, was of a tall and majestic stature, and of dignified and courteous manners. Still, however, he refused to communicate the substance of his errand in any place but that he had mentioned; and at the same time gave hints concerning the secret he would disclose, that awakened a degree of solemn curiosity in the baron, which at length induced him to consent to the stranger on certain conditions.

'Sir knight,' said he, 'I will attend you to the forest, and will take with me only four of my people, who shall witness our conference.'

To this, however, the knight objected.

'What I would disclose,' said he with solemnity, 'is to you alone. There are only three living persons to whom the circumstance is known: it is of more consequence to you and your house than I shall now explain. In future years you will look back to this night with satisfaction or repentance, accordingly as you now determine. As you would hereafter prosper, follow me; I pledge you the honour of a knight that no evil shall befall you. If you are contented to dare futurity, remain in your chamber, and I will depart as I came.'

'Sir knight,' replied the baron, 'how is it possible that my future peace can depend upon my present determination?'

'That is not now to be told,' said the stranger; 'I have explained myself to the utmost. It is late: if you follow me it must be quickly; you will do well to consider the alternative.'

The baron mused, and, as he looked upon the knight, he perceived his countenance assume a singular solemnity.

(Here Ludovico thought he heard a noise, and he threw a glance round the chamber, and then held up the lamp to assist his observation; but not perceiving anything to confirm his alarm, he took up the book again, and pursued the story.)

The baron paced his apartment for some time in silence, impressed by the words of the stranger, whose extraordinary request he feared to grant, and feared also to refuse. At length he said, 'Sir knight, you are utterly unknown to me; tell me, yourself, is it reasonable that I should trust myself alone with a stranger, at this hour, in the solitary forest? Tell me, at least, who you are, and who assisted to secrete you in this chamber.'

The knight frowned at these words, and was a moment silent;

then, with a countenance somewhat stern, he said, 'I am an English knight; I am called Sir Bevys of Lancaster, and my deeds are not unknown at the holy city, whence I was returning to my native land, when I was benighted in the forest.'

'Your name is not unknown to fame,' said the baron; 'I have heard of it.' (The knight looked haughtily.) 'But why, since my castle is known to entertain all true knights, did not your herald announce you? Why did you not appear at the banquet, where your presence would have been welcomed, instead of hiding yourself in my castle, and stealing to my chamber at midnight?'

The stranger frowned, and turned away in silence; but the baron repeated the questions.

'I come not,' said the knight, 'to answer inquiries, but to reveal facts. If you would know more, follow me; and again I pledge the honour of a knight that you shall return in safety. Be quick in your determination—I must be gone.'

After some farther hesitation, the baron determined to follow the stranger, and to see the result of his extraordinary request; he therefore again drew forth his sword, and, taking up a lamp, bade the knight lead on. The latter obeyed; and opening the door of the chamber, they passed into the ante-room, where the baron, surprised to find all his pages asleep, stopped, and with hasty violence was going to reprimand them for their carelessness, when the knight waved his hand, and looked so expressively at the baron, that the latter restrained his resentment, and passed on.

The knight, having descended a staircase, opened a secret door, which the baron had believed was only known to himself; and proceeding through several narrow and winding passages, came at length to a small gate that opened beyond the walls of the castle. Perceiving that these secret passages were so well known to a stranger, the baron felt inclined to turn back from an adventure that appeared to partake of treachery as well as danger. Then, considering that he was armed, and observing the courteous and noble air of his conductor, his courage returned, he blushed that it had failed him for a moment, and he resolved to trace the mystery to its source.

He now found himself on the healthy platform, before the great gates of his castle, where, on looking up, he perceived lights glimmering in the different casements of the guests, who were retiring to sleep; and while he shivered in the blast, and looked on the dark and desolate scene around him, he thought of the comforts of his warm chamber, rendered cheerful by the blaze of wood, and felt, for a moment, the full contrast of his present situation.

(Here Ludovico paused a moment, and, looking at his own fire, gave it a brightening stir.)

The wind was strong, and the baron watched his lamp with anxiety, expecting every moment, to see it extinguished; but though the flame wavered, it did not expire, and he still followed the stranger, who often sighed as he went, but did not speak.

When they reached the borders of the forest, the knight turned and raised his head, as if he meant to address the baron, but then closing his lips, in silence he walked on.

As they entered beneath the dark and spreading boughs, the baron, affected by the solemnity of the scene, hesitated whether to proceed, and demanded how much farther they were to go. The knight replied only by a gesture, and the baron, with hesitating steps and a suspicious eye, followed through an obscure and intricate path, till, having proceeded a considerable way, he again demanded whither they were going, and refused to proceed unless he was informed.

As he said this, he looked at his own sword and at the knight alternately, who shook his head, and whose dejected countenance disarmed the baron, for a moment, of suspicion.

'A little farther is the place whither I would lead you,' said the stranger; 'no evil shall befall you—I have sworn it on the honour of a knight.'

The baron, reassured, again followed in silence, and they soon arrived at a deep recess of the forest, where the dark and lofty chestnuts entirely excluded the sky, and which was so overgrown with underwood that they proceeded with difficulty.

The knight sighed deeply as he passed, and sometimes paused; and having at length reached a spot where the trees crowded into a knot, he turned, and with a terrific look, pointing to the ground, the baron saw there the body of a man, stretched at its length, and weltering in blood; a ghastly wound was on the forehead, and death appeared already to have contracted the features.

The baron, on perceiving the spectacle, started in horror, looked at the knight for explanation, and was then going to raise the body, and examine if there were any remains of life; but the stranger, waving his hand, fixed upon him a look so earnest and mournful, as not only much surprised him, but made him desist.

But what were the baron's emotions when, on holding the lamp near the features of the corpse, he discovered the exact resemblance of the stranger his conductor, to whom he now looked up in astonishment and inquiry! As he gazed he perceived the countenance of the knight change and begin to fade, till his whole form gradually vanished from his astonished sense! While the baron stood, fixed to the spot, a voice was heard to utter these words:

(Ludovico started, and laid down the book for he thought he heard a voice in the chamber, and he looked towards the bed, where, however, he saw only the dark curtain and the pall. He listened, scarcely daring to draw his breath, but heard only the distant roaring of the sea in the storm, and the blast that rushed by the casements; when, concluding that he had been deceived by its sighings, he took up his book to finish his story.)

While the baron stood, fixed to the spot, a voice was heard to utter these words:

'The body of Sir Bevys of Lancaster, a noble knight of England, lies before you. He was this night waylaid and murdered, as he journeyed from the holy city towards his native land. Respect the honour of knighthood, and the law of humanity; inter the body in christian ground, and cause his murderers to be punished. As ye observe or neglect this, shall peace and happiness, or war and misery, light upon you and your house for ever!'

The baron, when he recovered from the awe and astonishment into which this adventure had thrown him, returned to his castle, whither he caused the body of Sir Bevys to be removed; and on the following day it was interred, with the honours of knighthood, in the chapel of the castle, attended by all the noble knights and ladies who graced the court of Baron de Brunne.

Ludovico, having finished this story, laid aside the book, for he felt drowsy; and after putting more wood on the fire, and taking another glass of wine, he reposed himself in the armchair on the hearth. In his dream he still beheld the chamber where the rally was, and once or twice started from imperfect slumbers, imagining he saw a man's face looking over the high back of his armchair. This idea had so strongly impressed him, that, when he raised his eyes, he almost expected to meet other eyes fixed upon his own; and he quitted his seat, and looked behind the chair before he felt perfectly convinced that no person was there.

Thus closed the hour.

The count, who had slept little during the night, rose early, and, anxious to speak with Ludovico, went to the north apartment; but the outer door having been fastened on the preceding night, he was obliged to knock loudly for admittance. Neither the knocking nor his voice was heard: he renewed his calls more loudly than before; after which a total silence ensued; and the count, finding all his efforts to be heard ineffectual, at length began to fear that some accident had befallen Ludovico, whom terror of an imaginary being might have deprived of his senses. He therefore left the door with an intention of summoning his servants to force it open, some of whom he now heard moving in the lower part of the château.

To the count's inquiries whether they had seen or heard anything of Ludovico, they replied, in affright, that not one of them had ventured on the north side of the château since the preceding night.

'He sleeps soundly, then,' said the count, 'and is at such a distance from the outer door, which is fastened, that to gain admittance to the chambers it will be necessary to force it. Bring an instrument, and follow me.'

The servants stood mute and dejected, and it was not till nearly all the household were assembled, that the count's orders were obeyed. In the meantime, Dorothee was telling of a door that opened from a gallery leading from the great staircase into the last ante-room of the saloon, and this being much nearer to the bedchamber, it appeared probable that Ludovico might be easily awakened by an attempt to open it. Thither, therefore, the count went; but his voice was as ineffectual at this door as it had proved at the remoter one; and now, seriously interested for Ludovico, he was himself going to strike upon the door with the instrument, when he observed its singular beauty, and withheld the blow. It appeared on the first glance to be of ebony, so dark and close was its grain, and so high its polish; but it proved to be only of larch wood, of the growth of Provence, then famous for its forests of larch. The beauty of its polished hue, and of its delicate carvings, determined the count to spare this door, and he returned to that leading from the back staircase, which being at length forced, he entered the first ante-room, followed by Henri and a few of the most courageous of his servants, the rest waiting the event of the inquiry on the stairs and landing-place.

All was silence in the chambers through which the count passed, and, having reached the saloon, he called loudly upon Ludovico; after which, still receiving no answer, he threw open the door of the bedroom, and entered.

The profound stillness within confirmed his apprehensions for Ludovico, for not even the breathings of a person in sleep were heard; and his uncertainty was not soon terminated, since the shutters being all closed, the chamber was too dark for any object to be distinguished in it.

The count bade a servant open them, who, as he crossed the room to do so, stumbled over something, and fell to the floor, when his cry occasioned such a panic among the few of his fellows who had ventured thus far, that they instantly fled, and the count and Henri were left to finish the adventure.

Henri then sprang across the room, and, opening a window-shutter, they perceived that the man had fallen over a chair near the hearth, in which Ludovico had been sitting;—for he sat there no longer, nor could anywhere be seen by the imperfect light that was admitted into the apartment. The count, seriously alarmed, now opened other shutters, that he might be enabled to examine farther; and Ludovico not yet appearing, he stood for a moment suspended in astonishment, and scarcely trusting his senses, till his eyes glancing on the bed, he advanced to examine whether he was there asleep. No person, however, was in it; and he proceeded to the Oriel, where everything remained as on the preceding night; but Ludovico was nowhere to be found.

The count now checked his amazement, considering that Ludovico might have left the chambers during the night, overcome by the terrors which their lonely desolation and the recollected reports concerning them had inspired. Yet, if this had been the fact, the man would naturally have sought society, and his fellow-servants had all declared they had not seen him; the door of the outer room also had been found fastened, with the key on the inside; it was impossible, therefore, for him to have passed through that; and all the outer doors of this suite were found, on examination, to be bolted and locked, with the keys also within them. The count, being then compelled to believe that the lad had escaped through the casements, next examined them; but such as opened wide enough to admit the body of a man were found to be carefully secured either by iron bars or by shutters, and no vestige appeared of any person having attempted to pass them; neither was it probable that Ludovico would have incurred the risk of breaking his neck by leaping from a window, when he might have walked safely through a door.

The count's amazement did not admit of words; but he returned once more to examine the bedroom, where was no appearance of disorder, except that occasioned by the late overthrow of the chair, near which had stood a small table; and on this Ludovico's sword, his lamp, the book he had been reading, and the remains of his flask of wine, still remained. At the foot of the table, too, was the basket, with some fragments of provision and wood.

Henri and the servant now uttered their astonishment without reserve, and though the count said little, there was a seriousness in his manner that expressed much. It appeared that Ludovico must have quitted these rooms by some concealed passage, for the count could not believe that any supernatural means had occasioned this event; yet, if there was any such passage, it seemed inexplicable why he should retreat through it; and it was equally surprising, that not even the smallest vestige should appear by which his progress could be traced. In the rooms, everything remained as much in order as if he had just walked out by the common way.

The count himself assisted in lifting the arras with which the bedchamber, saloon, and one of the ante-rooms were hung, that he might discover if any door had been concealed behind it; but after a laborious search, none was found; and he at length quitted the apartments, having secured the door of the last antechamber the key of which he took into his own possession. He then gave orders that strict search should be made for Ludovico, not only in the château, but in the neighbourhood, and retiring with Henri to his closet, they remained there in conversation for a considerable time; and whatever was the subject of it, Henri from this hour lost much of his vivacity; and his manners were particularly grave and reserved, whenever the topic, which now agitated the count's family with wonder and alarm, was introduced.*

*The château had been inhabited before the count came into its possession. He was not aware that the apparently outward walls contained a series of passages and staircases, which led to unknown vaults underground, and, therefore, he never thought of looking for a door in those parts of the chamber which he supposed to be next to the air. In these was a communication with the room. The château (for we are not here in Udolpho) was on the sea-shore in Languedoc; its vaults had become the store-house of pirates, who did their best to keep up the supernatural delusions that hindered people from searching the premises; and these pirates had carried Ludovico away.

The Last Man

MARY WOLLSTONECRAFT SHELLEY

English novelist Mary Wollstonecraft Shelley (1797-1851) is best known for her Frankenstein; or, The Modern Prometheus, *published in 1818. Her highly romanticized personal life, however, has attracted almost as much attention as her famous tale of Dr. Frankenstein and his monster. Born to William Godwin and Mary Wollstonecraft, a radical feminist, Shelley suffered all her life from depression over her mother's untimely death a few days after bearing her. A month prior to her seventeenth birthday, she eloped with the then-married poet Percy Bysshe Shelley and carried on her liaison with him until his wife's death by suicide permitted them to marry two years later. The deaths in infancy of their first three children further deepened her depression, which perhaps accounts for the dark quality of* Frankenstein, *which was published when she was only twenty. Subsequent works—including* Valperga; or, The Life and Adventures of Castruccio, Prince of Lucca *(1823) and* Lodore *(1835)—proved disappointing in contrast to her first tale of the mad scientist and his horrible creation. "The Last Man" reveals an uncompromising realism in the face of the ultimate horror of man's annihilation from the planet.*

HAVE ANY of you, my readers, observed the ruins of an ant-hill immediately after its destruction? At first it appears entirely deserted of its former inhabitants; in a little time you see an ant struggling through the upturned mould; they reappear by twos and threes, running hither and thither in search of their lost companions. Such were we upon earth, wondering aghast at the effects of pestilence. Our empty habitations remained, but the dwellers were gathered to the shades of the tomb.

As the rules of order and pressure of laws were lost, some began with hesitation and wonder to transgress the accustomed uses of society. Palaces were deserted, and the poor man dared at length, unreproved, intrude into the splendid apartments, whose very furniture and decorations were an unknown world to him. It was found, that, though at first the stop put to all circulation of property, had reduced those before supported by the factitious wants of society to sudden and hideous poverty, yet when the boundaries of private possession were thrown down, the products of human labour at present existing were more, far more, than the thinned generation could possibly consume. To some among the poor this was matter of exultation. We were all equal now; magnificent dwellings, luxurious carpets, and beds of down, were afforded to all. Carriages and horses, gardens, pictures, statues, and princely libraries, there were enough of these even to superfluity; and there was nothing to prevent each from assuming possession of his share. We were all equal now; but near at hand was an equality still more levelling, a state where beauty and strength, and wisdom, would be as vain as riches and birth. The grave yawned beneath us all, and its prospect prevented any of us from enjoying the ease and plenty which in so awful a manner was presented to us.

We departed from Versailles fifteen hundred souls. We set out on the eighteenth of June.We made a long procession, in which was contained every dear relationship, or tie of love, that existed in human society. Fathers and husbands, with guardian care, gathered their dear relatives around them; wives and mothers looked for support to the manly form beside them, and then with tender anxiety bent their eyes on the infant troop around. They were sad, but not hopeless. Each thought that someone would be saved; each, with that pertinacious optimism, which to the last characterised our human nature, trusted that their beloved family would be the one preserved.

We passed through France, and found it empty of inhabitants. Some one or two natives survived in the larger towns, which they roamed through like ghosts; we received therefore small increase to our numbers, and such decrease through death, that at last it became easier to count the scanty list of survivors. As we never deserted any of the sick, until their death permitted us to commit the remains to the shelter of a grave, our journey was long, while every day a frightful gap was made in our troop—they died by tens, by fifties, by hundreds. No mercy was shewn by death; we ceased to expect it and every day welcomed the sun with the feeling that we might never see it rise again.

The nervous terrors and fearful visions which had scared us during the spring, continued to visit our coward troop during this sad journey. Every evening brought its fresh creation of spectres; a ghost was depicted by every blighted tree; and appalling shapes were manufactured from each shaggy bush. By degrees these common marvels pulled on us, and then other wonders were called into being. Once it was confidently asserted, that the sun rose an hour later than its seasonable time; again it was discovered that he grew paler and paler; that shadows took an uncommon appearance. It was impossible to have imagined, during the usual calm routine of life men had before experienced, the terrible effects produced by these extravagant delusions: in truth, of such little worth are our senses, when unsupported by concurring testimony, that it was with the utmost difficulty I kept myself free from the belief in supernatural events, to which the major part of our people readily gave credit. Being one sane amidst a crowd of the mad, I hardly dared assert to my own mind, that the vast luminary had undergone no change—that the shadows of night were unthickened by innumerable shapes of awe and terror; or that the wind, as it sung in the trees, or whistled round an empty building, was not pregnant with sounds of wailing and despair. Sometimes realities took ghostly shapes; and it was impossible for one's blood not to curdle at the perception of an evident mixture of what we knew to be true, with the visionary semblance of all that we feared.

Once, at the dusk of the evening, we saw a figure all in white, apparently of more than human stature, flourishing about the road, now throwing up its arms, now leaping to an astonishing height in the air, then turning round several times successively, then raising itself to its full height and gesticulating violently. Our troop, on the alert to discover and believe in the supernatural, made a halt at some distance from this shape; and, as it became darker, there was something appalling even to the incredulous, in the lonely spectre, whose gambols, if they hardly accorded with spiritual dignity, were beyond human powers. Now it leapt right up in the air, now sheer over a high hedge, and was again the moment after in the road before us. By the time I came up, the fright experienced by the spectators of this ghostly exhibition, began to manifest itself in the flight of some, and the close huddling together of the rest. Our goblin now perceived us; he approached, and, as we drew reverentially back, made a low bow. The sight was irresistibly ludicrous even to our hapless band, and his politeness was hailed by a shout of laughter;—then, again springing up, as a last effort, it sunk to the ground, and became almost invisible through the dusky night. This circumstance again spread silence and fear through the troop; the more courageous at length advanced, and, raising the dying wretch, discovered the tragic explanation of this wild scene. It was an opera-dancer, and had been one of the troop which deserted from Villeneuve la-Guiard: falling sick, he had been deserted by his companions; in an access of delirium he had fancied himself on the stage, and, poor fellow, his dying sense eagerly accepted the last human applause that could ever be bestowed on his grace and agility.

At another time we were haunted for several days by an apparition, to which our people gave the appellation of the Black Spectre. We never saw it except at evening, when his coal black steed, his mourning dress, and plume of black feathers, had a majestic and awe-striking appearance; his face, one said, who had seen it for a moment, was ashy pale; he had lingered far behind the rest of his troop, and suddenly at a turn in the road, saw the Black Spectre coming towards him; he hid himself in fear, and the horse and his rider slowly past, while the moonbeams fell on the face of the latter, displaying its unearthly hue. Sometimes at dead of night, as we watched the sick, we heard one galloping through the town; it was the Black Spectre come in token of inevitable death. He grew giant tall to vulgar eyes; an icy atmosphere, they said, surrounded him; when he was heard, all animals shuddered, and the dying knew that their last hour was come. It was Death himself, they declared, come visibly to seize on subject earth, and quell at once our decreasing numbers, sole rebels to his law. One day at noon, we saw a dark mass on the road before us, and, coming up, beheld the Black Spectre fallen from his horse, lying in the agonies of disease upon the ground. He did not survive many hours; and his last words disclosed the secret of his mysterious conduct. He was a French noble of distinction, who, from the effects of plague, had been left alone in his district; during many months, he had wandered from town to town, from province to province, seeking some survivor for a companion, and abhorring the loneliness to which he was condemned. When he discovered our troop, fear of contagion conquered his love of society. He dared not join us, yet he could not resolve to lose sight of us, sole human beings who besides himself existed in wide and fertile France; so he accompanied us in the spectral guise I have described, till pestilence gathered him to a larger congregation, even that of Dead Mankind.

It had been well, if such vain terrors could have distracted our thoughts from more tangible evils. But these were too dreadful and too many not to force themselves into every thought, every moment, of our lives. We were obliged to halt at different periods for days together, till another and yet another was consigned as a clod to the vast clod which had been once our living mother. Thus we continued travelling during the hottest season; and it was not till the first of August, that we, the emigrants,—reader, there were just eighty of us in number,—entered the gates of Dijon.

We had expected this moment with eagerness, for now we had accomplished the worst part of our dreary journey, and Switzerland was near at hand. Yet how could we congratulate ourselves on any event thus imperfectly fulfilled? Were these miserable beings, who, worn and wretched, passed in sorrowful procession, the sole remnants of the race of man, which, like a flood, had once spread over and possessed the whole earth? It had come down clear and unimpeded from its primal mountain source in Ararat, and grew from a puny streamlet to a vast perennial river, generation after generation flowing on ceaselessly. The same, but diversified, it grew and swept onwards towards the absorbing ocean, whose dim shores we now reached. It had been the mere plaything of nature, when first it crept out of uncreative void into light; but thought brought forth power and knowledge; and, clad with these, the race of man assumed dignity and authority. It was then no longer the mere gardener of earth, or the shepherd of her flocks; "it carried with it an imposing and majestic aspect; it had a pedigree and illustrating ancestors; it had its gallery of portraits, its monumental inscriptions, its records and titles."

This was all over, now that the ocean of death had sucked in the slackening tide, and its source was dried up. We first had bidden adieu to the state of things which having existed many thousand years, seemed eternal, such a state of government, obedience, traffic, and domestic intercourse, as had moulded our hearts and capacities, as far back as memory could reach. Then to patriotic zeal, to the arts, to reputation, to enduring fame, to the name of country, we had bidden farewell. We saw depart all hope of retrieving our ancient state—all expectation, except the feeble one of saving our individual lives from the wreck of the past. To preserve these we had quitted England—England no more; for without her children, what name could that barren island claim? With tenacious grasp we clung to such rule and order as could best save us; trusting that, if a little colony could be preserved, that would suffice at some remoter period to restore the lost community of mankind.

But the game is up! We must all die; nor leave survivor nor heir to the wide inheritance of earth. We must all die! The species of man must perish; his frame of exquisite workmanship; the wondrous mechanism of his senses; the noble proportion of his godlike limbs; his mind, the throned king of these; must perish. Will the earth still keep her place among the planets; will she still journey with unmarked regularity round the sun; will the seasons change, the trees adorn themselves with leaves, and flowers shed their fragrance, in solitude? Will the mountains remain unmoved, and streams still keep a downward course towards the vast abyss; will the tides rise and fall, and the winds fan universal-nature; will beasts pasture, birds fly, and fishes swim, when man, the lord, possessor, perceiver, and recorder of all these things, has passed away, as though he had never been? O, what mockery is this! Surely death is not death, and humanity is not extinct; but merely passed into other shapes, unsubjected to our perceptions. Death is a vast portal, an high road to life: let us hasten to pass; let us exist no more in this living death, but die that we may live!

We had longed with inexpressible earnestness to reach Dijon, since we had fixed on it, as a kind of station in our progress. But now we entered it with a torpor more painful than acute suffering. We had come slowly but irrevocably to the opinion, that our utmost efforts would not preserve one human being alive. We took our hands therefore away from the long grasped rudder; and the frail vessel on which we floated seemed, the government over her suspended, to rush, prow foremost, into the dark abyss of the billows. A gush of grief, a wanton profusion of tears, and vain laments, and overflowing tenderness, and passionate but fruitless clinging to the priceless few that remained, was followed by languor and recklessness.

After remaining a week at Dijon, until thirty of our number deserted the vacant ranks of life, we continued our way towards Geneva. At noon on the second day we arrived at the foot of Jura. We halted here during the heat of the day. Here fifty human beings—fifty, the only human beings that survived of the food-teeming earth, assembled to read in the looks of each other ghastly plague, or wasting sorrow, desperation, or worse, carelessness of future or present evil. Here we assembled at the foot of this mighty wall of mountain, under a spreading walnut tree; a brawling stream refreshed the green sward by its sprinkling; and the busy grasshopper chirped among the thyme. We clustered together a groupe of wretched sufferers. A mother cradled in her enfeebled arms the child, last of many, whose glazed eye was about to close for ever. Her beauty, late glowing in youthful lustre and consciousness, now wan and neglected, knelt fanning with uncertain motion the beloved, who lay striving to paint his features, distorted by illness, with a thankful smile. There an hard-featured, weather-worn veteran, having prepared his meal, sat, his head dropped on his breast, the useless knife falling from his grasp, his limbs utterly relaxed, as thought of wife and child, and dearest relative, all lost, passed across his recollection. There sat a man who for forty years had basked in fortune's tranquil sunshine; he held the hand of his last hope, his beloved daughter, who had just attained womanhood; and he gazed on her with anxious eyes, while she tried to rally her fainting spirit to comfort him. Here a servant, faithful to the last, though dying, waited on one, who, though still erect with health, gazed with gasping fear on the variety of woe around.

This evening was marked by another event. Passing through Ferney on our way to Geneva, unaccustomed sounds of music arose from the rural church which stood embosomed in trees, surrounded by smokeless, vacant cottages. The peal of an organ with rich swell awoke the mute air, lingering along, and mingling with the intense beauty that clothed the rocks and woods and waves around.

Music—the language of the immortals, disclosed to us as testimony of their existence—music, "Silver key of the fountain of tears," child of love, soother of grief, inspirer of heroism and radiant thoughts, O music, in this our desolation, we had forgotten thee! Nor pipe at eve cheered us, nor harmony of voice, nor linked thrill of string; thou camest upon us now, like the revealing of other forms of being; and transported as we had been by the loveliness of nature, fancying that we beheld the abode of spirits, now we might well imagine that we heard their melodious communings. We paused in such awe as would seize on a pale votarist, visiting some holy shrine at midnight; if she beheld animated and smiling, the image which she worshipped. We all stood mute; many knelt. In a few minutes however, we were recalled to human wonder and sympathy by a familiar strain. The air was Haydn's "New-Created World," and, old and drooping as humanity had become, the world yet fresh as at creation's day, might still be worthily celebrated by such an hymn of praise. Adrian and I entered the church; the nave was empty, though the smoke of incense rose from the altar, bringing with it the recollection of vast congregations, in once thronged cathedrals; we went into the loft. A blind old man sat at the bellows; his whole soul was ear; and as he sat in the attitude of attentive listening, a bright glow of pleasure was diffused over his countenance; for, though his lack-lustre eye could not reflect the beam, yet his parted lips, and every line of his face and venerable brow spoke delight. A young woman sat at the keys, perhaps twenty years of age. Her auburn hair hung on her neck, and her fair brow shone in its own beauty; but her drooping eyes let fall fast-flowing tears, while the constraint she exercised to suppress her sobs, and still her trembling, flushed her else pale cheek; she was thin; languor, and alas! sickness bent her form.

We stood looking at the pair, forgetting what we heard in the absorbing sight; till, the last chord struck, the peal died away in lessening reverberations. The mighty voice, inorganic we might call it, for we could in no way associate it with mechanism of pipe or key, stilled its sonorous tone, and the girl, turning to lend her assistance to her aged companion, at length perceived us.

It was her father; and she, since childhood, had been the guide of his darkened steps. They were Germans from Saxony, and, emigrating thither but a few years before, had formed new ties with the surrounding villagers. About the time that the pestilence had broken out, a young German student had joined them. Their simple history was easily divined. He, a noble, loved the fair daughter of the poor musician, and followed them in their flight from the persecutions of his friends; but soon the mighty leveller came with unblunted scythe to mow, together with the grass, the tall flowers of the field. The youth was an early victim. She preserved herself for her father's sake. His blindness permitted her to continue a delusion, at first the child of accident—and now solitary beings, sole survivors in the land, he remained unacquainted with the change, nor was aware that when he listened to his child's music, the mute mountains, senseless lake, and unconscious trees, were, himself excepted, her sole auditors.

The very day that we arrived she had been attacked by symptomatic illness. She was paralyzed with horror at the idea of leaving her aged, sightless father alone on the empty earth; but she had not courage to disclose the truth, and the very excess of her desperation animated her to surpassing exertions. At the accustomed vesper hour, she led him to the chapel; and, though trembling and weeping on his account, she played, without fault in time, or error in note, the hymn written to celebrate the creation of the adorned earth, soon to be her tomb.

We came to her like visitors from heaven itself; her high-wrought courage; her hardly sustained firmness, fled with the appearance of relief. With a shriek she rushed towards us, embraced the knees of Adrian, and uttering but the word, "O save my father!" with sobs and hysterical cries, opened the long-shut floodgates of her woe.

Poor girl!—she and her father now lie side by side, beneath the high walnut-tree where her lover reposes, and which in her dying moments she had pointed out to us. Her father, at length aware of his daughter's danger, unable to see the changes of her dear countenance, obstinately held her hand, till it was chilled and stiffened by death. Nor did he then move or speak, till, twelve hours after, kindly death took him to his breakless repose. They rest beneath the sod, the tree their monument;—the hallowed spot is distinct in my memory, paled in by craggy Jura, and the far, immeasurable Alps; the spire of the church they frequented still points from out the embosoming trees; and though her hand be cold, still methinks the sounds of divine music which they loved wander about, solacing their gentle ghosts.

The Yellow Wall Paper

CHARLOTTE PERKINS GILMAN

First published in the New England Magazine in 1895, "The Yellow Wall Paper" is widely considered today to be one of the classics of macabre fiction—a tale of terror and madness that mounts inexorably to a Poe-esque climax. Curiously, this story is the only notable one penned by Charlotte Perkins Gilman (1860–1935), an otherwise obscure San Francisco writer and early feminist leader. Her only other claim to literary distinction is that one of the primary targets of her feminist zeal was the confirmed misogynist, Ambrose Bierce, whom she bitterly denounced several times in print.

IT IS very seldom that mere ordinary people like John and myself secure ancestral halls for the summer.

A colonial mansion, a hereditary estate, I would say a haunted house, and reach the height of romantic felicity,—but that would be asking too much of fate!

Still I will proudly declare that there is something queer about it.

Else, why should it be let so cheaply? And why have stood so long untenanted?

John laughs at me, of course, but one expects that in marriage.

John is practical in the extreme. He has no patience with faith, an intense horror of superstition, and he scoffs openly at any talk of things not to be felt and seen and put down in figures.

John is a physician, and *perhaps*—(I would not say it to a living soul, of course, but this is dead paper and a great relief to my mind)—*perhaps* that is one reason I do not get well faster.

You see, he does not believe I am sick!

And what can one do?

If a physician of high standing, and one's own husband, assures friends and relatives that there is really nothing the matter with one but temporary nervous depression,—a slight hysterical tendency,—what is one to do?

My brother is also a physician, and also of high standing, and he says the same thing.

So I take phosphates or phosphites,—whichever it is,—and tonics, and journeys, and air, and exercise, and am absolutely forbidden to "work" until I am well again.

Personally I disagree with their ideas.

Personally I believe that congenial work, with excitement and change, would do me good.

But what is one to do?

I did write for a while in spite of them; but it *does* exhaust me a good deal—having to be so sly about it, or else meet with heavy opposition.

I sometimes fancy that in my condition if I had less opposition and more society and stimulus—but John says the very worst thing I can do is to think about my condition, and I confess it always makes me feel bad.

So I will let it alone and talk about the house.

The most beautiful place! It is quite alone, standing well back from the road, quite three miles from the village. It makes me think of English places that you read about, for there are hedges, and walls and gates that lock, and lots of separate little houses for the gardeners and people.

There is a *delicious* garden! I never saw such a garden—large and shady, full of box-bordered paths, and lined with long grape-covered arbors with seats under them.

There were greenhouses, too, but they are all broken now.

There was some legal trouble, I believe, something about the heirs and co-heirs; anyhow, the place has been empty for years.

That spoils my ghostliness, I am afraid; but I don't care—there is something strange about the house—I can feel it.

I even said so to John one moonlight evening, but he said what I felt was a *draught*, and shut the window.

I get unreasonably angry with John sometimes. I'm sure I never used to be so sensitive. I think it is due to this nervous condition.

But John says if I feel so I shall neglect proper self-control; so I take pains to control myself—before him, at least, and that makes me very tired.

I don't like our room a bit. I wanted one downstairs that opened on the piazza and had roses all over the window, and such pretty, old-fashioned chintz hangings! but John would not hear of it.

He said there was only one window and not room for two beds, and no near room for him if he took another.

He is very careful and loving, and hardly lets me stir without special direction.

I have a schedule prescription for each hour in the day; he takes all care from me, and so I feel basely ungrateful not to value it more.

He said we came here solely on my account, that I was to have perfect rest and all the air I could get. "Your exercise depends on your strength, my dear," said he, "and your food somewhat on your appetite; but air you can absorb all the time." So we took the nursery, at the top of the house.

It is a big, airy room, the whole floor nearly, with windows that look all ways, and air and sunshine galore. It was nursery first and then playground and gymnasium, I should judge; for the windows are barred for little children, and there are rings and things in the walls.

The paint and paper look as if a boy's school had used it. It is stripped off—the paper—in great patches all around the head of my bed, about as far as I can reach, and in a great place on the other side of the room low down. I never saw a worse paper in my life.

One of those sprawling flamboyant patterns committing every artistic sin.

It is dull enough to confuse the eye in following, pronounced enough to constantly irritate, and provoke study, and when you follow the lame, uncertain curves for a little distance they suddenly commit suicide—plunge off at outrageous angles, destroy themselves in unheard-of contradictions.

The color is repellent, almost revolting; a smouldering, unclean yellow, strangely faded by the slow-turning sunlight.

It is a dull yet lurid orange in some places, a sickly sulphur tint in others.

No wonder the children hated it! I should hate it myself if I had to live in this room long.

There comes John, and I must put this away,—he hates to have me write a word.

We have been here two weeks, and I haven't felt like writing before, since that first day.

I am sitting by the window now, up in this atrocious nursery, and there is nothing to hinder my writing as much as I please, save lack of strength.

John is away all day, and even some nights when his cases are serious.

I am glad my case is not serious!

But these nervous troubles are dreadfully depressing.

John does not know how much I really suffer. He knows there is no *reason* to suffer, and that satisfies him.

Of course it is only nervousness. It does weigh on me so not to do my duty in any way!

I meant to be such a help to John, such a real rest and comfort, and here I am a comparative burden already!

Nobody would believe what an effort it is to do what little I am able—to dress and entertain, and order things.

It is fortunate Mary is so good with the baby. Such a dear baby!

And yet I *cannot* be with him, it makes me so nervous.

I suppose John never was nervous in his life. He laughs at me so about this wall paper!

At first he meant to repaper the room, but afterwards he said that I was letting it get the better of me, and that nothing was worse for a nervous patient than to give way to such fancies.

He said that after the wall paper was changed it would be the heavy bedstead, and then the barred windows, and then that gate at the head of the stairs, and so on.

"You know the place is doing you good," he said, "and really, dear, I don't care to renovate the house just for a three months' rental."

"Then do let us go downstairs," I said, "there are such pretty rooms there."

Then he took me in his arms and called me a blessed little goose, and said he would go down cellar if I wished, and would have it whitewashed into the bargain.

But he is right enough about the beds and windows and things.

It is as airy and comfortable a room as any one need wish, and of course, I would not be so silly as to make him uncomfortable just for a whim.

I'm really getting quite fond of the big room, all but that horrid paper.

Out of one window I can see the garden, those mysterious deep-shaded arbors, the riotous old-fashioned flowers, and bushes and gnarly trees.

Out of another I get a lovely view of the bay and a little private wharf belonging to the estate. There is a beautiful shaded lane that runs down there from the house. I always fancy I see people walking in these numerous paths and arbors, but John has cautioned me not to give way to fancy in the least. He says that with my imaginative power and habit of story-making a nervous weakness like mine is sure to lead to all manner of excited fancies, and that I ought to use my will and good sense to check the tendency. So I try.

I think sometimes that if I were only well enough to write a little it would relieve the press of ideas and rest me.

But I find I get pretty tired when I try.

It is so discouraging not to have any advice and companionship about my work. When I get really well John says we will ask Cousin Henry and Julia down for a long visit; but he says he would as soon put fire-works in my pillow-case as to let me have those stimulating people about now.

I wish I could get well faster.

But I must not think about that. This paper looks to me as if it *knew* what a vicious influence it had!

There is a recurrent spot where the pattern lolls like a broken neck and two bulbous eyes stare at you upside-down.

I got positively angry with the impertinence of it and the everlastingness. Up and down and sideways they crawl, and those absurd, unblinking eyes are everywhere. There is one place where two breadths didn't match, and the eyes go all up and down the line, one a little higher than the other.

I never saw so much expression in an inanimate thing before, and we all know how much expression they have!

I used to lie awake as a child and get more entertainment and terror out of blank walls and plain furniture than most children could find in a toy-store.

I remember what a kindly wink the knobs of our big old bureau used to have, and there was one chair that always seemed like a strong friend.

I used to feel that if any of the other things looked too fierce I could always hop into that chair and be safe.

The furniture in this room is no worse than inharmonious, however, for we had to bring it all from downstairs. I suppose when this was used as a playroom they had to take the nursery things out, and no wonder! I never saw such ravages as the children have made here.

The wall paper, as I said before, is torn off in spots, and it sticketh closer than a brother—they must have had perseverance as well as hatred.

Then the floor is scratched and gouged and splintered, the plaster itself is dug out here and there, and this great heavy bed, which is all we found in the room, looks as if it had been through the wars.

But I don't mind it a bit—only the paper.

There comes John's sister. Such a dear girl as she is, and so careful of me! I must not let her find me writing.

She is a perfect, an enthusiastic housekeeper, and hopes for no better profession. I verily believe she thinks it is the writing which made me sick!

But I can write when she is out, and see her a long way off from these windows.

There is one that commands the road, a lovely, shaded, winding road, and one that just looks off over the country. A lovely country, too, full of great elms and velvet meadows.

This wall paper has a kind of sub-pattern in a different shade, a particularly irritating one, for you can only see it in certain lights, and not clearly then.

But in the places where it isn't faded, and where the sun is just so, I can see a strange, provoking, formless sort of figure, that seems to sulk about that silly and conspicuous front design.

There's sister on the stairs!

Well, the Fourth of July is over! The people are all gone and I am tired out. John thought it might do me good to see a little company, so we just had mother and Nellie and the children down for a week.

Of course I didn't do a thing. Jennie sees to everything now.

But it tired me all the same.

John says if I don't pick up faster he shall send me to Weir Mitchell in the fall.

But I don't want to go there at all. I had a friend who was in his hands once, and she says he is just like John and my brother, only more so!

Besides, it is such an undertaking to go so far.

I don't feel as if it was worth while to turn my hand over for anything, and I'm getting dreadfully fretful and querulous.

I cry at nothing, and cry most of the time.

Of course I don't when John is here, or anybody else, but when I am alone.

And I am alone a good deal just now. John is kept in town very often by serious cases, and Jennie is good and lets me alone when I want her to.

So I walk a little in the garden or down that lovely lane, sit on the porch under the roses, and lie down up here a good deal.

I'm getting really fond of the room in spite of the wall paper. Perhaps *because* of the wall paper.

It dwells in my mind so!

I lie here on this great immovable bed—it is nailed down, I believe—and follow that pattern about by the hour. It is as good as gymnastics, I assure you. I start, we'll say, at the bottom, down in the corner over there where it has not been touched, and I determine for the thousandth time that I *will* follow that pointless pattern to some sort of a conclusion.

I know a little of the principles of design, and I know this thing was not arranged on any laws of radiation, or alternation, or repetition, or symmetry, or anything else that I ever heard of.

It is repeated, of course, by the breadths, but not otherwise.

Looked at in one way, each breadth stands alone, the bloated curves and flourishes—a kind of "debased Romanesque" with *delirium tremens*—go waddling up and down in isolated columns of fatuity.

But, on the other hand, they connect diagonally, and the sprawling outlines run off in great slanting waves of optic horror, like a lot of wallowing seaweeds in full chase.

The whole thing goes horizontally, too, at least it seems so, and I exhaust myself in trying to distinguish the order of its going in that direction.

They have used a horizontal breadth for a frieze, and that adds wonderfully to the confusion.

There is one end of the room where it is almost intact, and there, when the cross-lights fade and the low sun shines directly upon it, I can almost fancy radiation, after all—the interminable grotesques seem to form around a common centre and rush off in headlong plunges of equal distraction.

It makes me tired to follow it. I will take a nap, I guess.

I don't know why I should write this.

I don't want to.

I don't feel able.

And I know John would think it absurd. But I *must* say what I feel and think in some way—it is such a relief!

But the effort is getting to be greater than the relief.

Half the time now I am awfully lazy, and lie down ever so much.

John says I mustn't lose my strength, and has me take cod-liver oil and lots of tonics and things, to say nothing of ale and wine and rare meat.

Dear John! He loves me very dearly, and hates to have me sick. I tried to have a real earnest reasonable talk with him the other day, and tell him how I wished he would let me go and make a visit to Cousin Henry and Julia.

But he said I wasn't able to go, nor able to stand it after I got there; and I did not make out a very good case for myself, for I was crying before I had finished.

It is getting to be a great effort for me to think straight. Just this nervous weakness, I suppose.

And dear John gathered me up in his arms, and just carried me upstairs and laid me on the bed, and sat by me and read to me till he tired my head.

He said I was his darling and his comfort and all he had, and that I must take care of myself for his sake, and keep well.

He says no one but myself can help me out of it, that I must use my will and self-control and not let my silly fancies run away with me.

There's one comfort, the baby is well and happy, and does not have to occupy this nursery with the horrid wall paper.

If we had not used it that blessed child would have! What a fortunate escape! Why, I wouldn't have a child of mine, an impressionable little thing, live in such a room for worlds.

I never thought of it before, but it is lucky that John kept me here, after all. I can stand it so much easier than a baby, you see.

Of course I never mention it to them any more,—I am too wise,—but I keep watch of it all the same.

There are things in that paper that nobody knows but me, or ever will.

Behind that outside pattern the dim shapes get clearer every day.

It is always the same shape, only very numerous.

And it is like a woman stooping down and creeping about behind that pattern. I don't like it a bit. I wonder—I begin to think—I wish John would take me away from here!

It is so hard to talk with John about my case, because he is so wise, and because he loves me so.

But I tried it last night.

It was moonlight. The moon shines in all around, just as the sun does.

I hate to see it sometimes, it creeps so slowly, and always comes in by one window or another.

John was asleep and I hated to waken him, so I kept still and watched the moonlight on that undulating wall paper till I felt creepy.

The faint figure behind seemed to shake the pattern, just as if she wanted to get out.

I got up softly and went to feel and see if the paper *did* move, and when I came back John was awake.

"What is it, little girl?" he said. "Don't go walking about like that—you'll get cold."

I thought it was a good time to talk, so I told him that I really was not gaining here, and that I wished he would take me away.

"Why, darling!" said he, "our lease will be up in three weeks, and I can't see how to leave before.

"The repairs are not done at home, and I cannot possibly leave town just now. Of course if you were in any danger I could and would, but you really are better, dear, whether you can see it or not. I am a doctor, dear, and I know. You are gaining flesh and color, your appetite is better. I feel really much easier about you."

"I don't weigh a bit more," said I, "nor as much; and my appetite may be better in the evening, when you are here, but it is worse in the morning, when you are away."

"Bless her little heart!" said he with a big hug; "she shall be as sick as she pleases. But now let's improve the shining hours by going to sleep, and talk about it in the morning."

"And you won't go away?" I asked gloomily.

"Why, how can I, dear? It is only three weeks more and then we will take a nice little trip of a few days while Jennie is getting the house ready. Really, dear, you are better!"

"Better in body, perhaps—" I began, and stopped short, for he sat up straight and looked at me with such a stern, reproachful look that I could not say another word.

"My darling," said he, "I beg of you, for my sake and for our child's sake, as well as for your own, that you will never for one instant let that idea enter your mind! There is nothing so dangerous, so fascinating, to a temperament like yours. It is a false and foolish fancy. Can you not trust me as a physician when I tell you so?"

So of course I said no more on that score, and we went to sleep before long. He thought I was asleep first, but I wasn't—I lay there for hours trying to decide whether that front pattern and the back pattern really did move together or separately.

On a pattern like this, by daylight, there is a lack of sequence, a defiance of law, that is a constant irritant to a normal mind.

The color is hideous enough, and unreliable enough, and infuriating enough, but the pattern is torturing.

You think you have mastered it, but just as you get well under way in following, it turns a back somersault, and there you are. It slaps you in the face, knocks you down, and tramples upon you. It is like a bad dream.

The outside pattern is a florid arabesque, reminding one of a fungus. If you can imagine a toadstool in joints, an interminable string of toadstools, budding and sprouting in endless convolutions,—why, that is something like it.

That is, sometimes!

There is one marked peculiarity about this paper, a thing nobody seems to notice but myself, and that is that it changes as the light changes.

When the sun shoots in through the east window—I always watch for that first long, straight ray—it changes so quickly that I never can quite believe it.

That is why I watch it always.

By moonlight—the moon shines in all night when there is a moon—I wouldn't know it was the same paper.

At night in any kind of light, in twilight, candlelight, lamplight, and worst of all by moonlight, it becomes bars! The outside pattern, I mean, and the woman behind it is as plain as can be.

I didn't realize for a long time what the thing was that showed behind,—that dim sub-pattern,—but now I am quite sure it is a woman.

By daylight she is subdued, quiet. I fancy it is the pattern that keeps her so still. It is so puzzling. It keeps me quiet by the hour.

I lie down ever so much now. John says it is good for me, and to sleep all I can.

Indeed, he started the habit my making me lie down for an hour after each meal.

It is a very bad habit, I am convinced, for, you see, I don't sleep.

And that cultivates deceit, for I don't tell them I'm awake,—oh, no!

The fact is, I am getting a little afraid of John.

He seems very queer sometimes, and even Jennie has an inexplicable look.

It strikes me occasionally, just as a scientific hypothesis, that perhaps it is the paper!

I have watched John when he did not know I was looking, and come into the room suddenly on the most innocent excuses, and I've caught him several times *looking at the paper!* And Jennie too. I caught Jennie with her hand on it once.

She didn't know I was in the room, and when I asked her in a quiet, a very quiet voice, with the most restrained manner possible, what she was doing with the paper she turned around as if she had been caught stealing, and looked quite angry—asked me why I should frighten her so!

Then she said that the paper stained everything it touched, and that she had found yellow smooches on all my clothes and John's, and she wished we would be more careful!

Did not that sound innocent? But I know she was studying that pattern, and I am determined that nobody shall find it out but myself!

Life is very much more exciting now than it used to be. You see I have something more to expect, to look forward to, to watch. I really do eat better, and am more quiet than I was.

John is so pleased to see me improve! He laughed a little the other day, and said I seemed to be flourishing in spite of my wall paper.

I turned it off with a laugh. I had no intention of telling him that it was *because* of the wall paper—he would make fun of me. He might even want to take me away.

I don't want to leave now until I have found it out. There is a week more, and I think that will be enough.

I'm feeling ever so much better! I don't sleep much at night, for it is so interesting to watch developments; but I sleep a good deal in the daytime.

In the daytime it is tiresome and perplexing.

There are always new shoots on the fungus, and new shades of yellow all over it. I cannot keep count of them, though I have tried conscientiously.

It is the strangest yellow, that wall paper! It makes me think of all the yellow things I ever saw—not beautiful ones like buttercups, but old foul, bad yellow things.

But there is something else about that paper—the smell! I noticed it the moment we came into the room, but with so much air and sun it was not bad. Now we have had a week of fog and rain, and whether the windows are open or not the smell is here.

It creeps all over the house.

I find it hovering in the dining-room, skulking in the parlor, hiding in the hall, lying in wait for me on the stairs.

It gets into my hair.

Even when I go to ride, if I turn my head suddenly and surprise it—there is that smell!

Such a peculiar odor, too! I have spent hours in trying to analyze it, to find what it smelled like.

It is not bad—at first, and very gentle, but quite the subtlest, most enduring odor I ever met.

In this damp weather it is awful. I wake up in the night and find it hanging over me.

It used to disturb me at first. I thought seriously of burning the house—to reach the smell.

But now I am used to it. The only thing I can think of that it is like is the *color* of the paper—a yellow smell!

There is a very funny mark on this wall, low down, near the mopboard. A streak that runs around the room. It goes behind every piece of furniture, except the bed, a long, straight, even *smooch,* as if it had been rubbed over and over.

I wonder how it was done and who did it, and what they did it for. Round and round and round—round and round and round—it makes me dizzy!

I really have discovered something at last.

Through watching so much at night, when it changes so, I have finally found out.

The front pattern *does* move—and no wonder! The woman behind shakes it!

Sometimes I think there are a great many women behind, and sometimes only one, and she crawls around fast, and her crawling shakes it all over.

Then in the very bright spots she keeps still, and in the very shady spots she just takes hold of the bars and shakes them hard.

And she is all the time trying to climb through. But nobody could climb through that pattern—it strangles so; I think that is why it has so many heads.

They get through, and then the pattern strangles them off and turns them upside-down, and makes their eyes white!

If those heads were covered or taken off it would not be half so bad.

I think that woman gets out in the daytime!

And I'll tell you why—privately—I've seen her!

I can see her out of every one of my windows!

It is the same woman, I know, for she is always creeping, and most women do not creep by daylight.

I see her in that long shaded lane, creeping up and down. I see her in those dark grape arbors, creeping all around the garden.

I see her on that long road under the trees, creeping along, and when a carriage comes she hides under the blackberry vines.

I don't blame her a bit. It must be very humiliating to be caught creeping by daylight!

I always lock the door when I creep by daylight. I can't do it at night, for I know John would suspect something at once.

And John is so queer, now, that I don't want to irritate him. I wish he would take another room! Besides, I don't want anybody to get that woman out at night but myself.

I often wonder if I could see her out of all the windows at once.

But, turn as fast as I can, I can only see out of one at one time.

And though I always see her she *may* be able to creep faster than I can turn!

I have watched her sometimes away off in the open country, creeping as fast as a cloud shadow in a high wind.

If only that top pattern could be gotten off from the under one! I mean to try it, little by little.

I have found out another funny thing, but I sha'n't tell it this time! It does not do to trust people too much.

There are only two more days to get this paper off, and I believe John is beginning to notice. I don't like the look in his eyes.

And I heard him ask Jennie a lot of professional questions about me. She had a very good report to give.

She said I slept a good deal in the daytime.

John knows I don't sleep very well at night, for all I'm so quiet!

He asked me all sorts of questions, too, and pretended to be very loving and kind.

As if I couldn't see through him!

Still, I don't wonder he acts so, sleeping under this paper for three months.

It only interests me, but I feel sure John and Jennie are secretly affected by it.

Hurrah! This is the last day, but it is enough. John is to stay in town over night, and won't be out until this evening.

Jennie wanted to sleep with me—the sly thing! but I told her I should undoubtedly rest better for a night all alone.

That was clever, for really I wasn't alone a bit! As soon as it was moonlight, and that poor thing began to crawl and shake the pattern, I got up and ran to help her.

I pulled and she shook, I shook and she pulled, and before morning we had peeled off yards of that paper.

A strip about as high as my head and half around the room.

And then when the sun came and that awful pattern began to laugh at me I declared I would finish it to-day!

We go away to-morrow, and they are moving all my furniture down again to leave things as they were before.

Jennie looked at the wall in amazement, but I told her merrily that I did it out of pure spite at the vicious thing.

She laughed and said she wouldn't mind doing it herself, but I must not get tired.

How she betrayed herself that time!

But I am here, and no person touches this paper but me—not *alive!*

She tried to get me out of the room—it was too patent! But I said it was so quiet and empty and clean now that I believed I would lie down again and sleep all I could; and not to wake me even for dinner—I would call when I woke.

So now she is gone, and the servants are gone, and the things are gone, and there is nothing left but that great bedstead nailed down, with the canvas mattress we found on it.

We shall sleep downstairs to-night, and take the boat home tomorrow.

I quite enjoy the room, now it is bare again.

How those children did tear about here!

This bedstead is fairly gnawed!

But I must get to work.

I have locked the door and thrown the key down into the front path.

I don't want to go out, and I don't want to have anybody come in, till John comes.

I want to astonish him.

I've got a rope up here that even Jennie did not find. If that woman does get out, and tries to get away, I can tie her!

But I forgot I could not reach far without anything to stand on!

This bed will *not* move!

I tried to lift and push it until I was lame, and then I got so angry I bit off a little piece at one corner—but it hurt my teeth.

Then I peeled off all the paper I could reach standing on the floor. It sticks horribly and the pattern just enjoys it! All those strangled heads and bulbous eyes and waddling fungus growths just shriek with derision!

I am getting angry enough to do something desperate. To jump out of the window would be admirable exercise, but the bars are too strong even to try.

Besides, I wouldn't do it. Of course not. I know well enough that a step like that is improper and might be misconstrued.

I don't like to *look* out of the windows even—there are so many of those creeping women, and they creep so fast.

I wonder if they all come out of that wall paper, as I did?

But I am securely fastened now by my well-hidden rope—you don't get *me* out in the road there!

I suppose I shall have to get back behind the pattern when it comes night, and that is hard!

It is so pleasant to be out in this great room and creep around as I please!

I don't want to go outside. I won't, even if Jennie asks me to.

For outside you have to creep on the ground, and everything is green instead of yellow.

But here I can creep smoothly on the floor, and my shoulder just fits in that long smooch around the wall, so I cannot lose my way.

Why, there's John at the door!

It is no use, young man, you can't open it!

How he does call and pound!

Now he's crying for an axe.

It would be a shame to break down that beautiful door!

"John, dear!" said I in the gentlest voice, "the key is down by the front steps, under a plantain leaf!"

That silenced him for a few moments.

Then he said—very quietly indeed, "Open the door, my darling!"

"I can't," said I. "The key is down by the front door, under a plantain leaf!"

And then I said it again, several times, very gently and slowly, and said it so often that he had to go and see, and he got it, of course, and came in. He stopped short by the door.

"What is the matter?" he cried. "For God's sake, what are you doing?"

I kept on creeping just the same, but I looked at him over my shoulder.

"I've got out at last," said I, "in spite of you and Jennie! And I've pulled off most of the paper, so you can't put me back!"

Now why should that man have fainted? But he did, and right across my path by the wall, so that I had to creep over him every time!

The Striding Place

GERTRUDE ATHERTON

A deceptive little shocker, whose last sentence is certain to give you a frisson d'horreur, *"The Striding Place" is typical of the macabre tales of Gertrude Atherton (1857–1948). Others may be found in her 1905 collection,* The Bell in the Fog and Other Stories. *She is best known, however, for her historical novels and stories about her native state of California* (The Splendid Idle Forties, The Californians), *and for such novels of then-contemporary society as* Black Oxen *(1923),* The Sophisticates *(1931), and* The Horn of Life *(1942).*

WEIGALL, continental and detached, tired early of grouse-shooting. To stand propped, against a sod fence while his host's workmen routed up the birds with long poles and drove them towards the waiting guns, made him feel himself a parody on the ancestors who had roamed the moors and forests of this West Riding of Yorkshire in hot pursuit of game worth the killing. But when in England in August he always accepted whatever proffered for the season, and invited his host to shoot pheasants on his estates in the South. The amusements of life, he argued, should be accepted with the same philosophy as its ills.

It had been a bad day. A heavy rain had made the moor so spongy that it fairly sprang beneath the feet. Whether or not the grouse had haunts of their own, wherein they were immune from rheumatism, the bag had been small. The women, too, were an unusually dull lot, with the exception of a new-minded *débutante* who bothered Weigall at dinner by demanding the verbal restoration of the vague paintings on the vaulted roof above them.

But it was no one of these things that sat on Weigall's mind as, when the other men went up to bed, he let himself out of the castle and sauntered down to the river. His intimate friend, the companion of his boyhood, the chum of his college days, his fellow-traveler in many lands, the man for whom he possessed stronger affection than for all men, had mysteriously disappeared two days ago, and his track might have sprung to the upper air for all trace he had left behind him. He had been a guest on the adjoining estate during the past week, shooting with the fervor of the true sportsman, making love in the intervals to Adeline Cavan, and apparently in the best of spirits. As far as was known there was nothing to lower his mental mercury, for his rent-roll was a large one, Miss Cavan blushed whenever he looked at her, and, being one of the best shots in England, he was never happier than in August. The suicide theory was preposterous, all agreed, and there was as little reason to believe him murdered. Nevertheless, he had walked out of March Abbey two nights ago without hat or overcoat, and had not been seen since.

The country was being patrolled night and day. A hundred keepers and workmen were beating the woods and poking the bogs on the moors, but as yet not so much as a handkerchief had been found.

Weigall did not believe for a moment that Wyatt Gifford was dead, and although it was impossible not to be affected by the general uneasiness, he was disposed to be more angry than frightened. At Cambridge Gifford had been an incorrigible practical joker, and by no means had outgrown the habit; it would be like him to cut across the country in his evening clothes, board a cattle-train, and amuse himself touching up the picture of the sensation in West Riding.

However, Weigall's affection for his friend was too deep to companion with tranquillity in the present state of doubt, and, instead of going to bed early with the other men, he determined to walk until ready for sleep. He went down to the river and followed the path through the woods. There was no moon, but the stars sprinkled their cold light upon the pretty belt of water flowing placidly past wood and ruin, between green masses of overhanging rocks or sloping banks tangled with tree and shrub, leaping occasionally over stones with the harsh notes of an angry scold, to recover its equanimity the moment the way was clear again.

It was very dark in the depths where Weigall trod. He smiled as he recalled a remark of Gifford's: "An English wood is like a good many other things in life—very promising at a distance, but a hollow mockery when you get within. You see daylight on both sides, and the sun freckles the very bracken. Our woods need the night to make them seem what they ought to be—what they once were, before our ancestors' descendants demanded so much more money, in these so much more various days."

Weigall strolled along, smoking, and thinking of his friend, his pranks—many of which had done more credit to his imagination than this—and recalling conversations that had lasted the night through. Just before the end of the London season they had walked the streets one hot night after a party, discussing the various theories of the soul's destiny. That afternoon they had met at the coffin of a college friend whose mind had been a blank for the past three years. Some months previously they had called at the asylum to see him. His expression had been senile, his face imprinted with the record of debauchery. In death the face was placid, intelligent, without ignoble lineation—the face of the man they had known at college. Weigall and Gifford had had no time to comment there, and the afternoon and evening were full; but, coming forth from the house of festivity together, they had reverted almost at once to the topic.

"I cherish the theory," Gifford had said, "that the soul sometimes lingers in the body after death. During madness, of course, it is an impotent prisoner, albeit a conscious one. Fancy its agony, and its horror! What more natural than that, when the life-spark goes out, the tortured soul should take possession of the vacant skull and triumph once more for a few hours while old friends look their last? It has had time to repent while compelled to crouch and behold the result of its work, and it has shrived itself into a state of comparative purity. If I had my way, I should stay inside my bones until the coffin had gone into its niche, that I might obviate for my poor old comrade the tragic impersonality of death. And I should like to see justice done to it, as it were—to see it lowered among its ancestors with the ceremony and solemnity that are its due. I am afraid that if I dissevered myself too quickly, I should yield to curiosity and hasten to investigate the mysteries of space."

"You believe in the soul as an independent entity, then—that it and the vital principle are not one and the same?"

"Absolutely. The body and soul are twins, life comrades—sometimes friends, sometimes enemies, but always loyal in the last instance. Some day, when I am tired of the world, I shall go to India and become a mahatma, solely for the pleasure of receiving proof during life of this independent relationship."

"Suppose you were not sealed up properly, and returned after one of your astral flights to find your earthly part unfit for habitation? It is an experiment I don't think I should care to try, unless even juggling with soul and flesh had palled."

"That would not be an uninteresting predicament. I should rather enjoy experimenting with broken machinery."

The high wild roar of water smote suddenly upon Weigall's ear and checked his memories. He left the wood and walked out on the huge slippery stones which nearly close the River Wharfe at this point, and watched the waters boil down into the narrow pass with their furious untiring energy. The black quiet of the woods rose high on either side. The stars seemed colder and whiter just above. On either hand the perspective of the river might have run into a rayless cavern. There was no lonelier spot in England, nor one which had the right to claim so many ghosts, if ghosts there were.

Weigall was not a coward, but he recalled uncomfortably the tales of those that had been done to death in the Strid.* Wordsworth's Boy of Egremond had been disposed of by the practical Whitaker; but countless others, more venturesome than wise, had gone down into that narrow boiling course, never to appear in the still pool a few yards beyond. Below the great rocks which form the walls of the Strid was believed to be a natural vault, on to whose shelves the dead were drawn. The spot had an ugly fascination. Weigall stood, visioning skeletons, uncoffined and green, the home of the eyeless things which had devoured all that had covered and filled that rattling symbol of man's mortality; then fell to wondering if any one had attempted

* "This striding place is called the 'Strid,'
A name which it took of yore;
A thousand years hath it borne the name,
And it shall a thousand more."

to leap the Strid of late. It was covered with slime; he had never seen it look so treacherous.

He shuddered and turned away, impelled, despite his manhood, to flee the spot. As he did so, something tossing in the foam below the fall—something as white, yet independent of it—caught his eye and arrested his step. Then he saw that it was describing a contrary motion to the rushing water—an upward backward motion. Weigall stood rigid, breathless; he fancied he heard the crackling of his hair. Was that a hand? It thrust itself still higher above the boiling foam, turned sidewise, and four frantic fingers were distinctly visible against the black rock beyond.

Weigall's superstitious terror left him. A man was there, struggling to free himself from the suction beneath the Strid, swept down, doubtless, but a moment before his arrival, perhaps as he stood with his back to the current.

He stepped as close to the edge as he dared. The hand doubled as if in imprecation, shaking savagely in the face of that force which leaves its creatures to immutable law; then spread wide again, clutching, expanding, crying for help as audibly as the human voice.

Weigall dashed to the nearest tree, dragged and twisted off a branch with his strong arms, and returned as swiftly to the Strid. The hand was in the same place, still gesticulating as wildly; the body was undoubtedly caught in the rocks below, perhaps already half-way along one of those hideous shelves. Weigall let himself down upon a lower rock, braced his shoulder against the mass beside him, then, leaning out over the water, thrust the branch into the hand. The fingers clutched it convulsively. Weigall tugged powerfully, his own feet dragged perilously near the edge. For a moment he produced no impression, then an arm shot above the waters.

The blood sprang to Weigall's head; he was choked with the impression that the Strid had him in her roaring hold, and he saw nothing. Then the mist cleared. The hand and arm were nearer, although the rest of the body was still concealed by the foam. Weigall peered out with distended eyes. The meager light revealed in the cuffs links of a peculiar device. The fingers clutching the branch were as familiar.

Weigall forgot the slippery stones, the terrible death if he stepped too far. He pulled with passionate will and muscle. Memories flung themselves into the hot light of his brain, trooping rapidly upon each other's heels, as in the thought of the drowning. Most of the pleasures of his life, good and bad, were identified in some way with this friend. Scenes of college days, of travel, where they had deliberately sought adventure and stood between one another and death upon more occasions than one, of hours of delightful companionship among the treasures of art, and others in the pursuit of pleasure, flashed like the changing particles of a kaleidoscope. Weigall had loved several women; but he would have flouted in these moments the thought that he had ever loved any woman as he loved Wyatt Gifford. There were so many charming women in the world, and in the thirty-two years of his life he had never known another man to whom he had cared to give his intimate friendship.

He threw himself on his face. His wrists were cracking, the skin was torn from his hands. The fingers still gripped the stick. There was life in them yet.

Suddenly something gave way. The hand swung about, tearing the branch from Weigall's grasp. The body had been liberated and flung outward, though still submerged by the foam and spray.

Weigall scrambled to his feet and sprang along the rocks, knowing that the danger from suction was over and that Gifford must be carried straight to the quiet pool. Gifford was a fish in the water and could live under it longer than most men. If he survived this, it would not be the first time that his pluck and science had saved him from drowning.

Weigall reached the pool. A man in his evening clothes floated on it, his face turned towards a projecting rock over which his arm had fallen, upholding the body. The hand that had held the branch hung limply over the rock, its white reflection visible in the black water. Weigall plunged into the shallow pool, lifted Gifford in his arms and returned to the bank. He laid the body down and threw off his coat that he might be the freer to practise the methods of resuscitation. He was glad of the moment's respite. The valiant life in the man might have been exhausted in that last struggle. He had not dared to look at his face, to put his ear to the heart. The hesitation lasted but a moment. There was no time to lose.

He turned to his prostrate friend. As he did so, something strange and disagreeable smote his senses. For a half-moment he did not appreciate its nature. Then his teeth clacked together, his feet, his outstretched arms pointed towards the woods. But he sprang to the side of the man and bent down and peered into his face. There was no face.

Afterward

EDITH WHARTON

One of America's most outstanding novelists, Edith Wharton (1862–1937) is known for her fine characterization, as demonstrated in such novels as Ethan Frome, *as well as in numerous mainstream and ghost stories. The survivor of a bitterly unhappy childhood and a troubled early marriage, Wharton displays uncommon sympathy for her characters and easily involves the reader in their lives and sufferings. It is proof of her skill that she is able to make the seemingly impossible disappearance in "Afterward" a reality to us; so much so, in fact, that we are caught up in the heroine's anxiety throughout the story and share in her horror when the terrifying conclusion is reached.*

I

"OH, there *is* one, of course, but you'll never know it." The assertion, laughingly flung out six months earlier in a bright June garden, came back to Mary Boyne with a new perception of its significance as she stood, in the December dusk, waiting for the lamps to be brought into the library.

The words had been spoken by their friend Alida Stair, as they sat at tea on her lawn at Pangbourne, in reference to the very house of which the library in question was the central, the pivotal, "feature." Mary Boyne and her husband, in quest of a country place in one of the southern or southwestern counties, had, on their arrival in England, carried their problem straight to Alida Stair, who had successfully solved it in her own case; but it was not until they had rejected, almost capriciously, several practical and judicious suggestions, that she threw out: "Well, there's Lyng, in Dorsetshire. It belongs to Hugo's cousins, and you can get it for a song."

The reason she gave for its being obtainable on these terms—its remoteness from a station, its lack of electric light, hot-water pipes, and other vulgar necessities—were exactly those pleasing in its favour with two romantic Americans perversely in search of the economic drawbacks which were associated, in their tradition, with unusual architectural felicities.

"I should never believe I was living in an old house unless I was thoroughly uncomfortable," Ned Boyne, the more extravagant of the two, had jocosely insisted; "the least hint of 'convenience' would make me think it had been bought out of an exhibition, with the pieces numbered, and set up again." And they had proceeded to enumerate, with humorous precision, their various doubts and demands, refusing to believe that the house their cousin recommended was *really* Tudor till they learned it had no heating system, or that the village church was literally in the grounds, and till she assured them of the deplorable uncertainty of the water-supply.

"It's too uncomfortable to be true!" Edward Boyne had continued to exult as the avowel of each disadvantage was successively wrung from her; but he had cut short his rhapsody to ask, with a relapse to distrust: "And the ghost? You've been concealing from us the fact that there is no ghost!"

Mary, at the moment, had laughed with him, yet almost with her laugh, being possessed of several sets of independent perceptions, had been struck by a note of flatness in Alida's answering hilarity.

"Oh, Dorsetshire's full of ghosts, you know."

"Yes, yes; but that won't do. I don't want to have to drive ten miles to see somebody else's ghost. I want one of my own on the premises. *Is* there a ghost at Lyng?"

His rejoinder had made Alida laugh again, and it was then that she had flung back tantalizing: "Oh, there *is* one, of course, but you'll never know it."

"Never know it?" Boyne pulled her up. "But what in the world constitutes a ghost except the fact of its being known for one?"

"I can't say. But that's the story."

"That there's a ghost, but that nobody know it's a ghost?"

"Well—not till afterward, at any rate."

"Till afterward?"

"Not till long, long afterward."

"But if it's once been identified as an unearthly visitant, why hasn't its *signalement* been handed down in the family? How has it managed to preserve its incognito?"

Alida could only shake her head. "Don't ask me. But it has."

"And then suddenly"—Mary spoke up as if from cavernous depths of divination—"suddenly, long afterward, one says to oneself, *'That was it!'* "

She was startled at the sepulchral sound with which her question fell on the banter of the other two, and she saw the shadow of the same surprise flit across Alida's pupils. "I suppose so. One just has to wait."

"Oh, hang waiting!" Ned broke in. "Life's too short for a ghost who can only be enjoyed in retrospect. Can't we do better than that, Mary?"

But it turned out that in the event they were not destined to, for within three months of their conversation with Mrs. Stair they were settled at Lyng, and the life they had yearned for, to the point of planning it in advance in all its daily details, had actually begun for them.

It was to sit, in the thick December dusk, by just such a wide-hooded fireplace, under just such black oak rafters, with the sense that beyond the mullioned panes the downs were darkened to a deeper solitude: it was for the ultimate indulgence of such sensations that Mary Boyne, abruptly exiled from New York by her husband's business, had endured for nearly fourteen years the soul-deadening ugliness of a Middle Western town, and that Boyne had ground on doggedly at his engineering till, with a suddenness that still made her blink, the prodigious windfall of the Blue Star Mine had put them at a stroke in possession of life and the leisure to taste it. They had never for a moment meant their new state to be one of idleness; but they meant to give themselves only to harmonious activities. She had her vision of painting and gardening (against a background of grey walls), he dreamed of the production of his long-planned book on the *Economic Basis of Culture;* and with such absorbing work ahead no existence could be too sequestered: they could not get far enough from the world, or plunge deep enough into the past.

Dorsetshire had attracted them from the first by an air of remoteness out of all proportion to its geographical position. But to the Boynes it was one of the ever-recurring wonders of the whole incredibly compressed island—a nest of counties, as they put it—that for the production of its effects so little of a given quality went so far: that so few miles made a distance, and so short a distance a difference.

"It's that," Ned had once enthusiastically explained, "that gives such depth to their efforts, such relief to their contrasts. They've been able to lay the butter so thick on every delicious mouthful."

The butter had certainly been laid on thick at Lyng: the old house hidden under a shoulder of the downs had almost all the finer marks of commerce with a protracted past. The mere fact that it was neither large nor exceptional made it, to the Boynes, abound the more completely in its special charm—the charm of having been for centuries a deep, dim reservoir of life. The life had probably not been of the most vivid order: for long periods, no doubt, it had fallen as noiselessly into the past as the quiet drizzle of autumn fell, hour after hour, into the fish-pond between the yews; but these back-waters of existence sometimes breed, in their sluggish depths, strange acuities of emotion, and Mary Boyne had felt from the first the mysterious stir of intenser memories.

The feeling had never been stronger than on this particular afternoon when, waiting in the library for the lamps to come, she rose from her seat and stood among the shadows of the hearth. Her husband had gone off, after luncheon, for one of his long tramps on the downs. She had noticed of late that he preferred to go alone; and, in the tried security of their personal relations, had been driven to conclude that his book was bothering him, and that he needed the afternoons to turn over in solitude the problems left from the morning's work. Certainly the book was not going as smoothly as she had thought it would, and there were lines of perplexity between his eyes such as had never been there in his engineering days. He had often, then, looked fagged to the verge of illness, but the native demon of "worry" had never branded his brow. Yet the few pages he had so far read to her—the introduction, and a summary of the opening chapter—showed a firm hold on his subject, and an increasing confidence in his powers.

The fact threw her into deeper perplexity, since, now that he had done with "business" and its disturbing contingencies, the one other possible source of anxiety was eliminated. Unless it were his health, then? But physically he had gained since they had come to Dorsetshire, grown robuster, ruddier and fresher-eyed. It was only within the last week that she had felt in him the undefinable change which made her restless in his absence, and as tongue-tied in his presence as though it were *she* who had a secret to keep from him!

The thought that there *was* a secret somewhere between them struck her with a sudden rap of wonder, and she looked about her down the long room.

"Can it be the house?" she mused.

The room itself might have been full of secrets. They seemed to be piling themselves up, as evening fell, like the layers and layers of velvet shadow dropping from the low ceiling, the row of books, the smoke-blurred sculpture of the hearth.

"Why, of course—the house is haunted!" she reflected.

The ghost—Alida's imperceptible ghost—after figuring, largely in the banter of their first month or two at Lyng, had been gradually left aside as too ineffectual for imaginative use. Mary had, indeed, as became the tenant of a haunted house, made the customary inquiries among her rural neighbours, but, beyond a vague "They du say so, ma'am," the villagers had nothing to impart. The elusive spectre had apparently never had sufficient identity for a legend to crystallize about it, and after a time the Boynes had set the matter down to their profit-and-loss account, agreeing that Lyng was one of the few houses good enough in itself to dispense with supernatural enhancements.

"And I suppose, poor ineffectual demon, that's why it beats its beautiful wings in vain in the void," Mary had laughingly concluded.

"Or, rather," Ned answered in the same strain, "why, amid so much that's ghostly, it can never affirm its separate existence as *the* ghost." And thereupon their visible housemate had finally dropped out of their references, which were numerous enough to make them soon unaware of the loss.

Now, as she stood on the hearth, the subject of their earlier curiosity revived in her with a new sense of its meaning—a sense gradually acquired through daily contact with the scene of the lurking mystery. It was the house itself, of course, that possessed the ghost-seeing faculty, that communed visually but secretly with its own past; if one could only get into close enough communion with the house one might surprise its secret, and acquire the ghost-sight on one's own account. Perhaps, in his long hours in this very room, where she never trespassed till the afternoon, her husband *had* acquired it already, and was silently carrying about the weight of whatever it had revealed to him. Mary was too well versed in the code of the spectral world not to know that one could not talk about the ghosts one saw: to do so was almost as great a breach of taste as to name a lady in a club. But this explanation did not really satisfy her. "What, after all, except for the fun of the shudder," she reflected, "would he really care for any of their old ghosts?" And thence she was thrown back once more on the fundamental dilemma: the fact that one's greater or less susceptibility to spectral influences had no particular bearing on the case, since, when one *did* see a ghost at Lyng, one did not know it.

"Not till long afterward," Alida Stair had said. Well, supposing Ned *had* seen one when they first came, and had known only within the last week what had happened to him? More and more under the spell of the hour, she threw back her thoughts to the early days of their tenancy, but at first only to recall a lively confusion of unpacking, settling, arranging of books, and calling to each other from remote corners of the house as, treasure after treasure, it revealed itself to them. It was in this particular connection that she presently recalled a certain soft afternoon of the previous October, when, passing from the first rapturous flurry of exploration to a detailed inspection of the old house, she had pressed (like a novel heroine) a panel that opened on a flight of corkscrew stairs leading to a flat ledge of the roof—the roof which, from below, seemed to slope away on all sides too abruptly for any but practised feet to scale.

The view from this hidden coign was enchanting, and she had

flown down to snatch Ned from his papers and give him the freedom of her discovery. She remembered still how, standing at her side, he had passed his arm about her while their gaze flew to the long tossed horizon-line of the downs, and then dropped contentedly back to trace the arabesque of yew hedges about the fish-pond, and the shadow of the cedar on the lawn.

"And now the other way," he had said, turning her about within his arm; and closely pressed to him, she had absorbed, like some long satisfying draught, the picture of the grey-walled court, the squat lions on the gates, and the lime-avenue reaching up to the high-road under the downs.

It was just then, while they gazed and held each other, that she had felt his arms relax, and heard a sharp "Hullo!" that made her turn to glance at him.

Distinctly, yes, she now recalled that she had seen, as she glanced, a shadow of anxiety, of perplexity, rather, fall across his face; and, following his eyes, had beheld the figure of a man—a man in loose greyish clothes, as it appeared to her—who was sauntering down the lime-avenue to the court with the doubtful gait of a stranger who seeks his way. Her short-sighted eyes had given her but a blurred impression of slightness and greyishness, with something foreign, or at least unlocal, in the cut of the figure or its dress; but her husband had apparently seen more—seen enough to make him push past her with a hasty "Wait!" and dash down the stairs without pausing to give her a hand.

A slight tendency to dizziness obliged her, after a provisional clutch at the chimney against which they had been leaning, to follow him first more cautiously; and when she had reached the landing she paused again, for a less definite reason, leaning over the banister to strain her eyes through the silence of the brown sun-flecked depths. She lingered there until, somewhere in those depths she heard the closing of a door; then, mechanically impelled, she went down the shallow flight of steps till she reached the lower hall.

The front door stood open on the sunlight of the court, and hall and court were empty. The library door was open, too, and after listening in vain for any sound of voices within, she crossed the threshold and found her husband alone, vaguely fingering the papers on his desk.

He looked up, as if surprised at her entrance, but the shadow of anxiety had passed from his face, leaving it even, as she fancied, a little brighter and clearer than usual.

"What was it? Who was it?" she asked.

"Who?" he repeated, with the surprise still all on his side.

"The man we saw coming toward the house."

He seemed to reflect. "The man? Why, I thought I saw Peters; I dashed after him to say a word about the stable drains, but he had disappeared before I could get down."

"Disappeared? But he seemed to be walking so slowly when we saw him."

Boyne shrugged his shoulders. "So I thought; but he must have got up steam in the interval. What do you say to our trying a scramble up Meldon Steep before sunset?"

That was all. At the time the occurrence had been less than nothing, had, indeed, been immediately obliterated by the magic of their first vision from Meldon Steep, a height which they had dreamed of climbing ever since they had first seen its bare spine rising above the roof of Lyng. Doubtless it was the mere fact of the other incident's having occurred on the very day of their ascent to Meldon that had kept it stored away in the fold of memory from which it now emerged; for in itself it had no mark of the portentous. At the moment there could have been nothing more natural than that Ned should dash down from the roof in pursuit of dilatory tradesmen. It was the period when they were always on the watch for one or the other of the specialists employed about the place; always lying in wait for them, and rushing out at them with questions, reproaches, or reminders. And certainly in the distance the grey figure had looked like Peters.

Yet now, as she reviewed the scene, she felt her husband's explanation of it to have been invalidated by the look of anxiety on his face. Why had the familiar appearance of Peters made him anxious? Why, above all, if it was of such prime necessity to confer with him on the subject of the stable drains, had the failure to find him produced such a look of relief? Mary could not say that any one of these questions had occurred to her at the time, yet, from the promptness with which they now marshalled themselves at her summons, she had a sense that they must all along have been there, waiting their hour.

II

Weary with her thoughts, she moved to the window. The library was now quite dark, and she was surprised to see how much faint light the outer world still held.

As she peered out into it across the court, a figure shaped itself far down the perspective of bare limes: it looked a mere blot of deeper grey in the greyness, and for an instant, as it moved toward her, her heart thumped to the thought, "It's the ghost!"

She had time, in that long instant, to feel suddenly that the man of whom, two months earlier, she had had a distant vision from the roof, was now, at his predestined hour, about to reveal himself as *not* having been Peters; and her spirit sank under the impending fear of the disclosure. But almost with the next tick of the clock the figure, gaining substance and character, showed itself even to her weak sight as her husband's; and she turned to meet him, as he entered, with the confession of her folly.

"It's really too absurd," she laughed out, "but I never *can* remember!"

"Remember what?" Boyne questioned as they drew together.

"That when one sees the Lyng ghost one never knows it."

Her hand was on his sleeve, and he kept it there, but with no response in his gesture or in the lines of his preoccupied face.

"Did you think you'd seen it?" he asked, after an appreciable interval.

"Why, I actually took *you* for it, my dear, in my mad determination to spot it!"

"Me—just now?" His arm dropped away, and he turned from

her with a faint echo of her laugh. "Really, dearest, you'd better give it up, if that's the best you can do."

"Oh yes, I give it up. Have *you*?" she asked, turning round on him abruptly.

The parlour-maid had entered with letters and a lamp, and the light struck up into Boyne's face as he bent above the tray she presented.

"Have *you*?" Mary perversely insisted, when the servant had disappeared on her errand of illumination.

"Have I what?" he rejoined absently, the light bringing out the sharp stamp of worry between his brows as he turned over the letters.

"Given up trying to see the ghost." Her heart beat a little at the experiment she was making.

Her husband, laying his letters aside, moved away into the shadow of the hearth.

"I never tried," he said, tearing open the wrapper of a newspaper.

"Well, of course," Mary persisted, "the exasperating thing is that there's no use trying, since one can't be sure until so long afterward."

He was unfolding the paper as if he had hardly heard her; but after a pause, during which the sheets rustled spasmodically between his hands, he looked up to ask, "Have you any idea *how long*?"

Mary had sunk into a low chair beside the fire-place. From her seat she glanced over, startled, at her husband's profile, which was projected against the circle of lamplight.

"No; none. Have *you*?" she retorted, repeating her former phrase with an added stress of intention.

Boyne crumpled the paper into a bunch, and then, inconsequently, turned back with it toward the lamp.

"Lord, no! I only meant," he explained, with a faint tinge of impatience, "is there any legend, any tradition as to that?"

"Not that I know of," she answered; but the impulse to add,

"What makes you ask?" was checked by the reappearance of the parlour-maid, with tea and a second lamp.

With the dispersal of shadows, and the repetition of the daily domestic office, Mary Boyne felt herself less oppressed by that sense of something mutely imminent which had darkened her afternoon. For a few moments she gave herself to the details of her task, and when she looked up from it she was struck to the point of bewilderment by the change in her husband's face. He had seated himself near the farther lamp, and was absorbed in the perusal of his letters; but was it something he had found in them, or merely the shifting of her own point of view, that had restored his features to their normal aspect? The longer she looked the more definitely the change affirmed itself. The lines of tension had vanished, and such traces of fatigue as lingered were of the kind easily attributable to steady mental effort. He glanced up, as if drawn by her gaze, and met her eyes with a smile.

"I'm dying for my tea, you know; and here's a letter for you," he said.

She took the letter he held out in exchange for the cup she proffered him, and, returning to her seat, broke the seal with the languid gesture of the reader whose interests are all enclosed in the circle of one cherished presence.

Her next conscious motion was that of starting to her feet, the letter falling to them as she rose, while she held out to her husband a newspaper clipping.

"Ned! What's this? What does it mean?"

He had risen at the same instant, almost as if hearing her cry before she uttered it; and for a perceptible space of time he and she studied each other, like adversaries watching for an advantage, across the space between her chair and his desk.

"What's what? You fairly made me jump!" Boyne said at length, moving toward her with a sudden half-exasperated laugh. The shadow of apprehension was on his face again, not now a look of fixed foreboding, but a shifting vigilance of lips and eyes that gave her the sense of feeling himself invisibly surrounded.

Her hand shook so that she could hardly give him the clipping.

"This article—from the *Waukesha Sentinel*—that a man named Elwell has brought suit against you—that there was something wrong about the Blue Star Mine. I can't understand more than half."

They continued to face each other as she spoke, and to her astonishment she saw that her words had the almost immediate effect of dissipating the strained watchfulness of his look.

"Oh, *that*!" He glanced down the printed slip, and then folded it with the gesture of one who handles something harmless and familiar. "What's the matter with you this afternoon, Mary? I thought you'd got bad news."

She stood before him with her undefinable terror subsiding slowly under the reassurance of his tone.

"You knew about this, then—it's all right?"

"Certainly I knew about it; and it's all right."

"But what *is* it? I don't understand. What does this man accuse you of?"

"Pretty nearly every crime in the calendar." Boyne had tossed the clipping down and thrown himself into an armchair near the fire. "Do you want to hear the story? It's not particularly interesting—just a squabble over interests in the Blue Star."

"But who is this Elwell? I don't know the name."

"Oh, he's a fellow I put into it—gave him a hand up. I told you all about him at the time."

"I dare say. I must have forgotten." Vainly she strained back among her memories. "But if you helped him, why does he make this return?"

"Probably some shyster lawyer got hold of him and talked him over. It's all rather technical and complicated. I thought that kind of thing bored you."

His wife felt a sting of compunction. Theoretically, she deprecated the American wife's detachment from her husband's professional interests, but in practice she had always found it difficult to fix her attention on Boyne's report of the transactions in which his varied interests involved him. Besides, she had felt during their years of exile, that, in a community where the amenities of living could be obtained only at the cost of efforts as arduous as her husband's professional labours, such brief leisure as he and she could command should be used as an escape from immediate preoccupations, a flight to the life they always dreamed of living. Once or twice, now that this new life had actually drawn its magic circle about them, she had asked herself if she had done right; but hitherto such conjectures had been no more than the retrospective excursions of an active fancy. Now, for the first time, it startled her a little to find how little she knew of the material foundation on which her happiness was built.

She glanced at her husband, and was again reassured by the composure of his face; yet she felt the need of more definite grounds for her reassurance.

"But doesn't this suit worry you? Why have you never spoken to me about it?"

He answered both questions at once. "I didn't speak of it at first because it *did* worry me—annoyed me, rather. But it's all ancient history now. Your correspondent must have got hold of a back number of the *Sentinel*."

She felt a quick thrill of relief. "You mean it's over? He's lost his case?"

There was a just perceptible delay in Boyne's reply. "The suit's been withdrawn—that's all."

But she persisted, as if to exonerate herself from the inward charge of being too easily put off. "Withdrawn it because he saw he had no chance?"

"Oh, he had no chance," Boyne answered.

She was still struggling with a dimly felt perplexity at the back of her thoughts.

"How long ago was it withdrawn?"

He paused, as if with a slight return of his former uncertainty.

"I've just had the news now; but I've been expecting it."

"Just now—in one of your letters?"

"Yes; in one of my letters."

She made no answer, and was aware only, after a short interval of waiting, that he had risen and, strolling across the room, had placed himself on the sofa at her side. She felt him, as he did so, pass an arm about her, she felt his hand seek hers and clasp it, and turning slowly, drawn by the warmth of his cheek, she met his smiling eyes.

"It's all right—it's all right?" she questioned, through the flood of her dissolving doubts; and, "I give you my word it was never righter!" he laughed back at her, holding her close.

III

One of the strangest things she was afterward to recall out of all the next day's strangeness was the sudden and complete recovery of her sense of security.

It was in the air when she awoke in her low-ceiled, dusky room; it went with her downstairs to the breakfast-table, flashed out at her from the fire, and reduplicated itself from the flanks of the urn and the sturdy flutings of the Georgian tea-pot. It was as if, in some roundabout way, all her diffused fears of the previous day, with their moment of sharp concentration about the newspaper article—as if this dim questioning of the future, and startled return upon the past, had between them liquidated the arrears of some haunting moral obligation. If she had indeed been careless of her husband's affairs, it was, her new state seemed to prove, because her faith in him instinctively justified such carelessness; and his right to her faith had now affirmed itself in the very face of menace and suspicion. She had never seen him more untroubled, more naturally and unconsciously himself, than after the cross-examination to which she had subjected him: it was almost as if he had been aware of her doubts, and had wanted the air cleared as much as she did.

It was as clear, thank heaven, as the bright outer light that surprised her almost with a touch of summer when she issued from the house for her daily round of the gardens. She had left Boyne at his desk, indulging herself, as she passed the library door, by a last peep at his quiet face, where he bent, pipe in mouth, above his papers; and now she had her own morning's task to perform. The task involved, on such charmed winter days, almost as much happy loitering about the different quarters of her demesne as if spring were already at work there. There were such endless possibilities still before her, such opportunities to bring out the latent graces of the old place, without a single irreverent touch of alteration, that the winter was all too short to plan what spring and autumn executed. And her recovered sense of safety gave, on this particular morning, a peculiar zest to her progress through the sweet, still place. She went first to the kitchen garden, where the espaliered pear trees drew complicated patterns on the walls, and pigeons were fluttering and preening about the silvery-slated roof of their cote.

There was something wrong about the piping of the hothouse and she was expecting an authority from Dorchester, who was to drive out between trains and make a diagnosis of the boiler. But when she dipped into the damp heat of the greenhouses, among the spiced scents and waxy pinks and reds of old-fashioned exotics—even the flora of Lyng was in the note!—she learned that the great man had not arrived, and, the day being too rare to waste in an artificial atmosphere, she came out again and paced along the springy turf of the bowling-green to the gardens behind the house. At their farther end rose a grass terrace, looking across the fish-pond and yew hedges to the long house-front with its twisted chimney-stacks and blue roof angles all drenched in the pale-gold moisture of the air.

Seen thus, across the level tracery of the gardens, it sent her, from open windows and hospitably smoking chimneys, the look of some warm human presence, of a mind slowly ripened on a sunny wall of experience. She had never before had such a sense of her intimacy with it, such a conviction that its secrets were all beneficent, kept, as they said to children, "for one's own good," such a trust in its power to gather up her life and Ned's into the harmonious pattern of the long, long story it sat there weaving in the sun.

She heard steps behind her, and turned, expecting to see the gardener accompanied by the engineer from Dorchester. But only one figure was in sight, that of a youngish, slightly built man, who, for reasons she could not on the spot have given, did not remotely resemble her notion of an authority on hothouse boilers. The new-comer, on seeing her, lifted his hat, and paused with the air of a gentleman—perhaps a traveller—who wishes to make it known that his intrusion is involuntary. Lyng occasionally attracted the more cultivated traveller, and Mary half expected to see the stranger dissemble a camera, or justify his presence by producing it. But he made no gesture of any sort, and after a moment she asked, in a tone responding to the courteous hesitation of his attitude: "Is there anyone you wish to see?"

"I came to see Mr. Boyne," he answered. His intonation, rather than his accent, was faintly American, and Mary, at the note, looked at him more closely. The brim of his soft felt hat cast a shade on his face, which, thus obscured, wore, to her short-sighted gaze, a look of seriousness, as of a person arriving "on business," and civilly but firmly aware of his rights.

Past experience had made her equally sensible to such claims; but she was jealous of her husband's morning hours, and doubtful of his having given anyone the right to intrude on them.

"Have you an appointment with my husband?" she asked.

The visitor hesitated, as if unprepared for the question.

"I think he expects me," he replied.

It was Mary's turn to hesitate. "You see, this is his time for work: he never sees anyone in the morning."

He looked at her a moment without answering; then, as if accepting her decision, he began to move away. As he turned, Mary saw him pause and glance up at the peaceful house-front. Something in his air suggested weariness and disappointment, the dejection of the traveller who has come from far off and whose hours are limited by the time-table. It occurred to her that if this were the case her refusal might have made his errand vain, and a sense of compunction caused her to hasten after him.

"May I ask if you have come a long way?"

He gave her the same grave look. "Yes—I have come a long way."

"Then, if you'll go to the house, no doubt my husband will see you now. You'll find him in the library."

She did not know why she had added the last phrase, except from a vague impulse to atone for her previous inhospitality. The visitor seemed about to express his thanks, but her attention was distracted by the approach of the gardener with a companion who bore all the marks of being the expert from Dorchester.

"This way," she said, waving the stranger to the house; and an instant later she had forgotten him in the absorption of her meeting with the boiler-maker.

The encounter led to such far-reaching results that the engineer ended by finding it expedient to ignore his train, and Mary was beguiled into spending the remainder of the morning in absorbed confabulation among the flower-pots. When the colloquy ended, she was surprised to find that it was nearly luncheon-time, and she half expected, as she hurried back to the house, to see her husband coming out to meet her. But she found no one in the court but an under-gardener raking the gravel, and the hall, when she entered it, was so silent that she guessed Boyne to be still at work.

Not wishing to disturb him, she turned into the drawing-room, and there, at her writing-table, lost herself in renewed calculations of the outlay to which the morning's conference had pledged her. The fact that she could permit herself such follies had not yet lost its novelty; and somehow, in contrast to the vague fears of the previous days, it now seemed an element of her recovered security, of the sense that, as Ned had said, things in general had never been "righter."

She was still luxuriating in a lavish play of figures when the parlour-maid, from the threshold, roused her with an inquiry as to the expediency of serving luncheon. It was one of their jokes that Trimmle announced luncheon as if she were divulging a State secret, and Mary, intent upon her papers, merely murmured an absent-minded assent.

She felt Trimmle wavering doubtfully on the threshold, as if in rebuke of such unconsidered assent; then her retreating steps sounded down the passage, and Mary, pushing away her papers, crossed the hall and went to the library door. It was still closed, and she wavered in her turn, disliking to disturb her husband, yet anxious that he should not exceed his usual measure of work. As she stood there, balancing her impulses, Trimmle returned with the announcement of luncheon, and Mary, thus impelled, opened the library door.

Boyne was not at his desk, and she peered about her, expecting to discover him before the book-shelves, somewhere down the length of the room; but her call brought no response, and gradually it became clear to her that he was not there.

She turned back to the parlour-maid.

"Mr. Boyne must be upstairs. Please tell him that luncheon is ready."

Trimmle appeared to hesitate between the obvious duty of obedience and an equally obvious conviction of the foolishness of the injunction laid on her. The struggle resulted in her saying: "If you please, madam, Mr. Boyne's not upstairs."

"Not in his room? Are you sure?"

"I'm sure, madam."

Mary consulted the clock. "Where is he, then?"

"He's gone out," Trimmle announced, with the superior air of one who has respectfully waited for the question that a well-ordered mind would have put first.

Mary's conjecture had been right, then; Boyne must have gone to the gardens to meet her, and since she had missed him, it was clear that he had taken the shorter way by the south door, instead of going round to the court. She crossed the hall to the french window opening directly on the yew garden, but the parlour-maid, after another moment of inner conflict, decided to bring out: "Please, madam, Mr. Boyne didn't go that way."

Mary turned back. "Where *did* he go? And when?"

"He went out of the front door, up the drive, madam." It was a matter of principle with Trimmle never to answer more than one question at a time.

"Up the drive? At this hour?" Mary went to the door herself and glanced across the court through the tunnel of bare limes. But its perspective was as empty as when she had scanned it on entering.

"Did Mr. Boyne leave no message?"

Trimmle seemed to surrender herself to a last struggle with the forces of chaos.

"No, madam. He just went out with the gentleman."

"The gentleman? What gentleman?" Mary wheeled about, as if to front this new factor.

"The gentleman who called, madam," said Trimmle resignedly.

"When did a gentleman call? Do explain yourself, Trimmle!"

Only the fact that Mary was very hungry, and that she wanted to consult her husband about the greenhouses, would have caused her to lay so unusual an injunction on her attendant; and even now she was detached enough to note in Trimmle's eye the dawning defiance of the respectful subordinate who has been pressed too hard.

"I couldn't exactly say the hour, madam, because I didn't let the gentleman in," she replied, with an air of discreetly ignoring the irregularity of her mistress's course.

"You didn't let him in?"

"No, madam. When the bell rang I was dressing, and Agnes—"

"Go and ask Agnes, then," said Mary.

Trimmle still wore her look of patient magnanimity. "Agnes would not know, madam, for she had unfortunately burnt her hand in trimming the wick of the new lamp from town"—Trimmle, as Mary was aware, had always been opposed to the new lamp—"and so Mrs. Dockett sent the kitchen-maid instead."

Mary looked again at the clock. "It's after two. Go and ask the kitchen-maid if Mr. Boyne left any word."

She went into luncheon without waiting, and Trimmle presently brought to her there the kitchen-maid's statement that the gentleman had called about eleven o'clock, and that Mr. Boyne had gone out with him without leaving any message. The kitchen-maid did not even know the caller's name, for he had written it on a slip of paper, which he had folded and handed to her, with the injunction to deliver it at once to Mr. Boyne.

Mary finished her luncheon, still wondering, and when it was over, and Trimmle had brought the coffee to the drawing-room, her wonder had deepened to a first faint tinge of disquietude. It was unlike Boyne to absent himself without explanation at so unwonted an hour, and the difficulty of identifying the visitor whose summons he had apparently obeyed made his disappearance the more unaccountable. Mary Boyne's experience as the wife of a busy engineer, subject to sudden calls and compelled to keep irregular hours, had trained her to the philosophic acceptance of surprises; but since Boyne's withdrawal from business he had adopted a Benedictine regularity of life. As if to make up for the dispersed and agitated years, with their "stand-up" lunches and dinners rattled down to the joltings of the dining-cars, he cultivated the last refinements of punctuality and monotony, discouraging his wife's fancy for the unexpected, and declaring that to a delicate taste there were infinite gradations of pleasure in the recurrences of habit.

Still, since no life can completely defend itself from the unforeseen, it was evident that all Boyne's precautions would sooner or later prove unavailable, and Mary concluded that he had cut short a tiresome visit by walking with his caller to the station, or at least accompanying him for part of the way.

This conclusion relieved her from farther preoccupation, and she went out herself to take up her conference with the gardener. Thence she walked to the village post office, a mile or so away; and when she turned toward home the early twilight was setting in.

She had taken a footpath across the downs, and as Boyne, meanwhile, had probably returned from the station by the high-road, there was little likelihood of their meeting. She felt sure, however, of his having reached the house before her; so sure that, when she entered it herself, without even pausing to inquire of Trimmle, she made directly for the library. But the library was still empty, and with an unwonted exactness of visual memory she observed that the papers on her husband's desk lay precisely as they had lain when she had gone in to call him to luncheon.

Then of a sudden she was seized by a vague dread of the unknown. She had closed the door behind her on entering, and as she stood alone in the long, silent room, her dread seemed to take shape and sound, to be there breathing and lurking among the shadows. Her short-sighted eyes strained through them, half discerning an actual presence, something aloof, that watched and knew; and in the recoil from that intangible presence she threw herself on the bell-rope and gave it a sharp pull.

The sharp summons brought Trimmle in precipitately with a lamp, and Mary breathed again at this sobering reappearance of the usual.

"You may bring tea if Mr. Boyne is in," she said, to justify her ring.

"Very well, madam. But Mr. Boyne is not in," said Trimmle, putting down the lamp.

"Not in? You mean he's come back and gone out again?"

"No, madam. He's never been back."

The dread stirred again, and Mary knew that now it had her fast.

"Not since he went out with—the gentleman?"

"Not since he went out with the gentleman."

"But who *was* the gentleman?" Mary insisted, with the shrill note of someone trying to be heard through a confusion of noises.

"That I couldn't say, madam." Trimmle, standing there by the lamp, seemed suddenly to grow less round and rosy, as though eclipsed by the same creeping shade of apprehension.

"But the kitchen-maid knows—wasn't it the kitchen-maid who let him in?"

"She doesn't know either, madam, for he wrote his name on a folded paper."

Mary, through her agitation, was aware that they were both designating the unknown visitor by a vague pronoun, instead of the conventional formula which, till then, had kept their allusions within the bounds of conformity. And at the same moment her mind caught at the suggestion of the folded paper.

"But he must have a name! Where's the paper?"

She moved to the desk and began to turn over the documents that littered it. The first that caught her eye was an unfinished letter in her husband's hand, with his pen lying across it, as though dropped there at a sudden summons.

My dear Parvis—who was Parvis?—*I have just received your letter announcing Elwell's death, and while I suppose there is now no further risk of trouble, it might be safer—*

She tossed the sheet aside, and continued her search; but no folded paper was discoverable among the letters and pages of manuscript which had been swept together in a heap, as if by a hurried or a startled gesture.

"But the kitchen-maid *saw* him. Send her here," she commanded, wondering at her dullness in not thinking sooner of so simple a solution.

Trimmle vanished in a flash, as if thankful to be out of the room, and when she reappeared, conducting the agitated underling, Mary had regained her self-possession and had her questions ready.

The gentleman was a stranger, yes—that she understood. But what had he said? And, above all, what had he looked like? The first question was easily enough answered, for the disconcerting reason that he had said so little—had merely asked for Mr. Boyne, and, scribbling something on a bit of paper, had requested that it should at once be carried in to him.

"Then you don't know what he wrote? You're not sure it *was* his name?"

The kitchen-maid was not sure, but supposed it was, since he had written it in answer to her inquiry as to whom she should announce.

"And when you carried the paper in to Mr. Boyne, what did he say?"

The kitchen-maid did not think that Mr. Boyne had said anything, but she could not be sure, for just as she had handed him the paper and he was opening it, she had become aware that the visitor had followed her into the library, and she had slipped out, leaving the two gentlemen together.

"But, then, if you left them in the library, how do you know that they went out of the house?"

This question plunged the witness into a momentary inarticulateness from which she was rescued by Trimmle, who, by means of ingenious circumlocutions, elicited the statement that before she could cross the hall to the back passage she had heard the two gentlemen behind her, and had seen them go out of the front door together.

"Then, if you saw the strange gentleman twice, you must be able to tell me what he looked like."

But with this final challenge to her powers of expression it became clear that the limit of the kitchen-maid's endurance had been reached. The obligation of going to the front door to "show in" a visitor was in itself so subversive of the fundamental order of things that it had thrown her faculties into hopeless disarray, and she could only stammer out, after various panting efforts: "His hat, mum, was different-like, as you might say—"

"Different? How different?" Mary flashed out, her own mind, in the same instant, leaping back to an image left on it that morning, and then lost under layers of subsequent impressions.

"His hat had a wide brim, you mean, and his face was pale—a youngish face?" Mary pressed her, with a white-lipped intensity of interrogation. But if the kitchen-maid found any adequate answer to this challenge, it was swept away for her listener down the rushing current of her own convictions. The stranger—the stranger in the garden! Why had not Mary thought of him before? She needed no one now to tell her that it was he who had called for her husband and gone away with him. But who was he, and why had Boyne obeyed him?

IV

It leaped out at her suddenly, like a grin out of the dark, that they had often called England so little—"such a confoundedly hard place to get lost in."

A confoundedly hard place to get lost in! That had been her husband's phrase. And now, with the whole machinery of official investigation sweeping its flashlights from shore to shore, and across the dividing straits; now, with Boyne's name blazing from the walls of every town and village, his portrait (how that wrung her!) hawked up and down the country like the image of a hunted criminal; now the little, compact, populous island, so policed, surveyed and administered, revealed itself as a Sphinx-like guardian of abysmal mysteries, staring back into his wife's anguished eyes as if with the wicked joy of knowing something they would never know!

In the fortnight since Boyne's disappearance there had been no word of him, no trace of his movements. Even the usual misleading reports that raise expectancy in tortured bosoms had been few and fleeting. No one but the kitchen-maid had seen Boyne leave the house, and no one else had seen the "gentleman" who accompanied him. All inquiries in the neighbourhood failed to elicit the memory of a stranger's presence that day in the neighbourhood of Lyng. And no one had met Edward Boyne, either alone or in company, in any of the neighbouring villages, or on the road across the downs, or at either of the local railway stations. The sunny English noon had swallowed him as completely as if he had gone out into Cimmerian night.

Mary, while every official means of investigation was working at its highest pressure, had ransacked her husband's papers for any trace of antecedent complications, of entanglements or obligations unknown to her, that might throw a ray into the darkness. But if any such had existed in the background of Boyne's life, they had vanished like the slip of paper on which the visitor had written his name. There remained no possible thread of guidance except—if it were indeed an exception—the letter which Boyne had apparently been in the act of writing when he received his mysterious summons. That letter, read and re-read by his wife, and submitted by her to the police, yielded little enough to feed conjecture.

"I have just heard of Elwell's death, and while I suppose there is now no further risk of trouble, it might be safer—" That was all. The "risk of trouble" was easily explained by the newspaper clipping which had apprised Mary of the suit brought against her husband by one of his associates in the Blue Star enterprise. The only new information conveyed by the letter was the fact of its showing Boyne, when he wrote it, to be still apprehensive of the results of the suit, though he had told his wife that it had been withdrawn, and though the letter itself proved that the plaintiff was dead. It took several days of cabling to fix the identity of the "Parvis" to whom the fragment was addressed, but even after these inquiries had shown him to be a Waukesha lawyer, no new facts concerning the Elwell suit were elicited. He appeared to have had no direct concern in it, but to have been conversant with the facts merely as an acquaintance, and possible intermediary; and he declared himself unable to guess with what object Boyne intended to seek his assistance.

This negative information, sole fruit of the first fortnight's search, was not increased by a jot during the slow weeks that followed. Mary knew that the investigations were still being carried on, but she had a vague sense of their gradually slackening, as the actual march of time seemed to slacken. It was as though the days, flying horror-struck from the shrouded image of the one inscrutable day, gained assurance as the distance lengthened, till at last they fell back into their normal gait. And so with the human imaginations at work on the dark event. No doubt it occupied them still, but week by week and hour by hour it grew less absorbing, took up less space, was slowly but inevitably crowded out of the foreground of consciousness by the new problems perpetually bubbling up from the cloudy cauldron of human experience.

Even Mary Boyne's consciousness gradually felt the same lowering of velocity. It still swayed with the incessant oscillations of conjecture; but they were slower, more rhythmical in their beat. There were even moments of weariness when, like the victim of some poison which leaves the brain clear, but holds the body motionless, she saw herself domesticated with the Horror, accepting its perpetual presence as one of the fixed conditions of life.

These moments lengthened into hours and days, till she passed into a phase of stolid acquiescence. She watched the routine of daily life with the incurious eye of a savage on whom the meaningless processes of civilization make but the faintest impression. She had come to regard herself as part of the routine, a spoke of the wheel, revolving with its motion; she felt almost like the furniture of the room in which she sat, an insensate object to be dusted and pushed about with the chairs and tables. And this deepening apathy held her fast at Lyng, in spite of the entreaties of friends and the usual medical recommendation of "change." Her friends supposed that her refusal to move was inspired by the belief that her husband would one day return to the spot from which he had vanished, and a beautiful legend grew up about this imaginary state of waiting. But in reality she had no such belief: the depths of anguish enclosing her were no longer lighted by flashes of hope. She was sure that Boyne would never come back, that he had gone out of her sight as completely as if death itself had waited that day on the threshold. She had even renounced, one by one, the various theories as to his disappearance which had been advanced by the Press, the police, and her own agonized imagination. In sheer lassitude her mind turned from these alternatives of horror, and sank back into the blank fact that he was gone.

No, she would never know what had become of him—no one would ever know. But the house *knew;* the library in which she spent her long, lonely evenings knew. For it was here that the last scene had been enacted, here that the stranger had come and spoken the word which had caused Boyne to rise and follow him. The floor she trod had felt his tread; the books on the shelves had seen his face; and there were moments when the intense consciousness of the old dusky walls seemed about to break out into some audible revelation of their secret. But the revelation never came, and she knew it would never come. Lyng was not one of the garrulous old houses that betray the secrets entrusted to them. Its very legend proved that it had always been the mute accomplice, the incorruptible custodian, of the mysteries it had surprised. And Mary Boyne, sitting face to face with its silence, felt the futility of seeking to break it by any human means.

V

"I don't say it *wasn't* straight, and yet I don't say it *was* straight. It was business."

Mary, at the words, lifted her head with a start and looked intently at the speaker.

When, half an hour before, a card with "Mr. Parvis" on it had been brought up to her, she had been immediately aware that the name had been a part of her consciousness ever since she had read it at the head of Boyne's unfinished letter. In the library she had found awaiting her a small, sallow man with a bald head and gold eye-glasses, and it sent a tremor through her to know that this was the person to whom her husband's last known thought had been directed.

Parvis, civilly, but without vain preamble—in the manner of a man who has his watch in his hand—had set forth the object of his visit. He had "run over" to England on business, and finding himself in the neighbourhood of Dorchester, had not wished to leave it without paying his respects to Mrs. Boyne; and without asking her, if the occasion offered, what she meant to do about Bob Elwell's family.

The words touched the spring of some obscure dread in Mary's bosom. Did her visitor, after all, know what Boyne had meant by his unfinished phrase? She asked for an elucidation of his question, and noticed at once that he seemed surprised at her continued ignorance of the subject. Was it possible that she really knew as little as she said?

"I know nothing—you just tell me," she faltered out; and her visitor thereupon proceeded to unfold his story. It threw, even to her confused perceptions and imperfectly initiated vision, a lurid glare on the whole hazy episode of the Blue Star Mine. Her husband had made his money in that brilliant speculation at the cost of "getting ahead" of someone less alert to seize the chance; and the victim of his ingenuity was young Robert Elwell, who had "put him on" to the Blue Star scheme.

Parvis, at Mary's first cry, had thrown her a sobering glance though his impartial glasses.

"Bob Elwell wasn't smart enough, that's all; if he had been, he might have turned round and served Boyne the same way. It's the kind of thing that happens every day in business. I guess it's what the scientists call the survival of the fittest—see?" said Mr. Parvis, evidently pleased with the aptness of his analogy.

Mary felt a physical shrinking from the next question she tried to frame: it was as though the words on her lips had a taste that nauseated her.

"But then—you accuse my husband of doing something dishonourable?"

Mr. Parvis surveyed the question dispassionately. "Oh no, I don't. I don't even say it wasn't straight." He glanced up and down the long lines of books, as if one of them might have supplied him with the definition he sought. "I don't say it *wasn't* straight, and yet I don't say it *was* straight. It was business."

After all, no definition in his category could be more comprehensive than that.

Mary sat staring at him with a look of terror. He seemed to her like the indifferent emissary of some evil power.

"But Mr. Elwell's lawyers apparently did not take your view, since I suppose the suit was withdrawn by their advice."

"Oh yes; they knew he hadn't a leg to stand on, technically. It was when they advised him to withdraw the suit that he got desperate. You see, he'd borrowed most of the money he lost in the Blue Star, and he was up a tree. That's why he shot himself when they told him he had no show."

The horror was sweeping over Mary in great deafening waves.

"He shot himself? He killed himself because of *that*?"

"Well, he didn't kill himself, exactly. He dragged on two months before he died." Parvis emitted the statement as unemotionally as a gramophone grinding out its "record."

"You mean that he tried to kill himself, and failed? And tried again?"

"Oh, he didn't have to *try* again," said Parvis grimly.

They sat opposite each other in silence, he swinging his eyeglasses thoughtfully about his finger, she motionless, her arms stretched along her knees in an attitude of rigid tension.

"But if you knew all this," she began at length, hardly able to force her voice above a whisper, "how is it that when I wrote you at the time of my husband's disappearance you said you didn't understand his letter?"

Parvis received this without perceptible embarrassment. "Why, I didn't understand it—strictly speaking. And it wasn't the time to talk about it, if I had. The Elwell business was settled when the suit was withdrawn. Nothing I could have told you would have helped you to find your husband."

Mary continued to scrutinize him. "Then why are you telling me now?"

Still Parvis did not hesitate. "Well, to begin with, I supposed you knew more than you appear to—I mean about the circumstances of Elwell's death. And then people are talking of it now;

the whole matter's been raked up again. And I thought if you didn't know you ought to."

She remained silent, and he continued: "You see, it's only come out lately what a bad state Elwell's affairs were in. His wife's a proud woman, and she fought on as long as she could, going out to work, and taking sewing at home when she got too sick—something with the heart, I believe. But she had his mother to look after, and the children, and she broke down under it, and finally had to ask for help. That called attention to the case, and the papers took it up, and a subscription was started. Everybody out there liked Bob Elwell, and most of the prominent names in the place are down on the list, and people began to wonder why—"

Parvis broke off to fumble in an inner pocket. "Here," he continued, "here's an account of the whole thing from the *Sentinel*—a little sensational, of course. But I guess you'd better look it over."

He held out a newspaper to Mary, who unfolded it slowly, remembering, as she did so, the evening when, in that same room, the perusal of a clipping from the *Sentinel* had first shaken the depths of her security.

As she opened the paper her eyes, shrinking from the glaring headlines, "Widow of Boyne's Victim Forced to Appeal for Aid," ran down the column of text to two portraits inserted in it. The first was her husband's, taken from a photograph made the year they had come to England. It was the picture of him that she liked best, the one that stood on the writing-table upstairs in her bedroom. As the eyes in the photograph met hers, she felt it would be impossible to read what was said of him, and closed her lids with the sharpness of the pain.

"I thought if you felt disposed to put your name down—" she heard Parvis continue.

She opened her eyes with an effort, and they fell on the other portrait. It was that of a youngish man, slightly built, with features somewhat blurred by the shadow of a projecting hat-brim.

Where had she seen that outline before? She stared at it confusedly, her heart hammering in her ears. Then she gave a cry.

"This is the man—the man who came for my husband!"

She heard Parvis start to his feet, and was dimly aware that she had slipped backward into the corner of the sofa, and that he was bending above her in alarm. She straightened herself and reached out for the paper, which she had dropped.

"It's the man! I should know him anywhere!" she persisted in a voice that sounded to her own ears like a scream.

Parvis's answer seemed to come to her from far off, down endless fog-muffled windings.

"Mrs. Boyne, you're not very well. Shall I call someone? Shall I get a glass of water?"

"No, no, no!" She threw herself toward him, her hand frantically clutching the newspaper. "I tell you, it's the man! I *know* him! He spoke to me in the garden!"

Parvis took the journal from her, directing his glasses to the portrait. "It can't be, Mrs. Boyne. It's Robert Elwell."

"Robert Elwell?" Her white stare seemed to travel into space. "Then it was Robert Elwell who came for him."

"Came for Boyne? The day he went away from here?" Parvis's voice dropped as hers rose. He bent over, laying a fraternal hand on her, as if to coax her gently back into her seat. "Why, Elwell was dead! Don't you remember?"

Mary sat with her eyes fixed on the picture, unconscious of what he was saying.

"Don't you remember Boyne's unfinished letter to me—the one you found on his desk that day? It was written just after he'd heard of Elwell's death." She noticed an odd shake in Parvis's unemotional voice. "Surely you remember!" he urged her.

Yes, she remembered: that was the profoundest horror of it. Elwell had died the day before her husband's disappearance; and this was Elwell's portrait; and it was the portrait of the man who had spoken to her in the garden. She lifted her head and looked slowly about the library. The library could have borne witness that it was also the portrait of the man who had come in that day to call Boyne from his unfinished letter. Through the misty surgings of her brain she heard the faint boom of half-forgotten words—words spoken by Alida Stair on the lawn at Pangbourne before Boyne and his wife had ever seen the house at Lyng, or had imagined that they might one day live there.

"This was the man who spoke to me," she repeated.

She looked again at Parvis. He was trying to conceal his disturbance under what he probably imagined to be an expression of indulgent commiseration; but the edges of his lips were blue. "He thinks me mad, but I'm not mad," she reflected; and suddenly there flashed upon her a way of justifying her strange affirmation.

She sat quiet, controlling the quiver of her lips, and waiting till she could trust her voice; then she said, looking straight at Parvis: "Will you answer me one question, please? When was it that Robert Elwell tried to kill himself?"

"When—when?" Parvis stammered.

"Yes; the date. Please try to remember."

She saw that he was growing still more afraid of her. "I have a reason," she insisted.

"Yes, yes. Only I can't remember. About two months before, I should say."

"I want the date," she repeated.

Parvis picked up the newspaper. "We might see here," he said, still humouring her. He ran his eyes down the page. "Here it is. Last October—the—"

She caught the words from him. "The 20th, wasn't it?" With a sharp look at her, he verified. "Yes, the 20th. Then you *did* know?"

"I know now." Her gaze continued to travel past him. "Sunday, the 20th—that was the day he came first."

Parvis's voice was almost inaudible. "Came *here* first?"

"Yes."

"You saw him twice, then?"

"Yes, twice." She just breathed it at him. "He came first on the 20th of October. I remember the date because it was the day we went up Meldon Steep for the first time." She felt a faint gasp of inward laughter at the thought that but for that she might have forgotten.

Parvis continued to scrutinize her, as if trying to intercept her gaze.

"We saw him from the roof," she went on. "He came down the lime-avenue toward the house. He was dressed just as he is in that picture. My husband saw him first. He was frightened, and ran down ahead of me; but there was no one there. He had vanished."

"Elwell had vanished?" Parvis faltered.

"Yes." Their two whispers seemed to grope for each other. "I couldn't think what had happened. I see now. He *tried* to come then; but he wasn't dead enough—he couldn't reach us. He had to wait for two months to die; and then he came back again—and Ned went with him."

She nodded at Parvis with the look of triumph of a child who has worked out a difficult puzzle. But suddenly she lifted her hands with a desperate gesture, pressing them to her temples.

"Oh, my God! I sent him to Ned—I told him where to go! I sent him to this room!" she screamed.

She felt the walls of books rush toward her, like inward falling ruins; and she heard Parvis, a long way off, through the ruins, crying to her and struggling to get at her. But she was numb to his touch, she did not know what he was saying. Through the tumult she heard but one clear note, the voice of Alida Stair speaking on the lawn at Pangbourne:

"You won't know till afterward," it said. "You won't know till long, long afterward."

Where Their Fire Is Not Quenched

MAY SINCLAIR

Actor Boris Karloff, who starred in dozens of horror films and knew whereof he spoke when it came to matters of the macabre, once said of May Sinclair's "Where Their Fire Is Not Quenched": *"[It] is as pretty a picture of Hell as I ever want to see." We can only add that the Hell it depicts in its quiet way is a particularly nasty one. May Sinclair (1865–1946) was a British writer (as well as a confirmed spiritualist and a tireless worker for women's suffrage) known during her lifetime primarily for such romances as* Divine Fire *(1904) and* The Three Sisters *(1914). But it is for her supernatural stories that she is remembered today, the best of which appear in two outstanding collections:* Uncanny Stories *(1923) and* The Intercessor and Other Stories *(1931).*

THERE was nobody in the orchard. Harriott Leigh went out, carefully, through the iron gate into the field. She had made the latch slip into its notch without a sound.

The path slanted widely up the field from the orchard gate to the stile under the elder tree. George Waring waited for her there.

Years afterwards, when she thought of George Waring she smelt the sweet, hot, wine-scent of the elder flowers. Years afterwards, when she smelt elder flowers she saw George Waring, with his beautiful, gentle face, like a poet's or a musician's, his black-blue eyes, and sleek, olive-brown hair. He was a naval lieutenant.

Yesterday he had asked her to marry him and she had consented. But her father hadn't, and she had come to tell him that and say good-bye before he left her. His ship was to sail the next day.

He was eager and excited. He couldn't believe that anything could stop their happiness, that anything he didn't want to happen could happen.

"Well?" he said.

"He's a perfect beast, George. He won't let us. He says we're too young."

"I was twenty last August," he said, aggrieved.

"And I shall be seventeen in September."

"And this is June. We're quite old, really. How long does he mean us to wait?"

"Three years."

"Three years before we can be engaged even—Why, we might be dead."

She put her arms round him to make him feel safe. They kissed; and the sweet, hot, wine-scent of the elder flowers mixed with their kisses. They stood, pressed close together, under the elder tree.

Across the yellow fields of charlock they heard the village clock strike seven. Up in the house a gong clanged.

"Darling, I must go," she said.

"Oh, stay—stay *five* minutes."

He pressed her close. It lasted five minutes, and five more. Then he was running fast down the road to the station, while Harriott went along the field-path, slowly, struggling with her tears.

"He'll be back in three months," she said. "I can live through three months."

But he never came back. There was something wrong with the engines of his ship, the *Alexandra*. Three weeks later she went down in the Mediterranean, and George with her.

Harriott said she didn't care how soon she died now. She was quite sure it would be soon, because she couldn't live without him.

Five years passed.

The two lines of beech trees stretched on and on, the whole length of the Park, a broad green drive between. When you came to the middle they branched off right and left in the form of a cross, and at the end of the right arm there was a white stucco pavilion with pillars and a three-cornered pediment like a Greek temple. At the end of the left arm, the west entrance to the Park, double gates and a side door.

Harriott, on her stone seat at the back of the pavilion, could see Stephen Philpotts the very minute he came through the side door.

He had asked her to wait for him there. It was the place he always chose to read his poems aloud in. The poems were a pretext. She knew what he was going to say. And she knew what she would answer.

There were elder bushes in flower at the back of the pavilion, and Harriott thought of George Waring. She told herself that George was nearer to her now than he could ever have been, living. If she married Stephen she would not be unfaithful, because she loved him with another part of herself. It was not as though Stephen were taking George's place. She loved Stephen with her soul, in an unearthly way.

But her body quivered like a stretched wire when the door opened and the young man came towards her down the drive under the beech trees.

She loved him; she loved his slenderness, his darkness and sallow whiteness, his black eyes lighting up with the intellectual flame, the way his black hair swept back from his forehead, the way he walked, tiptoe, as if his feet were lifted with wings.

He sat down beside her. She could see his hands tremble. She felt that her moment was coming; it had come.

"I wanted to see you alone because there's something I must say to you. I don't quite know how to begin. . . ."

Her lips parted. She panted lightly.

"You've heard me speak of Sybill Foster?"

Her voice came stammering, "N-no, Stephen. Did you?"

"Well, I didn't mean to, till I knew it was all right. I only heard yesterday."

"Heard what?"

"Why, that she'll have me. Oh, Harriott—do you know what it's like to be terribly happy?"

She knew. She had known just now, the moment before he told her. She sat there, stone-cold and stiff, listening to his raptures, listening to her own voice saying she was glad.

Ten years passed.

Harriott Leigh sat waiting in the drawing-room of a small house in Maida Vale. She had lived there ever since her father's death two years before.

She was restless. She kept on looking at the clock to see if it was four, the hour that Oscar Wade had appointed. She was not sure that he would come, after she had sent him away yesterday.

She now asked herself, why, when she had sent him away yesterday, she had let him come to-day. Her motives were not altogether clear. If she really meant what she had said then, she oughtn't to let him come to her again. Never again.

She had shown him plainly what she meant. She could see

herself, sitting very straight in her chair, uplifted by a passionate integrity, while he stood before her, hanging his head, ashamed and beaten; she could feel again the throb in her voice as she kept on saying that she couldn't, she couldn't; he must see that she couldn't; that no, nothing would make her change her mind; she couldn't forget he had a wife; that he must think of Muriel.

To which he had answered savagely: "I needn't. That's all over. We only live together for the look of the thing."

And she, serenely, with great dignity: "And for the look of the thing, Oscar, we must leave off seeing each other. Please go."

"Do you mean it?"

She was not sure whether she were glad or sorry. She had had her moment of righteous exaltation and she had enjoyed it. But there was no joy in the weeks that followed. She had given up Oscar Wade because she didn't want him very much; and now she wanted him furiously, perversely, because she had given him up. Though he had no resemblance to her ideal, she couldn't live without him.

She dined with him again and again, till she knew Schnebler's Restaurant by heart, the white panelled walls picked out with gold; the white pillars, and the curling gold fronds of their capitals; the Turkey carpets, blue and crimson, soft under her feet; the thick crimson velvet cushions, that clung to her skirts; the glitter of silver and glass on the innumerable white circles of the tables. And the faces of the diners, red, white, pink, brown, grey and sallow, distorted and excited; the curled mouths that twisted as they ate; the convoluted electric bulbs pointing, pointing down at them, under the red, crinkled shades. All shimmering in a thick air that the red light stained as wine stains water.

And Oscar's face, flushed with his dinner. Always, when he leaned back from the table and brooded in silence she knew what he was thinking. His heavy eyelids would lift; she would find his eyes fixed on hers, wondering, considering.

She knew now what the end would be. She thought of George Waring, and Stephen Philpotts, and of her life, cheated. She hadn't chosen Oscar, she hadn't really wanted him; but now he had forced himself on her she couldn't afford to let him go. Since George died no man had loved her, no other man ever would. And she was sorry for him when she thought of him going from her, beaten and ashamed.

She was certain, before he was, of the end. Only she didn't know when and where and how it would come. That was what Oscar knew.

It came at the close of one of their evenings when they had dined in a private sitting-room. He said he couldn't stand the heat and noise of the public restaurant.

She went before him, up a steep, red-carpeted stair to a white door on the second landing.

From time to time they repeated the furtive, hidden adventure. Sometimes she met him in the room above Schnebler's. Sometimes, when her maid was out, she received him at her house in Maida Vale. But that was dangerous, not to be risked too often.

"Yes. We must never see each other again."

And he had gone then, ashamed and beaten.

She could see him, squaring his broad shoulders to meet the blow. And she was sorry for him. She told herself she had been unnecessarily hard. Why shouldn't they see each other again, now he understood where they must draw the line? Until yesterday the line had never been very clearly drawn. To-day she meant to ask him to forget what he had said to her. Once it was forgotten, they could go on being friends as if nothing had happened.

It was four o'clock. Half-past. Five. She had finished tea and given him up when, between the half-hour and six o'clock, he came.

He came as he had come a dozen times, with his measured, deliberate, thoughtful tread, carrying himself well braced, with a sort of held-in arrogance, his great shoulders heaving. He was a man of about forty, broad and tall, lean-flanked and short-necked, his straight, handsome features showing small and even in the big square face and in the flush that swamped it. The close-clipped, reddish-brown moustache bristled forwards from the pushed-out upper lip. His small, flat eyes shone, reddish-brown, eager and animal.

She liked to think of him when he was not there, but always at the first sight of him she felt a slight shock. Physically, he was very far from her admired ideal. So different from George Waring and Stephen Philpotts.

He sat down, facing her.

There was an embarrassed silence, broken by Oscar Wade.

"Well, Harriott, you said I could come." He seemed to be throwing the responsibility to her.

"So I suppose you've forgiven me," he said.

"Oh, yes, Oscar, I've forgiven you."

He said she'd better show it by coming to dine with him somewhere that evening.

She could give no reason to herself for going. She simply went.

He took her to a restaurant in Soho. Oscar Wade dined well, even extravagantly, giving each dish its importance. She liked his extravagance. He had none of the mean virtues.

It was over. His flushed, embarrassed silence told her what he was thinking. But when he had seen her home, he left her at her garden gate. He had thought better of it.

Oscar declared himself unspeakably happy. Harriott was not quite sure. This was love, the thing she had never had, that she had dreamed of, hungered and thirsted for; but now she had it she was not satisfied. Always she looked for something just beyond it, some mystic, heavenly rapture, always beginning to come, that never came. There was something about Oscar that repelled her. But because she had taken him for her lover, she couldn't bring herself to admit that it was a certain coarseness. She looked another way and pretended it wasn't there. To justify herself, she fixed her mind on his good qualities, his generosities, his strength, the way he had built up his engineering business. She made him take her over his works, and show her his great dynamos. She made him lend her the books he read. But always, when she tried to talk to him, he let her see that *that* wasn't what she was there for.

"My dear girl, we haven't time," he said. "It's waste of our priceless moments."

She persisted. "There's something wrong about it all if we can't talk to each other."

He was irritated. "Women never seem to consider that a man can get all the talk he wants from other men. What's wrong is our meeting in this unsatisfactory way. We ought to live together. It's the only sane thing. I would, only I don't want to break up Muriel's home and make her miserable."

"I thought you said she wouldn't care."

"My dear, she cares for her home and her position and the children. You forget the children."

Yes. She had forgotten the children. She had forgotten Muriel. She had left off thinking of Oscar as a man with a wife and children and a home.

He had a plan. His mother-in-law was coming to stay with Muriel in October and he would get away. He would go to Paris, and Harriott should come to him there. He could say he went on business. No need to lie about it; he *had* business in Paris.

He engaged rooms in an hotel in the rue de Rivioli. They spent two weeks there.

For three days Oscar was madly in love with Harriott and Harriott with him. As she lay awake she would turn on the light and look at him as he slept at her side. Sleep made him beautiful and innocent; it laid a fine, smooth tissue over his coarseness; it made his mouth gentle; it entirely hid his eyes.

In six days reaction had set in. At the end of the tenth day, Harriott, returning with Oscar from Montmartre, burst into a fit of crying. When questioned, she answered wildly that the Hotel Saint Pierre was too hideously ugly; it was getting on her nerves. Mercifully Oscar explained her state as fatigue following excitement. She tried hard to believe that she was miserable because her love was purer and more spiritual than Oscar's; but all the time she knew perfectly well she had cried from pure boredom.

She was in love with Oscar, and Oscar bored her. Oscar was in love with her, and she bored him. At close quarters, day in and day out, each was revealed to the other as an incredible bore.

At the end of the second week she began to doubt whether she had ever been really in love with him.

Her passion returned for a little while after they got back to London. Freed from the unnatural strain which Paris had put on them, they persuaded themselves that their romantic temperaments were better fitted to the old life of casual adventure.

Then, gradually, the sense of danger began to wake in them. They lived in perpetual fear, face to face with all the chances of discovery. They tormented themselves and each other by imagining possibilities that they would never have considered in their first fine moments. It was as though they were beginning to ask themselves if it were, after all, worth while running such awful risks, for all they got out of it. Oscar still swore that if he had been free he would have married her. He pointed out that his intentions at any rate were regular. But she asked herself: Would I marry *him*? Marriage would be the Hotel Saint Pierre all over again, without any possibility of escape. But, if she wouldn't marry him, was she in love with him? That was the test. Perhaps it was a good thing he wasn't free. Then she told herself that these doubts were morbid, and that the question wouldn't arise.

One evening Oscar called to see her. He had come to tell her that Muriel was ill.

"Seriously ill?"

"I'm afraid so. It's pleurisy. May turn to pneumonia. We shall know one way or another in the next few days."

A terrible fear seized upon Harriott. Muriel might die of her pleurisy; and if Muriel died, she would have to marry Oscar. He was looking at her queerly, as if he knew what she was thinking, and she could see that the same thought had occurred to him and that he was frightened too.

Muriel got well again; but their danger had enlightened them.

Muriel's life was now inconceivably precious to them both; she stood between them and that permanent union, which they dreaded and yet would not have the courage to refuse.

After enlightenment the rupture.

It came from Oscar, one evening when he sat with her in her drawing-room.

"Harriott," he said, "do you know I'm thinking seriously of settling down?"

"How do you mean, settling down?"

"Patching it up with Muriel, poor girl. . . . Has it never occurred to you that this little affair of ours can't go on for ever?"

"You don't want it to go on?"

"I don't want to have any humbug about it. For God's sake, let's be straight. If it's done, it's done. Let's end it decently."

"I see. You want to get rid of me."

"That's a beastly way of putting it."

"Is there any way that isn't beastly? The whole thing's beastly. I should have thought you'd have stuck to it now you've made it what you wanted. When I haven't an ideal, I haven't a single illusion, when you've destroyed everything you didn't want."

"What didn't I want?"

"The clean, beautiful part of it. The part *I* wanted."

"My part at least was real. It was cleaner and more beautiful than all that putrid stuff you wrapped it up in. You were a hypocrite, Harriott, and I wasn't. You're a hypocrite now if you say you weren't happy with me."

"I was never really happy. Never for one moment. There was always something I missed. Something you didn't give me. Perhaps you couldn't."

"No. I wasn't spiritual enough," he sneered.

"You were not. And you made me what you were."

"Oh, I noticed that you were always very spiritual *after* you'd got what you wanted."

"What I wanted?" she cried. "Oh, my God—"

"If you ever knew what you wanted."

"What—I—wanted," she repeated, drawing out her bitterness.

"Come," he said, "why not be honest? Face facts. I was awfully gone on you. You were awfully gone on me—once. We got tired of each other and it's over. But at least you might own we had a good time while it lasted."

"A good time?"

"Good enough for me."

"For you, because for you love only means one thing. Everything that's high and noble in it you dragged down to that, till there's nothing left for us but that. *That's* what you made of love."

Twenty years passed.

It was Oscar who died first, three years after the rupture. He did it suddenly one evening, falling down in a fit of apoplexy.

His death was an immense relief to Harriott. Perfect security had been impossible as long as he was alive. But now there wasn't a living soul who knew her secret.

Still, in the first moment of shock, Harriott told herself that Oscar dead would be nearer to her than ever. She forgot how little she had wanted him to be near her, alive. And long before the twenty years had passed she had contrived to persuade herself that he had never been near to her at all. It was incredible that she had ever known such a person as Oscar Wade. As for their affair, she couldn't think of Harriott Leigh as the sort of woman to whom such a thing could happen. Schnebler's and the Hotel Saint Pierre ceased to figure among prominent images of her past. Her memories, if she had allowed herself to remember, would have clashed disagreeably with the reputation for sanctity which she had now acquired.

For Harriott at fifty-two was the friend and helper of the Reverend Clement Farmer, Vicar of St. Mary the Virgin, Maida Vale. She worked as a deaconess in his parish, wearing the uniform of a deaconess, the semi-religious gown, the cloak, the bonnet and veil, the cross and rosary, the holy smile. She was also secretary to the Maida Vale and Kilburn Home for Fallen Girls.

Her moments of excitement came when Clement Farmer, the lean, austere likeness of Stephen Philpotts, in his cassock and lace-bordered surplice, issued from the vestry, when he mounted the pulpit, when he stood before the altar rails and lifted up his arms in the Benediction; her moments of ecstasy when she received the Sacrament from his hands. And she had moments of calm happiness when his study door closed on their communion. All these moments were saturated with a solemn holiness.

And they were insignificant compared with the moment of her dying.

She lay dozing in her white bed under the black crucifix with the ivory Christ. The basins and medicine bottles had been cleared from the table by her pillow; it was spread for the last rites. The priest moved quietly about the room, arranging the candles, the Prayer Book and the Holy Sacrament. Then he drew a chair to her bedside and watched with her, waiting for her to come up out of her doze.

She woke suddenly. Her eyes were fixed upon him. She had a flash of lucidity. She was dying, and her dying made her supremely important to Clement Farmer.

"Are you ready?" he asked.

"Not yet. I think I'm afraid. Make me not afraid."

He rose and lit the two candles on the altar. He took down the crucifix from the wall and stood it against the foot-rail of the bed.

She sighed. That was not what she had wanted.

"You will not be afraid now," he said.

"I'm not afraid of the hereafter. I suppose you get used to it. Only it may be terrible just at first."

"Our first state will depend very much on what we are thinking of at our last hour."

"There'll be my—confession," she said.

"And after it you will receive the Sacrament. Then you will have your mind fixed firmly upon God and your Redeemer. . . . Do you feel able to make your confession now, Sister? Everything is ready."

Her mind went back over her past and found Oscar Wade there. She wondered: should she confess to him about Oscar Wade? One moment she thought it was possible; the next she knew that she couldn't. She could not. It wasn't necessary. For twenty years he had not been part of her life. No. She wouldn't confess about Oscar Wade. She had been guilty of other sins.

She made a careful selection.

"I have cared too much for the beauty of this world. . . . I have failed in charity to my poor girls. Because of my intense repugnance to their sin. . . . I have thought, often, about—people I love, when I should have been thinking about God."

After that she received the Sacrament.

"Now," he said, "there is nothing to be afraid of."

"I won't be afraid if—if you would hold my hand."

He held it. And she lay still a long time, with her eyes shut. Then he heard her murmuring something. He stooped close.

"This—is—dying. I thought it would be horrible. And it's bliss. . . . Bliss."

The priest's hand slackened, as if at the bidding of some wonder. She gave a weak cry."

"Oh—don't let me go."

His grasp tightened.

"Try," he said, "to think about God. Keep on looking at the crucifix."

"If I look," she whispered, "you won't let go my hand?"

"I will not let you go."

He held it till it was wrenched from him in the last agony.

She lingered for some hours in the room where these things had happened.

Its aspect was familiar and yet unfamiliar, and slightly repugnant to her. The altar, the crucifix, the lighted candles, suggested some tremendous and awful experience the details of which she was not able to recall. She seemed to remember that they had been connected in some way with the sheeted body on the bed; but the nature of the connection was not clear; and she did not associate the dead body with herself. When the nurse came in and laid it out, she saw that it was the body of a middle-aged woman. Her own living body was that of a young woman of about thirty-two.

Her mind had no past and no future, no sharp-edged, coherent memories, and no idea of anything to be done next.

Then, suddenly, the room began to come apart before her eyes, to split into shafts of floor and furniture and ceiling that shifted and were thrown by their commotion into different planes. They leaned slanting at every possible angle; they crossed and overlaid each other with a transparent mingling of dislocated perspectives, like reflections fallen on an interior seen behind glass.

The bed and the sheeted body slid away somewhere out of sight. She was standing by the door that still remained in position.

She opened it and found herself in the street, outside a building of yellowish-grey brick and freestone, with a tall slated spire. Her mind came together with a palpable click of recognition. This object was the Church of St. Mary the Virgin, Maida Vale. She could hear the droning of the organ. She opened the door and slipped in.

She had gone back into a definite space and time, and recovered a certain limited section of coherent memory. She remembered the rows of pitch-pine benches, with their Gothic peaks and mouldings; the stone-coloured walls and pillars with their chocolate stencilling; the hanging rings of lights along the aisles of the nave; the high altar with its lighted candles, and the polished brass cross, twinkling. These things were somehow permanent and real, adjusted to the image that now took possession of her.

She knew what she had come there for. The service was over. The choir had gone from the chancel; the sacristan moved before the altar, putting out the candles. She walked up the middle aisle to a seat that she knew under the pulpit. She knelt down and covered her face with her hands. Peeping sideways through her fingers, she could see the door of the vestry on her left at the end of the north aisle. She watched it steadily.

Up in the organ loft the organist drew out the Recessional, slowly and softly, to its end in the two solemn, vibrating chords.

The vestry door opened and Clement Farmer came out, dressed in his black cassock. He passed before her, close, close outside the bench where she knelt. He paused at the opening. He was waiting for her. There was something he had to say.

She stood up and went towards him. He still waited. He didn't move to make way for her. She came close, closer than she had ever come to him, so close that his features grew indistinct. She bent her head back, peering short-sightedly, and found herself looking into Oscar Wade's face.

He stood still, horribly still, and close, barring her passage.

She drew back; his heaving shoulders followed her. He leaned forward, covering her with his eyes. She opened her mouth to scream and no sound came.

She was afraid to move lest he should move with her. The heaving of his shoulders terrified her.

One by one the lights in the side aisles were going out. The lights in the middle aisle would go next. They had gone. If she didn't get away she would be shut up with him there, in the appalling darkness.

She turned and moved towards the north aisle, groping, steadying herself by the book ledge.

When she looked back, Oscar Wade was not there.

Then she remembered that Oscar Wade was dead. Therefore, what she had seen was not Oscar; it was his ghost. He was dead; dead seventeen years ago. She was safe from him for ever.

When she came out on to the steps of the church she saw that the road it stood in had changed. It was not the road she remembered. The pavement on this side was raised slightly and covered in. It ran under a succession of arches. It was a long gallery walled with glittering shop windows on the side; on the other a line of tall grey columns divided it from the street.

She was going along the arcades of the rue de Rivoli. Ahead of her she could see the edge of an immense grey pillar jutting out. That was the porch of the Hotel Saint Pierre. The revolving glass door swung forward to receive her; she crossed the grey, sultry vestibule under the pillared arches. She knew it. She knew the porter's shining, wine-coloured, mahogany pen on her left, and the shining, wine-coloured, mahogany barrier of the clerk's bureau on her right; she made straight for the great grey carpeted staircase; she climbed the endless flights that turned round and round the caged-in shaft of the well, past the latticed doors of the lift, and came up on to a landing that she knew, and into the long, ash-grey, foreign corridor lit by a dull window at one end.

It was there that the horror of the place came on her. She had no longer any memory of St. Mary's Church, so that she was unaware of her backward course through time. All space and time were here.

She remembered she had to go to the left, the left.

But there was something there; where the corridor turned by the window; at the end of all the corridors. If she went the other way she would escape it.

The corridor stopped there. A blank wall. She was driven back past the stairhead to the left.

At the corner, by the window, she turned down another long ash-grey corridor on her right, and to the right again where the night-light sputtered on the table-flap at the turn.

This third corridor was dark and secret and depraved. She knew the soiled walls, and the warped door at the end. There was a sharp-pointed streak of light at the top. She could see the number on it now, 107.

Something had happened there. If she went in it would happen again.

Oscar Wade was in the room waiting for her behind the closed door. She felt him moving about in there. She leaned forward, her ear to the key-hole, and listened. She could hear the measured, deliberate, thoughtful footsteps. They were coming from the bed to the door.

She turned and ran; her knees gave way under her; she sank and ran on, down the long grey corridors and the stairs, quick and blind, a hunted beast seeking for cover, hearing his feet coming after her.

The revolving doors caught her and pushed her out into the street.

The strange quality of her state was this, that it had no time. She remembered dimly that there had once been a thing called time; but she had forgotten altogether what it was like. She was aware of things happening and about to happen; she fixed them by the place they occupied, and measured their duration by the space she went through.

So now she thought: If I could only go back and get to the place where it hadn't happened.

To get back farther—

She was walking now on a white road that went between broad grass borders. To the right and left were the long raking lines of the hills, curve after curve, shimmering in a thin mist.

The road dropped to the green valley. It mounted the humped bridge over the river. Beyond it she saw the twin gables of the grey house pricked up over the high, grey garden wall. The tall iron gate stood in front of it between the ball-topped stone pillars.

And now she was in a large, low-ceilinged room with drawn blinds. She was standing before the wide double bed. It was her father's bed. The dead body, stretched out in the middle under the drawn white sheet, was her father's body.

The outline of the sheet sank from the peak of the upturned toes to the shin bone, and from the high bridge of the nose to the chin.

She lifted the sheet and folded it back across the breast of the dead man. The face she saw then was Oscar Wade's face, stilled and smoothed in the innocence of sleep, the supreme innocence of death. She stared at it, fascinated, in a cold, pitiless joy.

Oscar was dead.

She remembered how he used to lie like that beside her in the room in the Hotel Saint Pierre, on his back with his hands folded on his waist, his mouth half open, his big chest rising and falling. If he was dead, it would never happen again. She would be safe.

The dead face frightened her, and she was about to cover it up again when she was aware of a light heaving, a rhythmical rise and fall. As she drew the sheet up tighter, the hands under it began to struggle convulsively, the broad ends of the fingers appeared above the edge, clutching it to keep it down. The mouth opened; the eyes opened; the whole face stared back at her in a look of agony and horror.

Then the body drew itself forward from the hips and sat up, its eyes peering into her eyes; he and she remained for an instant motionless, each held there by the other's fear.

Suddenly she broke away, turned and ran, out of the room, out of the house.

She stood at the gate, looking up and down the road, not knowing by which way she must go to escape Oscar. To the right, over the bridge and up the hill and across the downs she would come to the arcades of the rue de Rivoli and the dreadful grey corridors of the hotel. To the left the road went through the village.

If she could get further back she would be safe, out of Oscar's reach. Standing by her father's death-bed she had been young, but not young enough. She must get back to the place where she was younger still, to the Park and the green drive under the beech trees and the white pavilion at the cross. She knew how to find it. At the end of the village the high road ran right and left, east and west, under the Park walls; the south gate stood there at the top looking down the narrow street.

She ran towards it through the village, past the long grey barns of Goodyer's farm, past the grocer's shop, past the yellow front and blue sign of the "Queen's Head," past the post office, with its one black window blinking under its vine, past the church and the yew-trees in the churchyard, to where the south gate made a delicate black pattern on the green grass.

These things appeared insubstantial, drawn back behind a sheet of air that shimmered over them like thin glass. They opened out, floated past and away from her; and instead of the high road and Park walls she saw a London street of dingy white façades, and instead of the south gate the swinging glass doors of Schnebler's Restaurant.

The glass doors swung open and she passed into the restaurant. The scene beat on her with the hard impact of reality: the white and gold panels, the white pillars and their curling gold capitals, the white circles of the tables, glittering, the flushed faces of the diners, moving mechanically.

She was driven forward by some irresistible compulsion to a table in the corner, where a man sat alone. The table napkin he was using hid his mouth, and jaw, and chest; and she was not sure of the upper part of the face above the straight, drawn edge. It dropped; and she saw Oscar Wade's face. She came to him, dragged, without power to resist; she sat down beside him, and he leaned to her over the table; she could feel the warmth of his red, congested face; the smell of wine floated towards her on his thick whisper.

"I knew you would come."

She ate and drank with him in silence, nibbling and sipping slowly, staving off the abominable moment it would end in.

At last they got up and faced each other. His long bulk stood before her, above her; she could almost feel the vibration of its power.

"Come," he said. "Come."

And she went before him, slowly, slipping out through the maze of the tables, hearing behind her Oscar's measured, deliberate, thoughtful tread. The steep, red-carpeted staircase rose up before her.

She swerved from it, but he turned her back.

"You know the way," he said.

At the top of the flight she found the white door of the room she knew. She knew the long windows guarded by drawn muslin blinds; the gilt looking-glass over the chimney-piece that reflected Oscar's head and shoulders grotesquely between two white porcelain babies with bulbous limbs and garlanded loins, she knew the sprawling stain on the drab carpet by the table, the shabby, infamous couch behind the screen.

They moved about the room, turning and turning in it like beasts in a cage, uneasy, inimical, avoiding each other.

At last they stood still, he at the window, she at the door, the length of the room between.

"It's no good your getting away like that," he said. "There couldn't be any other end to it—to what we did."

"But that *was* ended."

"Ended there, but not here."

"Ended for ever. We've done with it for ever."

"We haven't. We've got to begin again. And go on. And go on."

"Oh, no. No. Anything but that."

"There isn't anything else."

"We can't. We can't. Don't you remember how it bored us?"

"Remember? Do you suppose I'd touch you if I could help it? . . . That's what we're here for. We must. We must."

"No. No. I shall get away—now."

She turned to the door to open it.

"You can't," he said. "The door's locked."

"Oscar—what did you do that for?"

"We always did it. Don't you remember?"

She turned to the door again and shook it; she beat on it with her hands.

"It's no use, Harriott. If you got out now you'd only have to come back again. You might stave it off for an hour or so, but what's that in an immortality?"

"Immortality?"

"That's what we're in for."

"Time enough to talk about immortality when we're dead. . . . Ah—"

They were being drawn towards each other across the room, moving slowly, like figures in some monstrous and appalling dance, their heads thrown back over their shoulders, their faces turned from the horrible approach. Their arms rose slowly, heavy with intolerable reluctance; they stretched them out towards each other, aching, as if they held up an overpowering weight. Their feet dragged and were drawn.

Suddenly her knees sank under her; she shut her eyes; all her being went down before him in darkness and terror.

It was over. She had got away, she was going back, back, to the green drive of the Park, between the beech trees, where Oscar had never been, where he would never find her. When she passed through the south gate her memory became suddenly young and clean. She forgot the rue de Rivoli and the Hotel Saint Pierre; she forgot Schnebler's Restaurant and the room at the top of the stairs. She was back in her youth. She was Harriott Leigh going to wait for Stephen Philpotts in the pavilion opposite the west gate. She could feel herself, a slender figure moving fast over the grass between the lines of the great beech trees. The freshness of her youth was upon her.

She came to the heart of the drive where it branched right and left in the form of a cross. At the end of the right arm the white Greek temple, with its pediment and pillars, gleamed against the wood.

She was sitting on their seat at the back of the pavilion, watching the side door that Stephen would come in by.

The door was pushed open; he came towards her, light and young, skimming between the beech trees with his eager, tiptoeing stride. She rose up to meet him. She gave a cry.

"Stephen!"

It had been Stephen. She had seen him coming. But

the man who stood before her between the pillars of the pavilion was Oscar Wade.

And now she was walking along the field-path that slanted from the orchard door to the stile; further and further back, to where young George Waring waited for her under the elder tree. The smell of the elder flowers came to her over the field. She could feel on her lips and in all her body the sweet, innocent excitement of her youth.

"George, oh, George?"

As she went along the field-path she had seen him. But the man who stood waiting for her under the elder tree was Oscar Wade.

"I told you it's no use getting away, Harriott. Every path brings you back to me. You'll find me at every turn."

"But how did you get *here*?"

"As I got into the pavilion. As I got into your father's room, on to his death bed. Because I *was* there. I am in all your memories."

"My memories are innocent. How could you take my father's place, and Stephen's, and George Waring's? You?"

"Because I did take them."

"Never. My love for *them* was innocent."

"Your love for me was part of it. You think the past affects the future. Has it never struck you that the future may affect the past? In your innocence there was the beginning of your sin. You *were* what you *were to be*."

"I shall get away," she said.

"And, this time, I shall go with you."

The stile, the elder tree, and the field floated away from her. She was going under the beech trees down the Park drive towards the south gate and the village, slinking close to the right-hand row of trees. She was aware that Oscar Wade was going with her under the left-hand row, keeping even with her, step by step, and tree by tree. And presently there was grey pavement under her feet and a row of grey pillars on her right hand. They were walking side by side down the rue de Rivoli towards the hotel.

They were sitting together now on the edge of the dingy white bed. Their arms hung by their sides, heavy and limp, their heads drooped, averted. Their passion weighed on them with the unbearable, unescapable boredom of immortality.

"Oscar—how long will it last?"

"I can't tell you. I don't know whether *this* is one moment of eternity, or the eternity of one moment."

"It must end some time," she said. "Life doesn't go on for ever. We shall die."

"Die? We *have* died. Don't you know what this is? Don't you know where you are? This is death. We're dead, Harriott. We're in hell."

"Yes. There can't be anything worse than this."

"This isn't the worst. We're not quite dead yet, as long as we've life in us to turn and run and get away from each other; as long as we can escape into our memories. But when you've got back to the farthest memory of all and there's nothing beyond it—When there's no memory but this—

"In the last hell we shall not run away any longer; we shall find no more roads, no more passages, no more open doors. We shall have no need to look for each other.

"In the last death we shall be shut up in this room, behind that locked door, together. We shall lie here together, for ever and ever, joined so fast that even God can't put us asunder. We shall be one flesh and one spirit, one sin repeated for ever, and ever; spirit loathing flesh, flesh loathing spirit; you and I loathing each other."

"Why? Why?" she cried.

"Because that's all that's left us. That's what you made of love."

The darkness came down swamping, it blotted out the room. She was walking along a garden path between high borders of phlox and larkspur and lupin. They were taller than she was, their flowers swayed and nodded above her head. She tugged at the tall stems and had no strength to break them. She was a little thing.

She said to herself then that she was safe. She had gone back so far that she was a child again; she had the blank innocence of childhood. To be a child, to go small under the heads of the lupins, to be blank and innocent, without memory, was to be safe.

The walk led her out through a yew hedge on to a bright green lawn. In the middle of the lawn there was a shallow round pond in a ring of rockery cushioned with small flowers, yellow and white and purple. Gold-fish swam in the olive brown water. She would be safe when she saw the gold-fish swimming towards her. The old one with the white scales would come up first, pushing up his nose, making bubbles in the water.

At the bottom of the lawn there was a privet hedge cut by a broad path that went through the orchard. She knew what she would find there; her mother was in the orchard. She would lift her up in her arms to play with the hard red balls of the apples that hung from the tree. She had got back to the farthest memory of all; there was nothing beyond it.

There would be an iron gate in the wall of the orchard. It would lead into a field.

Something was different here, something that frightened her. An ash-grey door instead of an iron gate.

She pushed it open and came into the last corridor of the Hotel Saint Pierre.

The Lamp

AGATHA CHRISTIE

Agatha Christie is widely regarded as the grande dame of mystery fiction, and her characters such as Miss Jane Marple and Inspector Hercule Poirot have delighted readers for over half a century. Lesser known—but no less excellent—are her tales of the supernatural. A series of these, collected in The Mysterious Mr. Quin *(1930), features detection, but there the similarity to Poirot and Marple stops. The reader is confronted by a perplexity—is Harley Quin a supernatural being, or is he not?—and the answer is left ambiguous. In* "The Lamp," *a more generic, nonseries horror story, we encounter yet another Christie tradition—a distinguished old house—but it is different from the author's usual settings. There is no murderer lurking in this particular house, only a grieving presence that longs to be set free.*

IT WAS undoubtedly an old house. The whole square was old, with that disapproving dignified old age often met with in a cathedral town. But No. 19 gave the impression of an elder among elders; it had a veritable patriarchal solemnity; it towered greyest of the grey, haughtiest of the haughty, chillest of the chill. Austere, forbidding, and stamped with that particular desolation attaching to all houses that have been long untenanted, it reigned above the other dwellings.

In any other town it would have been freely labelled "haunted," but Weyminster was averse from ghosts and considered them hardly respectable except as the appanage of a "county family." So No. 19 was never alluded to as a haunted house; but nevertheless it remained, year after year, "To Be Let or Sold."

Mrs. Lancaster looked at the house with approval as she drove up with the talkative house agent, who was in an unusually hilarious mood at the idea of getting No. 19 off his books. He inserted the key in the door without ceasing his appreciative comments.

"How long has the house been empty?" inquired Mrs. Lancaster, cutting short his flow of language rather brusquely.

Mr. Raddish (of Raddish and Foplow) became slightly confused.

"Er—er—some time," he remarked blandly.

"So I should think," said Mrs. Lancaster dryly.

The dimly lighted hall was chill with a sinister chill. A more imaginative woman might have shivered, but this woman happened to be eminently practical. She was tall, with much dark brown hair just tinged with grey and rather cold blue eyes.

She went over the house from attic to cellar, asking a pertinent question from time to time. The inspection over, she came back into one of the front rooms looking out on the square and faced the agent with a resolute mien.

"What is the matter with the house?"

Mr. Raddish was taken by surprise.

"Of course, an unfurnished house is always a little gloomy," he parried feebly.

"Nonsense," said Mrs. Lancaster. "The rent is ridiculously low for such a house—purely nominal. There must be some reason for it. I suppose the house is haunted?"

Mr. Raddish gave a nervous little start but said nothing.

Mrs. Lancaster eyed him keenly. After a few moments she spoke again.

"Of course that is all nonsense. I don't believe in ghosts or anything of that sort, and personally it is no deterrent to my taking the house; but servants, unfortunately, are very credulous and easily frightened. It would be kind of you to tell me exactly what—what thing *is* supposed to haunt this place."

"I—er—really don't know," stammered the house agent.

"I am sure you must," said the lady quietly. "I cannot take the house without knowing. What was it? A murder?"

"Oh, no!" cried Mr. Raddish, shocked by the idea of anything so alien to the respectability of the square. "It's—it's—only a child."

"A child?"

"Yes."

"I don't know the story exactly," he continued reluctantly. "Of course, there are all kinds of different versions, but I believe that about thirty years ago a man going by the name of Williams took Number Nineteen. Nothing was known of him; he kept no servants; he had no friends; he seldom went out in the daytime. He had one child, a little boy. After he had been there about two months, he went up to London, and had barely set foot in the metropolis before he was recognized as being a man 'wanted' by the police on some charge—exactly what, I do not know. But it must have been a grave one, because, sooner than give himself up, he shot himself. Meanwhile, the child lived on here, alone in the house. He had food for a little time, and he waited day after day for his father's return. Unfortunately, it had been impressed upon him that he was never under any circumstances to go out of the house or to speak to anyone. He was a weak, ailing, little creature, and did not dream of disobeying this command. In the night, the neighbours, not knowing that his father had gone away, often heard him sobbing in the awful loneliness and desolation of the empty house.''

Mr. Raddish paused.

''And—er—the child starved to death,'' he concluded in the same tones as he might have announced that it had just begun to rain.

''And it is the child's ghost that is supposed to haunt the place?'' asked Mrs. Lancaster.

''It is nothing of consequence really,'' Mr. Raddish hastened to assure her. ''There's nothing *seen*, not *seen*, only people say, ridiculous, of course, but they do say they hear—the child—crying, you know.''

Mrs. Lancaster moved towards the front door.

''I like the house very much,'' she said. ''I shall get nothing as good for the price. I will think it over and let you know.''

''It really looks very cheerful, doesn't it, Papa?''

Mrs. Lancaster surveyed her new domain with approval. Gay rugs, well-polished furniture, and many knickknacks, had quite transformed the gloomy aspect of No. 19.

She spoke to a thin, bent old man with stooping shoulders and a delicate mystical face. Mr. Winburn did not resemble his daughter; indeed no greater contrast could be imagined than that presented by her resolute practicalness and his dreamy abstraction.

''Yes,'' he answered with a smile, ''no one would dream the house was haunted.''

''Papa, don't talk nonsense! On our first day, too.''

Mr. Winburn smiled.

"Very well, my dear, we will agree that there are no such things as ghosts."

"And please," continued Mrs. Lancaster, "don't say a word before Geoff. He's so imaginative."

Geoff was Mrs. Lancaster's little boy. The family consisted of Mr. Winburn, his widowed daughter, and Geoffrey.

Rain had begun to beat against the window—pitter-patter, pitter-patter.

"Listen," said Mr. Winburn. "Is it not like little footsteps?"

"It's more like rain," said Mrs. Lancaster, with a smile.

"But *that, that* is a footstep," cried her father, bending forward to listen.

Mrs. Lancaster laughed outright.

"That's Geoff coming downstairs."

Mr. Winburn was obliged to laugh, too. They were having tea in the hall, and he had been sitting with his back to the staircase. He now turned his chair round to face it.

Little Geoffrey was coming down, rather slowly and sedately, with a child's awe of a strange place. The stairs were of polished oak, uncarpeted. He came across and stood by his mother. Mr. Winburn gave a slight start. As the child was crossing the floor, he distinctly heard another pair of footsteps on the stairs, as of someone following Geoffrey. Dragging footsteps, curiously painful they were. Then he shrugged his shoulders incredulously. "The rain, no doubt," he thought.

"I'm looking at the sponge cakes," remarked Geoff with the admirably detached air of one who points out an interesting fact.

His mother hastened to comply with the hint.

"Well, Sonny, how do you like your new home?" she asked.

"Lots," replied Geoffrey with his mouth generously filled. "Pounds and pounds and pounds." After this last assertion, which was evidently expressive of the deepest contentment, he relapsed into silence, only anxious to remove the sponge cake from the sight of man in the least time possible.

Having bolted the last mouthful, he burst forth into speech.

"Oh! Mummy, there's attics here, Jane says; and can I go at once and eggzplore them? And there might be a secret door. Jane says there isn't, but I think there must be, and, anyhow, I know there'll be pipes, water pipes (with a face full of ectasy), and can I play with them, and, oh! can I go and see the boi-i-ler?" He spun out the last word with such evident rapture that his grandfather felt ashamed to reflect that this peerless delight of childhood only conjured up to his imagination the picture of hot water that wasn't hot, and heavy and numerous plumber's bills.

"We'll see about the attics tomorrow, darling," said Mrs. Lancaster. "Suppose you fetch your bricks and build a nice house, or an engine."

"Don't want to build an 'ouse."

"House."

"House, or h'engine h'either."

"Build a boiler," suggested his grandfather.

Geoffrey brightened.

"With pipes?"

"Yes, lots of pipes."

Geoffrey ran away happily to fetch his bricks.

The rain was still falling. Mr. Winburn listened. Yes, it must have been the rain he had heard; but it did sound like footsteps.

He had a queer dream that night.

He dreamt that he was walking through a town, a great city it seemed to him. But it was a children's city; there were no grown-up people there, nothing but children, crowds of them. In his dream they all rushed to the stranger crying: "Have you brought him?" It seemed that he understood what they meant and shook his head sadly. When they saw this, the children turned away and began to cry, sobbing bitterly.

The city and the children faded away and he awoke to find himself in bed, but the sobbing was still in his ears. Though wide awake, he heard it distinctly; and he remembered that Geoffrey slept on the floor below, while this sound of a child's sorrow descended from above. He sat up and struck a match. Instantly the sobbing ceased.

Mr. Winburn did not tell his daughter of the dream or its sequel. That it was no trick of his imagination, he was convinced; indeed soon afterwards he heard it again in the daytime. The wind was howling in the chimney but *this* was a separate sound—distinct, unmistakable: pitiful little heartbroken sobs.

He found out, too, that he was not the only one to hear them. He overheard the housemaid saying to the parlour-maid that she "didn't think as that there nurse was kind to Master Geoffrey, she'd 'eard 'im crying 'is little 'eart out only that very morning." Geoffrey had come down to breakfast and lunch beaming with health and happiness; and Mr. Winburn knew that it was not Geoff who had been crying, but that other child whose dragging footsteps had startled him more than once.

Mrs. Lancaster alone never heard anything. Her ears were not perhaps attuned to catch sounds from another world.

Yet one day she also received a shock.

"Mummy," said Geoff plaintively. "I wish you'd let me play with that little boy."

Mrs. Lancaster looked up from her writing table with a smile.

"What little boy, dear?"

"I don't know his name. He was in an attic, sitting on the floor crying, but he ran away when he saw me. I suppose he was shy (with slight contempt), not like a big boy, and then, when I was in the nursery building, I saw him standing in the door watching me build, and he looked so awful lonely and as though he wanted to play wiv me. I said: 'Come and build a h'engine,' but he didn't say nothing, just looked as—as though he saw a lot of chocolates, and his mummy had told him not to touch them." Geoff sighed, sad personal reminiscences evidently recurring to him. "But when I asked Jane who he was and told her I wanted to play wiv him, she said there wasn't no little boy in the 'ouse and not to tell naughty stories. I don't love Jane at all."

Mrs. Lancaster got up.

"Jane was right. There was no little boy."

"But I saw him. Oh! Mummy, do let me play wiv him, he did look so awful lonely and unhappy. I do want to do something to 'make him better.' "

Mrs. Lancaster was about to speak again, but her father shook his head.

"Geoff," he said very gently, "that poor little boy *is* lonely, and perhaps you may do something to comfort him; but you must find out how by yourself—like a puzzle—do you see?"

"Is it because I am getting big I must do it all my lone?"

"Yes, because you are getting big."

As the boy left the room, Mrs. Lancaster turned to her father impatiently.

"Papa, this is absurd. To encourage the boy to believe the servants' idle tales!"

"No servant has told the child anything," said the old man gently. "He's seen—what I hear, what I could see perhaps if I were his age."

"But it's such nonsense! Why don't I see it or hear it?"

Mr. Winburn smiled, a curiously tired smile, but did not reply.

"Why?" repeated his daughter. "And why did you tell him he could help—the—thing. It's—it's all so impossible."

The old man looked at her with his thoughtful glance.

"Why not?" he said. "Do you remember these words:

"What Lamp has Destiny to guide
Her little Children stumbling in the Dark?"
"A Blind Understanding," Heaven replied.

"Geoffrey has that—a blind understanding. All children possess it. It is only as we grow older that we lose it, that we cast it away from us. Sometimes, when we are quite old, a faint gleam comes back to us, but the Lamp burns brightest in childhood. That is why I think Geoffrey may help."

"I don't understand," murmured Mrs. Lancaster feebly.

"No more do I. That—that child is in trouble and wants—to be set free. But how? I do not know, but—it's awful to think of it—sobbing its heart out—a *child.*"

A month after this conversation Geoffrey fell very ill. The east wind had been severe, and he was not a strong child. The doctor shook his head and said that it was a grave case. To Mr. Winburn he divulged more and confessed that the case was quite hopeless. "The child would never have lived to grow up, under any circumstances," he added. "There has been serious lung trouble for a long time."

It was when nursing Geoff that Mrs. Lancaster became aware of that—other child. At first the sobs were an indistinguishable part of the wind, but gradually they became more distinct, more unmistakable. Finally she heard them in moments of dead calm: a child's sobs—dull, hopeless, heartbroken.

Geoff grew steadily worse and in his delirium he spoke of the "little boy" again and again. "I do want to help him get away, I do!" he cried.

Succeeding the delirium there came a state of lethargy. Geoffrey lay very still, hardly breathing, sunk in oblivion. There was nothing to do but wait and watch. Then there came a still night, clear and calm, without one breath of wind.

Suddenly the child stirred. His eyes opened. He looked past his mother towards the open door. He tried to speak and she bent down to catch the half-breathed words.

"All right, I'm comin'," he whispered; then he sank back.

The mother felt suddenly terrified; she crossed the room to her father. Somewhere near them the other child was laughing. Joyful, contented, triumphant, the silvery laughter echoed through the room.

"I'm frightened; I'm frightened," she moaned.

He put his arm round her protectingly. A sudden gust of wind made them both start, but it passed swiftly and left the air quiet as before.

The laughter had ceased and there crept to them a faint sound, so faint as hardly to be heard, but growing louder till they could distinguish it. Footsteps—light footsteps, swiftly departing.

Pitter-patter, pitter-patter, they ran—those well-known halting little feet. Yet—surely—now *other* footsteps suddenly mingled with them, moving with a quicker and a lighter tread.

With one accord they hastened to the door.

Down, down, down, past the door, close to them, pitter-patter, pitter-patter, went the unseen feet of the little children together.

Mrs. Lancaster looked up wildly.

"There are *two* of them—*two!*"

Grey with sudden fear, she turned towards the cot in the corner, but her father restrained her gently and pointed away.

"There," he said simply.

Pitter-patter, pitter-patter—fainter and fainter.

And then—silence.

The Gray Men

REBECCA WEST

Rebecca West (1892-1983) enjoyed a long and distinguished career as a novelist, critic, journalist, and political analyst. (She was also a socialist and an ardent feminist and was made Dame Commander of the British Empire in 1959.) She published numerous books, including the novels The Thinking Reed *(1936) and* The Fountain Overflows *(1956); such nonfiction works as* Black Lamb and Grey Falcon *(1941), a study of Yugoslavia; and such collections of essays and other short nonfiction works as* The Meaning of Treason *(1947),* A Train of Powder *(1955), and* The New Meaning of Treason *(1964). "The Gray Men," which was first published early in her career, in 1927, and which shows a markedly different side to her literary nature, is a chilly little excursion into the realm of the supernatural.*

I MUST begin the account of my experience by setting down my misfortunes, not in order that I may enjoy the delights of querulousness, but because I would not have had this experience if I had not been in a peculiar physical state. At the end of August I went down for a holiday to a remote village in Cornwall, and after a few days was taken ill with blood-poisoning and transported to a nursing home in one of the largest mining towns. I was in a state to respond extravagantly to the infection, because I had been in bad health for some years and for the last eighteen months I had been more or less continuously ill; and when I caught the germ I could not get well. My temperature sank to normal but the rate of my pulse and respiration was greatly excessive, amounting sometimes to twice what it ought to have been. I suffered from persistent insomnia; very often I would not fall asleep till after the mine hooters had gone, and an hour and a half later I would be awakened for breakfast by the implacable routine of the nursing home. So I fell into a curious state. I lost my power of suppressing irrelevant impressions and co-ordinating those that remained. I felt obliged to watch the trees outside my window and their behaviour in the sunshine and wind, to note the characteristics of every person who spoke to me, with a quite disagreeable intensity, and I was so fatigued by this constant effort of apprehension that there was no continuity in the working of my brain. Every moment of consciousness was distinct and unrelated to any other. Instead of being a stream my mental life was a string of disparate beads.

There came a Monday when I was told I could go back to London two days later; and in the afternoon I was sent out to take a little walk round the town. The walk I chose was one straight up the face of a high heathery hill, with an obelisk and a tower on the humps of its saddleback, which stands a mile or so outside the town. I knew it was unwise, but I had heard there was a fine view of the North Coast from the obelisk, and I was sick of being prevented from doing things by my health. But when I got to the top I realised that the ascent had, as they say, put the lid on it. I could not see the view. I could see it in bits but not as a whole. It was like trying to take a photograph of a view with a non-panoramic camera. And what I saw seemed like meaningless painting on glass. The patchwork of colours carried no suggestion of textures and contours. I had to work hard to interpret it, to see, for example, that that spattered rhomboidal patch was a cornfield, starred with arrish mows, that rolled its fourth corner over the bend of the hill. But I did not look at it for long, because two miners and their dogs came up onto the plateau round the obelisk, and my exaggerated disordered perceptions took too much notice of them. This hill was certainly large enough to support these four inoffensive creatures as well as myself, but I felt as irritated and uncomfortable as if I were being jostled by a dense crowd. I went down the hill and walked home, realising at every step that my mechanism was hopelessly out of gear, and that I was in a thoroughly abnormal condition.

This feeling of strangeness remained throughout the evening till I fell asleep about midnight; and about three hours later I began to dream. I thought I awoke with a sense of imminent danger, and that I got out of bed and ran to the window. The nursing home consisted of two three-storeyed semi-detached villas knocked into one; the two porches had been left as they were in the middle of the frontage, and the two broad gravel walks that had run from the gate of each villa-garden to its porch had been joined and now formed a semi-circular drive. I was sleeping in the ground-floor room to the right of the porches and, as it was built on a half-basement that rose out of its well to an exceptional height, I had a good view over the garden from my large bay-window. To my surprise, for vehicles were supposed to stop in the road outside the gate lest they should disturb the patients, a large grey limousine was drawn up in front of the porch. As I looked at it I began to shake with fear, for sitting in the front seat were two men of terrifying appearance. They were dressed in a uniform which was rather like that of the A. A. scouts, but cut very tightly of midnight blue cloth, and their heads were covered with aviators' helmets. They sat there with an inhuman immobility. They were the most sinister people I had ever seen. They were not diabolical, but they were inexorable. And I realised they had come here with the intention of abducting somebody from the home, and I began to run to the door so that I could rouse the household.

But as I crossed the floor I saw, not with the physical eye, for there was a wall and a door of frosted glass and wood in between, but with what the saints and mystics have called "the eye of the mind," that there was another man like these, standing on the balcony that opened off my room on the side that was at right angles to the frontage. I stood a moment wondering how he had got there, for no steps led to it from the garden, and it stood on smooth iron pillars rather above the height of a man, and I then went to the door. But I could not open it because there was a similar watchman guarding the other side of the door. I was conscious, somehow, of a thin cold stream of breath coming from between his lips. At that I realised that I could do nothing. I could not help the poor creature who was even now being laid hands on by the confederates of these people.

There was something very sinister about the way these sentinels were standing with their backs to the entrances they guarded. It suggested that they did not need to keep their fists ready to prevent my escape but could rely on some invisible emanation from their bodies.

Then, high up on the staircase of the other villa there sounded muffled, thudding noises which became recognisable while they descended from third flight to second flight, from second flight to first, as the footsteps of men carrying an unwieldly burthen.

I became aware that they were carrying a man or woman wrapped in some kind of envelope from which he or she was partly protruding. I visualized it that two of these men were carrying downstairs a person who had been put into one of these large unbleached calico bags in which one keeps one's fur coat, and who had succeeded in getting his head above the drawstring at the top. I knew that this wasn't exactly what the men were carrying, that it was merely a metaphorical image for something I did not like my mind to perceive directly. Here for the first time I detected myself trying to interfere with the dream; to forget it, as it were. I went on trying to recognise the person in the bag as a friend of mine whom I knew to be in very dangerous circumstances, obviously with the intention of explaining away the dream by interpreting it symbolically. But I could not keep it up. And I gave up the attempt when they passed through the hall and the captured person cried out to them—"Say something to me" and then sobbed softly, "Oh, if they would only tell me who they are and where they are taking me."

They did not reply. In silence they carried the person down the steep stone steps of the porch and lifted him or her into the car which immediately started. I followed it for a little way along the road, watching the poor thing as it turned to its immobile captors and, flapping its pinioned arms, pleaded to know what was going to happen to it.

I half awoke; and in that borderland state tossed about and tried to pretend that it was not really a terrifying dream.

"What a situation for the movies," I muttered and tried to work out a plot to lead up to it. Then I really woke up and realised the dream had been one of the most horrible things that had ever happened to me and I then passed immediately into a vivid recollection of an incident of my childhood.

I was eight or nine. I was having tea, in a room with folding doors, with two women. Behind the folding doors an old lady lay dead. We heard the padding of a cat about the room, the sound of its spring onto the creaking bedstead.

"Naughty kitty's jumped onto the bed. Go in and fetch kitty dear." I had never liked the old lady's obese body, and when I was told to go into the room where she lay dead it appeared to me possible that death might have given her new resources of ugliness. She was probably looking dreadful. I cried so much that they did not make me go, but my imagination had been set working. . . .

I shuddered out of this memory, but found myself obsessed by thoughts of death as a harsh abduction to a place of decay. I remembered a thousand threats I had noticed, that the other side of death might be torment and petrifaction. I felt that I was going to die soon, and I was possessed by fear and by resentments against the people who had wasted my life by their demands. Then I burst into the exhausted weeping that follows prolonged pain and lay crying till it was broad daylight.

I woke with the worst headache I have ever had in my life. All the morning I was heavy with it, and in the afternoon it had grown so intolerable that they gave me a heavy dose of aspirin. In the evening I became very restless and could not bring myself to undress and go to bed. At half-past ten I was sitting wondering when the night nurse would come and rebuke me for my late hours, when I heard the sound of one of the gates being opened and wheels coming along the drive.

"That is the car I dreamed of last night," I said to myself.

The horror did not revisit me; I even felt what psychologists call the pleasure of recognition. I was on the point of going to the window when my natural scepticism reasserted itself and I sat down again.

"Nonsense, that was a dream. Besides . . . it was a car I saw. This is something drawn by a horse."

I heard people coming up the stone steps and going through the hall. I tried to pretend that really all this was not of the slightest importance and began to undress; but presently I was compelled to go to the window and look out. There was nothing but a little low cart drawn by a sturdy pony. I said to myself that the most probable explanation of its presence there was a late delivery of the washing. But all the time I knew with absolute certainty that I was watching the incident of which my dream had been the fantastic rehearsal, and I was not surprised when I heard those muffled footsteps coming down the staircase of the other villa and passing through the hall as I heard them the night before. I was not surprised when two men carried out a coffin and laid it in the cart.

I have the intensest desire to believe that the soul is mortal and perishes with the body. But it is really very difficult for me not to suspect that I became aware of the death of this woman who had died the previous evening in a room on the third storey, by supernatural means. I had not come in contact with anyone who had been present at her death or was aware of it, as I had seen none of the day-nurses after tea-time. She had not been expected to die; therefore I could not have derived my sense of the corpse in the house from anything in the conversation or manner of the people about me. And as I believed that only nurses slept on the third storey, I had not the slightest reason for my accurate location of the deathbed. I am forced to go a little further than this. I cannot deny that all my emotions are convinced that I overheard the tribulation of a soul that was terrified at finding itself stripped of the flesh in a world not this earth.

I wish greatly that I had not had this experience. I am amazed at the temerity of those people, spiritualists and the like, who try to force these unnatural contacts with life after it has been subjected to the extreme change of death. For the human mind, exquisitely adapted as it is to the task of carrying its possessor through the material world, is, I think, unable to handle life in that altered state. My mechanism, having gone out of gear, intercepted the emotions of a person who had passed into that different world; emotions that no doubt, if I could have understood them, were not more significant, not more incompatible with the scheme of a kindly universe, than the weeping of a newborn child. But my earthly mind could not deal with it. The special weakness that had made me liable to this revelation made me link it up with childish fears and clothe it in symbolism inspired by an infantile conception of death that I knew to be untrue. I am quite sure that it is untrue; for though there is, as I have learned, much that is disagreeable in this universe and an almost profligate abundance of pain, I have never found any scrap of evidence in support of the existence of bogeys. But the reality that was contained in my experience gives a sanction to the rubbish with which my imagination surrounded it and has therefore made that infantile conception take fresh root in my mind. I was degraded; I am more subject to terror than I was. To me, for some little time to come, till I find my footing again, it will seem as if death has its sting and the grave its victory. I can imagine no more rash challenge to fear than the voluntary seeking of such an experience.

The Cyprian Cat

DOROTHY L. SAYERS

Dorothy L. Sayers (1893–1957) was an extremely prolific writer, having published poetry, plays, religious essays, and, of course, the well-known series of detective novels featuring Lord Peter Wimsey. Although Ms. Sayers is best remembered for her tales of the foppish nobleman, his efficient manservant Bunter, and mystery writer Harriet Vane, she also published three volumes of short stories, only four of which are about Wimsey and friends. In addition, she edited three volumes of detective, mystery, and horror stories (1929, 1931, and 1935). "The Cyprian Cat" is a tale of the ordinary vacation of an ordinary man, which turns into a nightmare of torment and violence. Sayers utilizes the elements of horror to weave a suspenseful tale best not read while alone at night.

IT'S extraordinarily decent of you to come along and see me like this, Harringay. Believe me, I do appreciate it. It isn't every busy K.C. who'd do as much for such a hopeless sort of client. I only wish I could spin you a more workable kind of story, but honestly, I can only tell you exactly what I told Peabody. Of course, I can see he doesn't believe a word of it, and I don't blame him. He thinks I ought to be able to make up a more plausible tale than that—and I suppose I could, but where's the use? One's almost bound to fall down somewhere if one tries to swear to a lie. What I'm going to tell you is the absolute truth. I fired one shot and one shot only, and that was at the cat. It's funny that one should be hanged for shooting at a cat.

Merridew and I were always the best of friends; school and college and all that sort of thing. We didn't see very much of each other after the war, because we were living at opposite ends of the country; but we met in town from time to time and wrote occasionally and each of us knew that the other was there in the background, so to speak. Two years ago, he wrote and told me he was getting married. He was just turned forty and the girl was fifteen years younger, and he was tremendously in love. It gave me a bit of a jolt—you know how it is when your friends marry. You feel they will never be quite the same again; and I'd got used to the idea that Merridew and I were cut out to be old bachelors. But of course I congratulated him and sent him a wedding present, and I did sincerely hope he'd be happy. He was obviously over head and ears; almost dangerously so, I thought, considering all things. Though except for the difference of age it seemed suitable enough. He told me he had met her at—of all places—a rectory garden-party down in Norfolk, and that she had actually never been out of her native village. I mean, literally—not so much as a trip to the nearest town. I'm not trying to convey that she wasn't pukka, or anything like that. Her father was some queer sort of recluse—a mediaevalist, or something desperately poor. He died shortly after their marriage.

I didn't see anything of them for the first year or so. Merridew is a civil engineer, you know, and he took his wife away after the honeymoon to Liverpool, where he was doing something in connection with the harbour. It must have been a big change for her from the wilds of Norfolk. I was in Birmingham, with my nose kept pretty close to the grindstone, so we only exchanged occasional letters. His were what I can only call deliriously happy, especially at first. Later on, he seemed a little worried about his wife's health. She was restless; town life didn't suit her; he'd be glad when he could finish up his Liverpool job and get her away into the country. There wasn't any doubt about their happiness, you understand—she'd got him body and soul as they say, and as far as I could make out it was mutual. I want to make that perfectly clear.

Well, to cut a long story short, Merridew wrote to me at the beginning of last month and said he was just off to a new job—a waterworks extension scheme down in Somerset; and he asked if I could possibly cut loose and join them there for a few weeks. He wanted to have a yarn with me, and Felice was longing to make my acquaintance. They had got rooms at the village inn. It was rather a remote spot, but there was fishing and scenery and so forth, and I should be able to keep Felice company while he was working up at the dam. I was about fed up with Birmingham, what with the heat and one thing and another, and it looked pretty good to me, and I was due for a holiday anyhow, so I fixed up to go. I had a bit of business to do in town, which I calculated would take me about a week, so I said I'd go down to Little Hexham on June 20th.

As it happened, my business in London finished itself off unexpectedly soon, and on the sixteenth I found myself absolutely free and stuck in an hotel with road-drills working just under the windows and a tar-spraying machine to make things livelier. You remember what a hot month it was—flaming June and no mistake about it. I didn't see any point in waiting, so I sent off a wire to Merridew, packed my bag and took the train for Somerset the same evening. I couldn't get a compartment to myself, but I found a first-class smoker with only three seats occupied, and stowed myself thankfully into the fourth corner. There was a military-looking old boy, an elderly female with a lot of bags and baskets, and a girl. I thought I should have a nice peaceful journey.

So I should have, if it hadn't been for the unfortunate way I'm built. It was quite all right at first—as a matter of fact, I think I was half asleep, and I only woke up properly at seven o'clock, when the waiter came to say that dinner was on. The other people weren't taking it, and when I came back from the restaurant car I found that the old boy had gone, and there were only the two women left. I settled down in my corner again, and gradually, as we went along, I found a horrible feeling creeping over me that there was a cat in the compartment somewhere. I'm one of those wretched people who can't stand cats. I don't mean just that I prefer dogs—I mean that the presence of a cat in the same room with me makes me feel like nothing on earth. I can't describe it, but I believe quite a lot of people are affected that way. Something to do with electricity, or so they tell me. I've read that very often the dislike is mutual, but it isn't so with me. The brutes seem to find me abominably fascinating—make a bee-line for my legs every time. It's a funny sort of complaint, and it doesn't make me at all popular with dear old ladies.

Anyway, I began to feel more and more awful and I realized that the old girl at the other end of the seat must have a cat in one of her innumerable baskets. I thought of asking her to put it out in the corridor, or calling the guard and having it removed, but I knew how silly it would sound and made up my mind to try and stick it. I couldn't say the animal was misbehaving itself or anything, and she looked a pleasant old lady; it wasn't her fault that I was a freak. I tried to distract my mind by looking at the girl.

She was worth looking at, too—very slim, and dark with one of those dead-white skins that make you think of magnolia blossom. She had the most astonishing eyes, too—I've never seen eyes quite like them; a very pale brown, almost amber, set wide apart and a little slanting, and they seemed to have a kind of luminosity of their own, if you get what I mean. I don't know if this sounds—I don't want you to think I was bowled over, or anything. As a matter of fact she held no sort of attraction for me, though I could imagine a different type of man going potty about her. She was just unusual, that was all. But however much I tried to think of other things I couldn't get rid of the uncomfortable feeling, and eventually I gave it up and went out into the corridor. I just mention this because it will help you to understand the rest of the story. If you can only realize how perfectly awful I feel when there's a cat about—even when it's shut up in a basket—you'll understand better how I came to buy the revolver.

Well, we got to Hexham Junction, which was the nearest station to Little Hexham, and there was old Merridew waiting on the platform. The girl was getting out too—but not the old lady with the cat, thank goodness—and I was just handing her traps out after her when he came galloping up and hailed us.

"Hullo!" he said. "Why, that's splendid! Have you introduced yourselves?" So I tumbled to it then that the girl was Mrs. Merridew, who'd been up to Town on a shopping expedition, and I explained to her about my change of plans and she said how jolly it was that I could come—the usual things. I noticed what an attractive low voice she had and how graceful her movements were, and I understood—though, mind you, I didn't share—Merridew's infatuation.

We got into his car—Mrs. Merridew sat in the back and I got up beside Merridew, and was very glad to feel the air and to get rid of the oppressive electric feeling I'd had in the train. He told me the place suited them wonderfully, and had given Felice an absolutely new lease of life, so to speak. He said he was very fit, too, but I thought myself that he looked rather fagged and nervy.

You'd have liked that inn, Harringay. The real, old-fashioned stuff, as quaint as you make 'em, and everything genuine—none of your Tottenham Court Road antiques. We'd all had our grub, and Mrs. Merridew said she was tired; so she went up to bed early and Merridew and I had a drink and went for a stroll round the village. It's a tiny hamlet quite at the other end of nowhere; lights out at ten, little thatched houses with pinched-up attic windows like furry ears—the place purred in its sleep. Merridew's working gang didn't sleep there, of course—they'd run up huts for them at the dam, a mile beyond the village.

The landlord was just locking up the bar when we came in—a block of a man with an absolutely expressionless face. His wife was a thin, sandy-haired woman who looked as though she was too downtrodden to open her mouth. But I found out afterwards that was a mistake, for one evening when he'd taken one or two over the eight and showed signs of wanting to make a night of it, his wife sent him off upstairs with a gesture and a look that took the heart out of him. That first night she was sitting in the porch, and hardly glanced at us as we passed her. I always thought her an uncomfortable kind of woman, but she certainly kept her house most exquisitely neat and clean.

They'd given me a noble bedroom, close under the eaves with a long, low casement window overlooking the garden. The sheets smelt of lavender, and I was between them and asleep almost before you could count ten. I was tired, you see. But later in the night I woke up. I was too hot, so took off some of the blankets and then strolled across to the window to get a breath of air. The garden was bathed in moonshine and on the lawn I could see something twisting and turning oddly. I stared a bit before I made it out to be two cats. They didn't worry me at that distance, and I watched them for a bit before I turned in again. They were rolling over one another and jumping away again and chasing their own shadows on the grass, intent on their own mysterious business—taking themselves seriously, the way cats always do. It looked like a kind of ritual dance. Then something seemed to startle them, and they scampered away.

I went back to bed, but I couldn't get to sleep again. My nerves seemed to be all on edge. I lay watching the window and listening to a kind of soft rustling noise that seemed to be going on in the big wisteria that ran along my side of the house. And then something landed with a soft thud on the sill—a great Cyprian cat.

What did you say? Well, one of those striped grey and black cats. Tabby, that's right. In my part of the country they call them Cyprus cats, or Cyprian cats. I'd never seen such a monster. It stood with its head cocked sideways, staring into the room and rubbing its ears very softly against the upright bar of the casement.

Of course, I couldn't do with that. I shooed the brute away, and it made off without a sound. Heat or no heat, I shut and fastened the window. Far out in the shrubbery I thought I heard a faint miauling; then silence. After that, I went straight off to sleep again and lay like a log till the girl came in to call me.

The next day, Merridew ran us up in his car to see the place where they were making the dam, and that was the first time I realized that Felice's nerviness had not been altogether cured. He showed us where they had diverted part of the river into a swift little stream that was to be used for working the dynamo of an electrical plant. There were a couple of planks laid across the stream, and he wanted to take us over to show us the engine. It wasn't extraordinarily wide or dangerous, but Mrs. Merridew peremptorily refused to cross it, and got quite hysterical when he tried to insist. Eventually he and I went over and inspected the machinery by ourselves. When we got back she had recovered her temper and apologized for being so silly. Merridew abased himself, of course, and I began to feel a little *de trop*. She told me afterwards that she had once fallen into the river as a child, and been nearly drowned, and it had left her with a what d'ye call it—complex about running water. And but for this one trifling episode, I never heard a single sharp word pass between them all the time I was there; nor, for a whole week, did I notice anything else to suggest a flaw in Mrs. Merridew's radiant health. Indeed, as the days wore on to midsummer and the heat grew more intense, her whole body seemed to glow with vitality. It was as though she was lit up from within.

Merridew was out all day and working very hard. I thought he was overdoing it and asked him if he was sleeping badly. He told me that, on the contrary, he fell asleep every night the moment his head touched the pillow, and—what was most unusual with him—had no dreams of any kind. I myself felt well enough, but the hot weather made me languid and disinclined for exertion. Mrs. Merridew took me out for long drives in the car. I would sit for hours, lulled into a half-slumber by the rush of warm air and the purring of the engine, and gazing at my driver, upright at the wheel, her eyes fixed unwaveringly upon the spinning road. We explored the whole of the country to the south and east of Little Hexham, and once or twice went as far north as Bath. Once I suggested that we should turn eastward over the bridge and run down into what looked like rather beautiful wooded country, but Mrs. Merridew didn't care for the idea; she said it was a bad road and that the scenery on that side was disappointing.

Altogether, I spent a pleasant week at Little Hexham, and if it had not been for the cats I should have been perfectly comfortable. Every night the garden seemed to be haunted by them—the Cyprian cat that I had seen the first night of my stay, and a little ginger one and a horrible stinking black Tom were especially tiresome, and one night there was a terrified white kitten that mewed for an hour on end under my window. I flung boots and books at my visitors till I was heartily weary, but they seemed determined to make the inn garden their rendezvous. The nuisance grew worse from night to night; on one occasion I counted fifteen of them, sitting on their hinder-ends in a circle, while the Cyprian cat danced her shadow-dance among them, working in and out like a weaver's shuttle. I had to keep my window shut, for the Cyprian cat evidently made a habit of climbing up by the wisteria. The door, too; for once when I had gone down to fetch something from the sitting room, I found her on my bed, kneading the coverlet with her paws—pr'rp, pr'rp, pr'rp—with her eyes closed in a sensuous ecstasy. I beat her off, and she spat at me as she fled into the dark passage.

I asked the landlady about her, but she replied rather curtly that they kept no cat at the inn, and it is true that I never saw any of the beasts in the daytime; but one evening about dusk I caught the landlord in one of the outhouses. He had the ginger cat on his shoulder, and was feeding her with something that looked like strips of liver. I remonstrated with him for encouraging the cats about the place and asked whether I could have a different room, explaining that the nightly caterwauling disturbed me. He half opened his slits of eyes and murmured that he would ask his wife about it; but nothing was done, and in fact I believe there was no other bedroom in the house.

And all this time the weather got hotter and heavier, working up for thunder, with the sky like brass and the earth like iron, and the air quivering over it so that it hurt your eyes to look at it.

All right, Harringay—I am trying to keep to the point. And I'm not concealing anything from you. I say that my relations with Mrs. Merridew were perfectly ordinary. Of course I saw a good deal of her, because as I explained Merridew was out all day. We went up to the dam with him in the morning and brought the car back, and naturally we had to amuse one another as best we could till the evening. She seemed quite pleased to be in my company, and I couldn't dislike her. I can't tell you what we talked about—nothing in particular. She was not a talkative woman. She would sit or lie for hours in the sunshine, hardly speaking—only stretching out her body to the light and heat. Sometimes she would spend a whole afternoon playing with a twig or a pebble, while I sat by and smoked. Restful! No. No—I shouldn't call her a restful personality, exactly. Not to me, at any rate. In the evening she would liven up and talk a little more, but she generally went up to bed early, and left Merridew and me to yarn together in the garden.

Oh! about the revolver. Yes. I bought that in Bath, when I had been at Little Hexham exactly a week. We drove over in the morning, and while Mrs. Merridew got some things for her husband, I prowled round the second-hand shops. I had intended to get an air-gun or a pea-shooter or something of that kind, when I saw this. You've seen it, of course. It's very tiny—what people in books describe as "little more than a toy," but quite deadly enough. The old boy who sold it to me didn't seem to know much about firearms. He'd taken it in pawn some time back, he told me, and there were ten rounds of ammunition with it. He made no bones about a license or anything—glad enough to make a sale, no doubt, without putting difficulties in a customer's way. I told him I knew how to handle it, and mentioned by way of a joke that I meant to take a potshot or two at the cats. That seemed to wake him up a bit. He was a dried-up little fellow, with a scrawny grey beard and a stringy neck. He asked me where I was staying. I told him at Little Hexham.

"You better be careful, sir," he said. "They think a heap of their cats down there, and it's reckoned unlucky to kill them." And then he added something I couldn't quite catch, about a silver bullet. He was a doddering old fellow, and he seemed to have some sort of scruple about letting me take the parcel away, but I assured him that I was perfectly capable of looking after it and myself. I left him standing in the door of his shop, pulling at his beard and staring after me.

That night the thunder came. The sky had turned to lead before evening, but the dull heat was more oppressive than the sunshine. Both the Merridews seemed to be in a state of nerves—he sulky and swearing at the weather and the flies, and she wrought up to a queer kind of vivid excitement. Thunder affects some people that way. I wasn't much better, and to make things worse I got the feeling that the house was full of cats. I couldn't see them but I knew they were there, lurking behind the cupboards and flitting noiselessly about the corridors. I could scarcely sit in the parlour and I was thankful to escape to my room. Cats or no cats, I had to open the window, and I sat there with my pyjama jacket unbuttoned, trying to get a breath of air. But the place was like the inside of a copper furnace. And pitch-dark. I could scarcely see from my window where the bushes ended and the lawn began. But I could hear and feel the cats. There were little scrapings in the wisteria and scufflings among the leaves, and about eleven o'clock one of them started the concert with a loud and hideous wail. Then another and another joined in—I'll swear there were fifty of them. And presently I got that foul sensation of nausea, and the flesh crawled on my bones, and I knew that one of them was slinking close to me in the darkness. I looked round quickly, and there she stood, the great Cyprian, right against my shoulder, her eyes glowing like green lamps. I yelled and struck out at her, and she snarled as she leaped out and down. I heard her thump the gravel, and the yowling burst out all over the garden with renewed vehemence. And then all in a moment there was utter silence, and in the far distance there came a flickering blue flash and then another. In the first of them I saw the far garden wall, topped along all its length with cats, like a nursery frieze. When the second flash came the wall was empty.

At two o'clock the rain came. For three hours before that I had sat there, watching the lightning as it spat across the sky and exulting in the crash of the thunder. The storm seemed to carry off all the electrical disturbance in my body; I could have shouted with excitement and relief. Then the first heavy drops fell; then a steady downpour; then a deluge. It struck the iron-baked garden with a noise like steel rods falling. The smell of the ground came up intoxicatingly, and the wind rose and flung the rain in against my face. At the other end of the passage I heard a window thrown to and fastened, but I leaned out into the tumult and let the water drench my head and shoulders. The thunder still rumbled intermittently, but with less noise and farther off, and in an occasional flash I saw the white grille of falling water drawn between me and the garden.

It was after one of these thunder-peals that I became aware of a knocking at my door. I opened it, and there was Merridew. He had a candle in his hand, and his face was terrified.

"Felice!" he said abruptly. "She's ill. I can't wake her. For God's sake, come and give me a hand."

I hurried down the passage after him. There were two beds in his room—a great four-poster, hung with crimson damask, and a small camp bedstead drawn up near to the window. The small bed was empty, the bedclothes tossed aside; evidently he had just risen from it. In the four-poster lay Mrs. Merridew, naked, with only a sheet upon her. She was stretched flat upon her back, her long black hair in two plaits over her shoulders. Her face was waxen and shrunk, like the face of a corpse, and her pulse, when I felt it, was so faint that at first I could scarcely feel it. Her breathing was very slow and shallow and her flesh cold. I shook her, but there was no response at all. I lifted her eyelids, and noticed how the eyeballs were turned up under the upper lid, so that only the whites were visible. The touch of my finger-tip upon the sensitive ball evoked no reaction. I immediately wondered whether she took drugs.

Merridew seemed to think it necessary to make some explanation. He was babbling about the heat—she couldn't bear so much as a silk nightgown—she had suggested that he should occupy the other bed—he had slept heavily—right through the thunder. The rain blowing in on his face had aroused him. He had got up and shut the window. Then he called to Felice to know if she was all right—he thought the storm might have frightened her. There was no answer. He had struck a light. Her condition had alarmed him—and so on.

I told him to pull himself together and to try whether, by chafing his wife's hands and feet, we could restore the circulation. I had it firmly in my mind that she was under the influence of some opiate. We set to work, rubbing and pinching and slapping her with wet towels and shouting her name in her ear. It was like handling a dead woman, except for the very slight but perfectly regular rise and fall of her bosom, on which—with a kind of surprise that there should be any flaw on its magnolia whiteness—I noticed a large brown mole, just over the heart. To my perturbed fancy it suggested a wound and a menace. We had been hard at it for some time, with the sweat pouring off us, when we became aware of something going on outside the window—a stealthy bumping and scraping against the panes. I snatched up the candle and looked out.

On the sill, the Cyprian cat sat and clawed at the casement.

Her drenched fur clung limply to her body, her eyes glared into mine, her mouth was opened in protest. She scrabbled furiously at the latch, her hind claws slipping and scratching on the woodwork. I hammered on the pane and bawled at her, and she struck back at the glass as though possessed. As I cursed her and turned away she set up a long, despairing wail.

Merridew called to me to bring back the candle and leave the brute alone. I returned to the bed, but the dismal crying went on and on incessantly. I suggested to Merridew that he should wake the landlord and get hot-water bottles and some brandy from the bar and see if a messenger could not be sent for a doctor. He departed on this errand, while I went on with my massage. It seemed to me that the pulse was growing still fainter. Then I suddenly recollected that I had a small brandy-flask in my bag. I ran out to fetch it, and as I did so the cat suddenly stopped its howling.

As I entered my own room the air blowing through the open window struck gratefully upon me. I found my bag in the dark and was rummaging for the flask among my shirts and socks when I heard a loud, triumphant mew, and turned round in time to see the Cyprian cat crouched for a moment on the sill, before it sprang in past me and out at the door. I found the flask and hastened back with it, just as Merridew and the landlord came running up the stairs.

We all went into the room together. As we did so, Mrs. Merridew stirred, sat up, and asked us what in the world was the matter.

I have seldom felt quite such a fool.

Next day the weather was cooler; the storm had cleared the air. What Merridew had said to his wife I do not know. None of us made any public allusion to the night's disturbance, and to all appearance Mrs. Merridew was in the best of health and spirits. Merridew took a day off from the waterworks, and we all went for a long drive and picnic together. We were on the best of terms with one another. Ask Merridew—he will tell you the same thing. He would not—he could not, surely—say otherwise. I can't believe, Harringay, I simply cannot believe that he would imagine or suspect me—I say, there was nothing to suspect. Nothing.

Yes—this is the important date—the 24th of June. I can't tell you any more details; there is nothing to tell. We came back and had dinner just as usual. All three of us were together all day, till bedtime. On my honour I had no private interview of any kind that day, either with him or with her. I was the first to go to bed, and I heard the others come upstairs about half an hour later. They were talking cheerfully.

It was a moonlight night. For once, no caterwauling came to trouble me. I didn't even bother to shut the window or the door. I put the revolver on the chair beside me before I lay down. Yes, it was loaded. I had no special object in putting it there, except that I meant to have a go at the cats if they started their games again.

I was desperately tired, and thought I should drop off to sleep at once, but I didn't. I must have been overtired, I suppose. I lay and looked at the moonlight. And then, about midnight, I heard what I had been half expecting: a stealthy scrabbling in the wisteria and a faint miauling sound.

I sat up in bed and reached for the revolver. I heard the "plop" as the big cat sprang up on to the window-ledge; I saw her black and silver flanks, and the outline of her round head, pricked ears and upright tail. I aimed and fired, and the beast let out one frightful cry and sprang down into the room.

I jumped out of bed. The crack of the shot had sounded terrific in the silent house, and somewhere I heard a distant voice call out. I pursued the cat into the passage, revolver in hand—with some idea of finishing it off, I suppose. And then, at the door of the Merridews' room, I saw Mrs. Merridew. She stood with one hand on each door-post, swaying to and fro. Then she fell down at my feet. Her bare breast was all stained with blood. And as I stood staring at her clutching the revolver, Merridew came out and found us—like that.

Well, Harringay, that's my story, exactly as I told it to Peabody. I'm afraid it won't sound very well in Court, but what can I say? The trail of blood led from my room to hers; the cat must have run that way; I *know* it was the cat I shot. I can't offer any explanation. I don't know who shot Mrs. Merridew, or why. I can't help it if the people at the inn say they never saw the Cyprian cat; Merridew saw it that other night, and I know he wouldn't lie about it. Search the house, Harringay—that's the only thing to do. Pull the place to pieces, till you find the body of the Cyprian cat. It will have my bullet in it.

A Haunted House

VIRGINIA WOOLF

Virginia Woolf (1882–1941) was one of the most prolific and acclaimed writers of her day, producing such novels as The Voyage Out *(1915),* Mrs. Dalloway *(1925),* To the Lighthouse *(1927), and* Orlando *(1928); as well as numerous short stories, essays, and works of literary criticism. A member of London's intellectual Bloomsbury set, she was also a publisher, operating the Hogarth Press with her husband, Leonard Woolf. "A Haunted House" is Woolf's only supernatural story; and it reveals the author's feeling that ghosts are merely benign spirits reliving their own bittersweet memories.*

WHATEVER hour you woke there was a door shutting. From room to room they went, hand in hand, lifting here, opening there, making sure—a ghostly couple.

"Here we left it," she said. And he added, "Oh, but here too!" "It's upstairs," she murmured. "And in the garden," he whispered. "Quietly," they said, "or we shall wake them."

But it wasn't that you woke us. Oh, no. "They're looking for it; they're drawing the curtain," one might say, and so read on a page or two. "Now they've found it," one would be certain, stopping the pencil on the margin. And then, tired of reading, one might rise and see for oneself, the house all empty, the doors standing open, only the wood pigeons bubbling with content and the hum of the threshing machine sounding from the farm. "What did I come in here for? What did I want to find?" My hands were empty. "Perhaps it's upstairs then?" The apples were in the loft. And so down again, the garden still as ever, only the book had slipped into the grass.

But they had found it in the drawing-room. Not that one could ever see them. The window panes reflected apples, reflected roses; all the leaves were green in the glass. If they moved in the drawing-room, the apple only turned its yellow side. Yet, the moment after, if the door was opened, spread about the floor, hung upon the walls, pendant from the ceiling—what? My hands were empty. The shadow of a thrush crossed the carpet; from the deepest wells of silence the wood pigeon drew its bubble of sound. "Safe, safe, safe," the pulse of the house beat softly. "The treasure buried; the room . . ." the pulse stopped short. Oh, was that the buried treasure?

A moment later the light had faded. Out in the garden then? But the trees spun darkness for a wandering beam of sun. So fine, so rare, coolly sunk beneath the surface the beam I sought always burnt behind the glass. Death was the glass; death was between us; coming to the woman first, hundreds of years ago, leaving the house, sealing all the windows; the rooms were darkened. He left it, left her, went North, went East, saw the stars turned in the Southern sky; sought the house, found it dropped beneath the Downs. "Safe, safe, safe," the pulse of the house beat gladly. "The Treasure yours."

The wind roars up the avenue. Trees stoop and bend this way and that. Moonbeams splash and spill wildly in the rain. But the beam of the lamp falls straight from the window. The candle burns stiff and still. Wandering through the house, opening the windows, whispering not to wake us, the ghostly couple seek their joy.

"Here we slept," she says. And he adds, "Kisses without number." "Waking in the morning—" "Silver between the trees—" "Upstairs—" "In the garden—" "When summer came—" "In winter snowtime—" The doors go shutting far in the distance, gently knocking like the pulse of a heart.

Nearer they come; cease at the doorway. The wind falls, the rain slides silver down the glass. Our eyes darken; we hear no steps beside us; we see no lady spread her ghostly cloak. His hands shield the lantern. "Look," he breathes. "Sound asleep. Love upon their lips."

Stooping, holding their silver lamp above us, long they look and deeply. Long they pause. The wind drives straightly; the flame stoops slightly. Wild beams of moonlight cross both floor and wall, and, meeting, stain the faces bent; the faces pondering; the faces that search the sleepers and seek their hidden joy.

"Safe, safe, safe," the heart of the house beats proudly. "Long years—" he sighs. "Again you found me." "Here," she murmurs, "sleeping; in the garden reading; laughing, rolling apples in the loft. Here we left our treasure—" Stooping, their light lifts the lids upon my eyes. "Safe! safe! safe!" the pulse of the house beats wildly. Waking, I cry, "Oh, is this *your* buried treasure? The light in the heart."

The Idol of the Flies

JANE RICE

In "The Idol of the Flies," a much-respected work in the field of the macabre, Jane Rice initially portrays the horror of a twisted human soul, but this soon escalates to another kind of horror on a more cosmic scale. Ms. Rice has been publishing her imaginative and excellent stories since the 1940s, in such magazines as Unknown, Astounding, *the* Magazine of Fantasy & Science Fiction, Ladies' Home Journal, Cosmopolitan, *and* Charm.

PRUITT watched a fly on the corner of the table. He held himself very still. The fly cleaned its wings with short, back-stroke motions of its legs. It looked, Pruitt thought, like Crippled Harry—cook's husband. He hated Aunt Mona. But he hated Miss Bittner most of all.

He lifted his head and bared his teeth at the nape of Miss Bittner's neck. He hated the way she stood there erasing the blackboard in great, sweeping circles. He hated the way her shoulder blades poked out. He hated the big horn comb thrust into her thin hair—thrust not quite far enough—so that some of the hair flapped. And he hated the way she arranged it around her sallow face and low on her neck, to conceal the little button that nestled in one large-lobed ear. The button and the narrow black cord that ran down the back of her dress under her starched collar.

He liked the button and the cord. He liked them because Miss Bittner hated them. She pretended she didn't care about being deaf. But she did. And she pretended she liked him. But she didn't.

He made her nervous. It was easy. All he had to do was open his eyes wide and stare at her without batting. It was delightfully simple. Too simple. It wasn't fun any more. He was glad he had found out about the flies.

Miss Bittner placed the eraser precisely in the center of the blackboard runnel, dusted her hands and turned toward Pruitt. Pruitt opened his eyes quite wide and gimleted her with an unblinking stare.

Miss Bittner cleared her throat nervously. "That will be all, Pruitt. Tomorrow we will begin on derivatives."

"Yes, Miss Bittner," Pruitt said loudly, meticulously forming the words with his lips.

Miss Bittner flushed. She straightened the collar of her dress. "Your aunt said you might take a swim."

"Yes, Miss Bittner."

"Good afternoon, Pruitt. Tea at five."

"Yes, Miss Bittner. Good afternoon, Miss Bittner." Pruitt lowered his gaze to a point three inches below Miss Bittner's knees. He allowed a faint expression of controlled surprise to wrinkle his forehead.

Involuntarily, Miss Bittner glanced down. Quick as a flash, Pruitt swept his hand across the table and scooped up the fly. When Miss Bittner again raised her head, Pruitt was regarding her blandly. He arose.

"There's some lemonade on top of the back porch icebox. Can I have some?"

"*May* I have some, Pruitt."

"*May* I have some?"

"Yes, Pruitt, you may."

Pruitt crossed the room to the door.

"Pruitt—"

Pruitt stopped, swiveled slowly on his heel and stared unwinkingly at his tutor. "Yes, Miss Bittner?"

"Let's remember not to slam the screen door, shall we? It disturbs your auntie, you know." Miss Bittner twitched her pale lips into what she mistakenly believed was the smile of a friendly conspirator.

Pruitt gazed at her steadily. "Yes, Miss Bittner."

"That's fine," said Clara Bittner with false heartiness.

"Is that all, Miss Bittner?"

"Yes, Pruitt."

Pruitt, without relaxing his basilisklike contemplation of his unfortunate tutor, counted up to twelve, then he turned and quitted the room.

Clara Bittner looked at the empty doorway a long while and then she shuddered. Had she been pressed for an explanation of that shudder she couldn't have given a satisfactory answer. In all probability, she would have said, with a vague conciliatory gesture, "I don't know. I think, perhaps, it's a bit difficult for a child to warm up to a teacher." And, no doubt, she would have added brightly, "the psychology of the thing, you know."

Miss Bittner was a stanch defender of psychology. She had taken a summer course in it—ten years ago—and had, as she was fond of repeating, received the highest grades in the class. It never occurred to Miss Bittner that this was due to her aptitude at memorizing whole paragraphs and being able to transpose these onto her test papers without ever having digested the kernels of thought contained therein.

Miss Bittner stooped and unlaced one oxford. She breathed a sigh of relief. She sat erect, pulled down her dress in back and then felt with her fingertips the rubbery, black cord dangling against her neck. Miss Bittner sighed again. A buzzing at one of the windows claimed her attention.

She went to a cupboard which yielded up a wire fly swatter. Grasping this militantly, she strode to the window, drew back, closed her eyes, and swatted. The fly, badly battered, dropped to the sill, lay on its wings, its legs curled.

She unhooked the screen and with the end of the swatter delicately urged the corpse outside.

"*Ugh*," said Miss Bittner. And had Miss Bittner been pressed for an explanation of that *ugh* she, likewise, would have been at a loss for a satisfactory answer. It was strange how she felt about flies. They affected her much as rattlesnakes would have. It wasn't that they were germy, or that their eyes were a reddish orange and, so she had heard, reflected everything in the manner of prisms; it wasn't that they had the odious custom of regurgitating a drop of their last meal before beginning on a new one; it wasn't the crooked hairy legs, nor the probing proboscis; it was—well, it was just the creatures themselves. Possibly, Miss Bittner might have said, simpering to show that she really didn't *mean* it, "I have flyophobia."

The truth was, she did. She was afraid of them. Deathly afraid. As some people are afraid of inclosed areas, as others are afraid of height, so Miss Bittner was afraid of flies. Childishly, senselessly, but horribly, afraid.

She returned the swatter to the cupboard and forthwith

scrubbed her hands thoroughly at the sink. It was odd, she thought, how many flies she had encountered lately. It almost seemed as if someone were purposely diverting a *channel* of flies her way. She smiled to herself at this foolish whimsy, wiped her hands and tidied her hair. Now, for some of that lemonade. She was pleased that Pruitt had mentioned it. If he hadn't she might not have known it was there and she did *so* love lemonade.

Pruitt stood at the head of the stairwell. He worked his jaws convulsively, then he pursed his mouth, leaned far over the polished banister and spat. The globule of spittle elongated into a pear-shaped tear and flattened with a wet smack on the floor below.

Pruitt went on down the stairs. He could feel the fly bumbling angrily in its hot, moist prison. He put his tightly curled hand to his lips and blew into the tunnel made by his thumb and forefinger. The fly clung for dear life to his creased palm.

At the foot of the stairs Pruitt paused long enough to squeeze each one of the tiny green balls on the ends of the fern that was potted in an intricate and artistic copper holder.

Then he went through a hallway into the kitchen.

"Give me a glass," he said to the ample-bosomed woman who sat on a stool picking nut meats and putting them into a glass bowl.

The woman heaved herself to her feet.

" 'Please' won't hurt you," the woman said.

"I don't have to say 'please' to you. You're the help."

The cook put her hands on her hips. "What you need is a thrashing," she said grimly. "A good, sound thrashing."

By way of reply, Pruitt snatched the paper sack of cracked hulls and deliberately up-ended the bag into the bowl of nut meats.

The woman made a futile grab. Her heavy face grew suffused with a wave of rich color. She opened her hand and brought it up in a swinging arc.

Pruitt planted his feet firmly on the linoleum and said low, "I'll scream. You know what that'll do to aunt."

The woman held her hand poised so for a second and then let it fall to her aproned side. "You brat," she hissed; "you sneaking, pink-eyed brat!"

"Give me a glass."

The woman reached up on a shelf of the cabinet, took down a glass and wordlessly handed it to the boy.

"I don't want that one," Pruitt said, "I want *that* one." He pointed to the glass' identical twin on the topmost shelf.

Silently, the woman padded across the floor and pushed a short kitchen ladder over to the cabinet. Silently, she climbed it. Silently, she handed down the designated glass.

Pruitt accepted it. "I'm going to tell Aunt Mona you took your shoes off."

The woman climbed down the ladder, put it away and returned to the bowl.

"Harry is a dirty you-know-what," Pruitt said.

The woman went on lifting out the nut hulls.

"He stinks."

The woman went on lifting out the nut hulls.

"So do you," finished Pruitt. He waited.

The woman went on lifting out the nut hulls.

The boy took his glass and repaired to the back porch. It spoiled the fun when they didn't talk back. Cook was "on to" him. But she wouldn't complain. Aunt Mona let them stay through the winter rent free with nobody but themselves to see to and Harry was a cripple and couldn't make a living. She wouldn't *dast* complain.

Pruitt lifted the pitcher of lemonade from the lid of the icebox and poured himself a glassful. He drank half of it and let the rest dribble along a crack, holding the glass close to the floor so it wouldn't make a trickling noise. When it dried it would be sweet and sticky. Lots of flies.

He relaxed his hand ever so slightly and dexterously extricated his shopworn captive. It hummed furiously. Pruitt pulled off one of its wings and dropped the mutilated insect into the lemonade. It kicked ineffectually, was quiet, kicked again, and was quiet—drifting on the surface of the liquid, sagging to one side, its remaining wing outstretched like a useless sail.

The boy caught it and pushed it under. "I christen you Miss Bittner," he said. He released his hold and the fly popped to the top—a piece of lemon pulp on its back. It kicked again—feebly—and was quiet.

Pruitt replaced the lemonade and opened the screen door. He pulled it so that the spring twanged protestingly. He let go and leaped down the steps. The door came to with a mighty bang behind him. *That* was the finish of Aunt Mona's nap.

He crouched on his haunches and listened. A cloud shadow floated across the grass. A butterfly teetered uncertainly on a waxy leaf, and fluttered away following an erratic air trail of its own. A June bug drummed through the warm afternoon, its armored belly a shiny bottle-green streak in the sunlight. Pruitt crumbled the cone of an ant hill and watched the excited maneuvers of its inhabitants.

There was the slow drag of footsteps somewhere above—the opening of a shutter. Pruitt grinned. His ears went up and back with the broadness of it. Cook would puff up two flights of stairs "out of the goodness of her heart," Aunt Mona said—"out of dumbness," if you asked him. Whyn't she let "Miss Mona" fill her own bloody icebag? There'd be time to go in and mix the nut shells up again. But no, he might run into Miss Bittner beating a thirsty course to the lemonade. She might guess about the fly. Besides he'd dallied too long as it was. He had business to attend to. Serious business.

He got up, stretched, scrunched his heel on the ant hill and walked away in the direction of the bathhouse.

Twice he halted to shy stones at a plump robin and once he froze into a statue as there was a movement in the path before him. His quick eyes fastened on a toad squatted in the dust, its bulgy sides going in and out, in and out, in and out, like a miniature bellows. Stealthily, Pruitt broke off a twig. In and out, in and out, in and out. Pruitt eased forward. In and out, in and out, in and out. He could see its toes spread far apart, the dappling of spots on its cool, froggy skin. In and out, in and out, the leg muscles tensed as the toad prepared to make another hop. Pantherlike, Pruitt leaped, his hand descending. The toad emitted an agonized, squeaking scream.

Pruitt stood up and looked at the toad with amusement. The twig protruded from its sloping back. In and out, in and out went the toad's sides. In—and out, in—and out. It essayed an unstable hop, leaving a darkish stain in its wake. Again it hopped. The twig remained stanchly upright. The third hop was shorter. Barely its own length. Pruitt nosed it over into the grass with his shoe. In—and—out went the toad's sides, in—and—out, in—and—out, in—

Pruitt walked on.

The crippled man mending his fishing net on the wooden pier sensed his approaching footsteps. With as much haste as his wracked spine would permit, the man got to his feet. Pruitt heard the scrambling and quickened his pace.

"Hello," he said innocently.

The man bobbed his head. " 'Do, Mr. Pruitt."

"Mending your nets?"

"Yes, Mr. Pruitt."

"I guess the dock is a good place to do it."

"Yes, Mr. Pruitt." The man licked his tongue across his lips and his eyes made rapid sortees to the right and left, as if seeking a means of escape.

Pruitt scraped his shoe across the wooden planking. "Excepting that it gets fish scales all over everything," he said softly, "and I don't *like* fish scales."

The man's Adam's apple jerked up and down as he swallowed thrice in rapid succession. He wiped his hands on his pants.

"I said I don't *like* fish scales."

"Yes, Mr. Pruitt, I didn't mean to—"

"So I guess maybe I better fix it so there won't *be* any fish scales any more."

"Mr. Pruitt, please, I didn't—" His voice petered out as the boy picked up a corner of the net.

"Not ever any more fish scales," said Pruitt.

"Don't pull it," the man begged, "it'll snag on the dock."

"I won't snag it," Pruitt said; "I wouldn't snag it for anything." He smiled at Harry. "Because if I just snagged it, you'd just mend it again and then there'd be more fish scales, and I don't *like* fish scales." Bunching the net in his fists, he dragged it to the edge of the dock. "So I'll just throw it in the water and then I guess there won't ever be any more fish scales."

Harry's jaw went slack with shocked disbelief. "Mr. Pruitt—" he began.

"Like this," said Pruitt. He held the net out at arm's length over the pier and relinquished his clasp.

With an inarticulate cry the man threw himself awkwardly on the planking in a vain attempt to retrieve his slowly vanishing property.

"Now there won't ever be any more fish scales," Pruitt said. "Not every any more."

Harry hefted himself to his knees. His face was white. For one dull, weighted minute he looked at his tormentor. Then he struggled to his feet and limped away without a word.

Pruitt considered his deformed posture with the eye of a connoisseur. "Harry is a hunchback," he sang after him in a lilting childish treble. "Harry is a hunchback, Harry is a hunchback."

The man limped on, one shoulder dipping sharply with each successive step, his coarse shirt stretched over his misshapen back. A bend in the path hid him from view.

Pruitt pushed open the door of the bathhouse and went inside. He closed the door behind him and bolted it. He waited until his eyes had become accustomed to the semi-gloom, whereupon he went over to a cot against the wall, lifted up its faded chintz spread, felt underneath and pulled out two boxes. He sat down and delved into their contents.

From the first he produced a section of a bread board, four pegs, and six half-burned birthday candles screwed into nibbled-looking pink candy rosettes. The bread board he placed on top the pegs, the candles he arranged in a semicircle. He surveyed the result with squint-eyed approval.

From the second box he removed a grotesque object composed of coal tar. It perched shakily on pipestem legs, two strips of Cellophane were pasted to its flanks and a black rubber band dangled downward from its head in which was embedded—one on each side—a red cinnamon drop.

The casual observer would have seen in this sculpture a child's crude efforts to emulate the characteristics of the common housefly. The casual observer—if he had been inclined to go on with his observing—also would have seen that Pruitt was in a "mood." He might even have observed aloud, "That child looks positively feverish and he *shouldn't* be allowed to play with matches."

But at the moment there was no casual observer. Only Pruitt absorbed in lighting the birthday candles. The image of the fly he deposited square in the middle of the bread board.

Cross-legged he sat, chin down, arms folded. He rocked himself back and forth. He began to chant. Singsong. Through his nose. Once in a while he rolled his eyes around in their sockets, but merely once in a while. He had found, if he did that too often, it made him dizzy.

"O Idol of the Flies," intoned Pruitt, "hahneemahneemo." He scratched his ankle ruminatively. "Hahnee*wee*mahneemo," he improved, "make the lemonade dry in the crack on the back porch, and make Miss Bittner find the scrooched up fly *after* she's already drunk some, and make cook go down in the cellar for some marmalade and make her not turn on the light and make her fall over the string I've got tied between the posts, and make aunt get a piece of nutshell in her bread and cough like hell.'' Pruitt thought this over. ''Hell,'' he said, ''hell, hell, hell, hell, HELL.''

He meditated in silence. ''I guess that's all,'' he said finally, ''except maybe you'd better fill up my fly catcher in case we have currant cookies for tea. Hahnee*wee*mahneemo, O Idol of the Flies, you are free to GO!''

Pruitt fixed his gaze in the middle distance and riveted it there. Motionless, scarcely breathing, his lips parted, he huddled on the bare boards—a small sphinx in khaki shorts.

This was what Pruitt called ''not-thinking-time.'' Pretty soon, entirely without volition on his part, queer, half-formed dream things would float through his mind. Like dark, polliwogs. Propelling themselves along with their tails, hinting at secrets that nobody knew, not even grown-ups. Some day he would be able to catch one, quickly, before it wriggled off into the inner hidden chamber where They had a nest and, then, he would *know*. He would catch it in a net of thought, like Harry's net caught fishes, and no matter how it squirmed and threshed about he would pin it flat against his skull until he *knew*. Once, he had almost caught one. He had been on the very rim of *knowing* and Miss Bittner had come down to bring him some peanut butter sandwiches and it had escaped back into that deep, strange place in his mind where They lived. He had only had it for a split second but he remembered it had blind, weepy eyes and was smooth.

If Miss Bittner hadn't come—He had vomited on her stockings. Here came one of Them now—fast, it was coming fast, too fast to catch. It was gone, leaving behind it a heady exhilaration. Here came another, revolving, writhing like a sea snake, indistinct, shadowy. Let it go, the next one might be lured into the net. Here it came, two of them, roiling in the sleep hollows. Easily now, easily, easily, close in, easily, so there wouldn't be any warning ripples, closer, they weren't watching, murmuring to each other—*there! He had them!*

''Pru-itt. Oh, Pru-itt.''

The things veered away, their tails whipping his intellect into a spinning mass of chaotic frenzy.

"Pru-itt. Where are you? Pru-itt."

The boy blinked.

"Pru-itt. Oh, Pru-itt."

His mouth distorted like that of an enraged animal. He stuck out his tongue and hissed at the locked door. The handle turned.

"Pruitt, are you in there?"

"Yes, Miss Bittner." The words were thick and meaty in his mouth. If he bit down, Pruitt thought, he could bite one in two and chew it up and it would squish out between his teeth like an eclair.

"Unlock the door."

"Yes, Miss Bittner."

Pruitt blew out the candles and swept his treasures under the cot. He reconsidered this action, shoved his hand under the chintz skirt, snaffled the coal tar fly and stuffed it in his shirt.

"Do you hear me, Pruitt? Unlock this door." The knob rattled.

"I'm coming fast as I can," he said. He rose, stalked over to the door, shot back the bolt and stood, squinting, in the brilliant daylight before Miss Bittner.

"What on *earth* are you doing in there?"

"I guess I must've fallen asleep."

Miss Bittner peered into the murky confines of the bathhouse. She sniffed inquisitively.

"Pruitt," she said, "have you been smoking?"

"No, Miss Bittner."

"We mustn't tell a falsehood, Pruitt. It is far better to tell the truth and accept the consequences."

"I haven't been smoking." Pruitt could feel his stomach moving inside him. He was going to be sick again. Like he was the last time. Miss Bittner was wavering in front of him. Her outside edges were all blurry. His stomach gave a violent lurch. Pruitt looked at Miss Bittner's stockings. They were messy. Awfully messy. Miss Bittner looked at them, too.

"Run along up to the house, Pruitt," she said kindly. "I'll be up presently."

"Yes, Miss Bittner."

"And we won't say anything about smoking to your auntie. I think you've been sufficiently punished."

"Yes, Miss Bittner."

"Run along, now."

Pruitt were languidly up the path, conscious of Miss Bittner's eyes boring into him. When he turned the bend, he stopped and crept slyly into the bushes. He made his way back toward the boathouse, pressing the branches away from him and easing them cautiously to prevent them from snapping.

Miss Bittner sat on the steps taking off her stockings. She rinsed her legs in the water and dried them with her handkerchief. Pruitt could see an oval corn plaster on her little toe. She put her bony feet into her patent-leather Health Eases, got up, brushed her dress and disappeared into the bathhouse.

Pruitt inched nearer.

Miss Bittner came to the doorway and examined something she held in her hands. She looked puzzled. From his vantage point, Pruitt glimpsed the pink of the candy rosettes, the stubby candle wicks.

"I hate you," Pruitt whispered venomously, "I hate you, I *hate* you." Tenderly, he withdrew the coal tar image from his shirt. He cuddled it against his cheek. "Break her ear thing," he muttered. "Break it all to pieces so's she'll have to act deaf. Break it, break it, hahnee*wee*mahneemo, break it good." Warily he crawled backward until he regained the path.

He trudged onward, pausing only twice. Once, at a break in the hedge where he reached into the aperture and drew forth a cone-shaped contraption smeared with sirup. Five flies clung to this, their wings sticky, their legs gluey. These he disengaged, ignoring the lesser fry of gnats and midges that had met a similar fate, and returned the flycatcher to its lair. The second interruption along his line of march was a sort of interlude during which he cracked the two-inch spine of a garden lizard and hung it on a bramble where it performed incredibly tortuous convolutions with the lower half of its body.

Mona Eagleston came out of her bedroom and closed the door gently behind her. Everything about Mona was gentle from the top of her wren brown head threaded with gray to the slippers on her ridiculously tiny feet. She was rather like a fawn. An aging fawn with liquid eyes that, despite the encroaching years, had failed to lose their tiptoe look of expectancy.

One knew instinctively that Mona Eagleston was that rare phenomenon—a lady to the manor born. If, occasionally, when in close proximity with her nephew, a perplexed look overshadowed that delicate face, it was no more than a passing cloud. Children were inherently good. If they appeared otherwise, it was simply because their actions were misunderstood. They—he—Pruitt didn't *mean* to do things. He couldn't *know* that—well, that slamming the screen door, for instance, could send a sickening stab of pain through a head racked with migraine. He couldn't be *expected* to know, the poor orphan lamb. The poor, dear, orphan lamb.

If only she didn't have to pour at teatime. If only she could lie quiet and still with a cold compress on her head and the shutters pulled to. How selfish she was. Teatimes to a child were lovely, restful periods. Moments to be forever cherished in the pattern of memory. Like colorful loops of embroidery floss embellishing the whole. A skein of golden, shining teatimes with the sunset staining the windows and high-lighting the fat-sided Delft milk jug. The taste of jam, the brown crumbles left on the cookie plate, the teacups—eggshell frail—with handles like wedding rings. All of these were precious to a child. Deep down inside, without quite knowing why, they absorbed such things as sponges absorbed water—and, like sponges, they could wring these memories out when they were growing old. As she did, sometimes. What a wretched person she was to begrudge a teatime to Pruitt, dear, little Pruitt, her own dead brother's child.

She went on down the stairs, one white hand trailing the banister. The fern, she noticed, was dying. This was the third fern. She'd always had so much luck with ferns, until lately. Her goldfish, too. They had died. It was almost an omen. And Pruitt's turtles. She had bought them at the village. So cunning they were with enameled pictures on their hard, tree-barky shells. They had died. She mustn't think about dying. The doctor had said it was bad for her.

She crossed the great hall and entered the drawing room.

"Dear Pruitt," she said to the boy swinging his legs from the edge of a brocaded chair. She kissed him. She had intended to kiss his sunwarm cheek but he had moved, suddenly, and the kiss had met an unresponsive ear. Children were jumpy little things.

"Did you have a nice day?"

"Yes, aunt."

"And you, Miss Bittner? Did you have a nice day? And how did the conjugations go this morning? Did our young man . . . why, my dear, whatever is the matter?"

"She broke her ear thing," Pruitt said. He turned toward his tutor and enunciated in an exaggerated fashion, "Didn't you, Miss Bittner?"

Miss Bittner reddened. She spoke in the unnaturally loud, toneless voice of the deaf, "I dropped my hearing-aid," she explained. "On the bathroom floor. I'm afraid, until I get it fixed, that you'll have to bear with me." She smiled a tight strained smile to show that it was really quite a joke on her.

"What a shame," said Mona Eagleston, "but I daresay it can be repaired in the village. Harry can take it in tomorrow."

Miss Bittner followed the movement of Mona Eagleston's lips almost desperately.

"No," she said hesitantly, "Harry didn't do it. I did it. The bathroom tile, you know. It was frightfully clumsy of me."

"And she drank some lemonade that had a fly in it. Didn't you, Miss Bittner? I said you drank some lemonade that had a fly in it, didn't you?"

Miss Bittner nodded politely. Her eyes focused on Pruitt's mouth.

"Cry?" she ventured. "No, I didn't cry."

Mona Eagleston seated herself behind the teacaddy and prepared to pour. She must warn cook, hereafter, to put an oiled cover over the lemonade. One couldn't be too particular where children were concerned. They were susceptible to all sorts of diseases and flies were notorious carriers. If Pruitt were taken ill because of her lack of forethought, she would never forgive herself. Never.

"Could I have some marmalade?" Pruitt asked.

"We have currant cookies, dear, and nut bread. Do you think we need marmalade?"

"I do *so* love marmalade, aunt. Miss Bittner does, too. Don't you, Miss Bittner?"

Miss Bittner smiled stoically on and accepted her cup with a pleasant noncommittal murmur that she devoutly hoped would serve as an appropriate answer to whatever Pruitt was asking.

"Very well, dear." Mona tinkled a bell.

"I'll pass the cookies, aunt."

"Thank you, Pruitt. You are very thoughtful."

The boy took the plate and carried it over to Miss Bittner and an expression of acute suffering swam across the Bittner countenance as the boy trod heavily on her foot.

"Have some cookies." Pruitt thrust the plate at her.

"That's quite all right," Miss Bittner said, thinking he had apologized and congratulating herself on the fact that she hadn't moaned aloud. If he had *known* she had a corn, he couldn't have selected the location with more exactitude. She looked at the cookies. After the lemonade episode, she had felt she couldn't eat again—but they were tempting. Gracious, how that corn ached.

"Here's a nice curranty one." Pruitt popped a cookie on her plate.

"Thank you, Pruitt."

Cook waddled into the room. "Did you ring, Miss Mona?"

"Yes, Bertha. Would you get Pruitt some marmalade, please?"

Bertha shot a poisonous glance at Pruitt. "There's none up, ma'am. Will the jam do?"

Pruitt managed a sorrowful sigh. "I do *so* love marmalade, aunt," and then happily, as if it were an afterthought, "Isn't there some in the basement cubby?"

Mona Eagleston made a helpless moue at cook. "Would you mind terribly, Bertha? You know how children are."

"Yes, ma'am, I know how children are," cook said in a flat voice.

"Thank you, Bertha. The pineapple will do."

"Yes, ma'am." Bertha plodded away.

"*She* was walking around in her bare feet again today," Pruitt said.

His aunt shook her head sadly. "I don't know what to do," she said to Miss Bittner. "I dislike being cross, but ever since she stepped on that nail"—Mona Eagleston smiled quickly at her nephew—"not that you meant to leave it there, darling, but . . . well . . . will you have a slice of nut bread, Miss Bittner?"

Pruitt licked back a grin. "Aunt said would you like a slice of nut bread, Miss Bittner," he repeated ringingly.

Miss Bittner paid no heed. She seemed to be in a frozen trance sitting as she did rigidly upright staring at her plate with horror. She arose.

"I . . . I don't feel well," she said, "I think . . . I think I'd better go lie down."

Pruitt hopped off his chair and took her plate. Mona Eagleston made a distressed *tching* sound. "Is there anything I can do—" She half rose but Miss Bittner waved her back.

"It's nothing," Miss Bittner said hoarsely. "I . . . I think it's just something I . . . I ate. Don't let me distrub your t-t-teatime." She put her napkin over her mouth and hastily hobbled from the room.

"I should see that she—" began Mona Eagleston worriedly.

"Oh, don't let's ruin teatime," Pruitt interposed hurriedly. "Here, have some nut bread. It looks dreadfully good."

"Well—"

"Please, Aunt Mona, Not *tea*time."

"Very well, Pruitt," Mona chose a slice of bread. "Does teatime mean a great deal to you? It did to me when I was a little girl."

"Yes, aunt." He watched her break a morsel of bread, butter it and put it in her mouth.

"I used to live for teatime. It was such a cozy—" Mona Eagleston lifted a pale hand to her throat. She began to cough. Her eyes filled with tears. She looked wildly around for water. She tried to say "water" but couldn't get the word past the choking in her lungs. If Pruitt would only—but he was just a child. He couldn't be expected to know what to do for a coughing spell. Poor, dear Pruitt, he looked so . . . so—perturbed. Handing her the tea like that, his face all puckery. She gulped down a great draught of the scalding liquid. Her slight frame was seized with a paroxysm of coughing. Mercy! She must have mistakenly put salt in it, instead of sugar.

She wiped her brimming eyes. "Nutshell," she wheezed, gaining her feet. "Back . . . presently—" Coughing violently she, too, quitted the room.

From somewhere beneath Pruitt's feet, deep in the bowels of the house, came a faint faraway thud.

Pruitt picked the flies off of Miss Bittner's cookie. Where there had been five, there was now four and a half. He put the remains in his pocket. They might come in handy.

Dimly he heard cook calling for help. It was a smothered, hysterical calling. If Aunt Mona didn't return, it could go on quite a while before it was heeded. Cook could yell herself blue around the gills by then.

"Hahnee*wee*mahneemo," he crooned. "O Idol of the Flies, you have served me true, yea, yea, double yea, forty-five, thirty-two."

Pruitt helped himself to a heaping spoonful of sugar.

The pinkish sky was filled with cawing rocks. They pivoted and wheeled, they planed their wings into black fans and settled in the great old beeches to shout gossip at one another.

Pruitt scuffed his shoe on the stone steps and wished he had an air rifle. He would ask for one on his birthday. He would ask for a lot of impossible things first and then—pitifully—say, "Well, then, could I just have a little old air rifle?" Aunt would fall for that. She was as dumb as his mother had been. Dumber. His mother had been "simple" dumb, which was pretty bad—going in, as she had, for treacly bedtime stories and lap sitting. Aunt was "sick" dumb, which was very dumb indeed. "Sick" dumb people always looked at the "bright side." They were the dumbest of all. They were push-overs, "sick" dumb people were. Easy, little old push-overs.

Pruitt shifted his position as there came to his ears the scrape of footsteps in the hall.

That dragging sound would be cook. He wondered if she really *had* pulled the muscles loose in her back. Here came Harry with the car. They must be going to the doctor. Harry's hunch made him look like he had a pillow behind him.

"We mustn't let Pruitt know about the string," he heard his aunt say. "It would make him feel badly to learn that he had been the cause."

Cook made a low, unintelligible reply.

"Purposely!" his aunt exclaimed aghast. "Why, Bertha, I'm ashamed of you. He's only a *child.*"

Pruitt drew his lips into a thin line. If she told about the nut hulls, he'd fix her. He scrambled up the steps and held open the screen door.

But cook didn't tell about the nut hulls. She was too busy gritting her teeth against the tearing pull in her back.

"Can I help?" Pruitt let a troubled catch into his voice.

His aunt patted his check. "We can manage, dear, thank you."

Miss Bittner smiled on him benevolently. "You can take care of me while they're gone," she said. "We'll have a picnic supper. Won't that be fun?"

"Yes, Miss Bittner. *Oodles* of fun."

He watched the two women assist their injured companion down the steps with Harry collaborating. He kissed his fingers to his aunt as the car drove away and linked his arm through Miss Bittner's. He gazed cherubically up at her.

"You are a filthy mess," he said caressingly, "and I hate your guts."

Miss Bittner beamed on him. It wasn't often that Pruitt was openly loving to her. "I'm sorry, Pruitt, but I can't hear very well now, you know. Perhaps you'd like me to read to you for a while."

Pruitt shook his head. "I'll just play," he said loudly and distinctly and then, softly, "you liverless, old hyena."

"Play?" said Miss Bittner.

Pruitt nodded.

"All right, darling. But don't go far. It'll be supper time soon."

"Yes, Miss Bittner." He ran lightly down the steps. "Good-by," he called, "you homely, dear, old hag, you."

"Good-by," said Miss Bittner, nodding and smiling.

Pruitt placed the bread board on the pegs and arranged the candles in a semicircle. One of them refused to stay vertical. It had been stepped on.

Pruitt examined it angrily. You'd think *she'd* be particular with other people's property. The sniveling fool. He'd fix *her.* He ate the candy rosette with relish and, after it was completely devoured, chewed up the candle, spitting out the wick when it had reached a sufficiently malleable state. He delved into his shirt front and extracted the coal tar fly which had developed a decided list to starboard. He compressed it into shape, re-anchored a wobbly pipestem leg, and established the figure in the center of the bread board.

He folded his arms and began to rock back and forth, the swealing candles spreading his shadow behind him like a thick, dark cloak.

"Hahnee*wee*mahneemo. O Idol of the Flies, hear, hear, O hear, come close and *hear.* Miss Bittner scrooched one of your candles. So send me lots of flies, lots and lots of flies, millions, trillions, skillions of flies. Quadrillions and skintillions. Make them also no-color so's I can mix them up in soup and things without them showing much. Black ones show. Send me pale ones that don't buzz and have feelers. Hear me, hear me, hear me, O Idol of the Flies, come close and *hear!*"

Pruitt chewed his candle and contemplated. His face lighted, as he was struck with a brilliant thought. "And make a thinking-time-dream-thing hold still so's I can get it. So's I'll *know.* I guess that's all. Hahnee*wee*mahneemo, O Idol of the Flies, you are free to GO!"

As he had done earlier in the afternoon, Pruitt became quiescent. His eyes, catlike, were set and staring, staring, staring, staring fixedly at nothing at all.

He didn't look excited. He looked like a small boy engaged in some innocuous small-boyish pursuit. But he *was* excited. Excitement coursed through his veins and rang in his ears. The pit of his stomach was cold with it and the palms of his hands were as moist as the inside of his mouth was dry.

This was the way he felt when he knew his father and mother were going to die. He had known it with a sort of clear, glittering lucidity—standing there in the white Bermuda sunlight, waving good-by to them. He had seen the plumy feather on his mother's hat, the sprigged organdy dress, his father's pointed mustache and his slender, artist's hands grasping the driving reins. He had seen the gleaming harness, the high-spirited shake of the horse's head, its stamping foot. His father wouldn't have a horse that wasn't high-spirited. Ginger had been its name. He had seen the bobbing fringe on the carriage top and the pin in the right rear wheel—the pin that he had diligently and with patient perseverance, worked loose with the screwdriver out of his toy tool chest. He had seen them roll away, down the drive, out through the wrought-iron gates. He had wondered if they would turn over when they rounded the bend and what sort of a crash they would make. They had turned over but he hadn't heard the crash. He had been in the house eating the icing off the cake.

But he *had* known they were going to die. The knowledge had been almost more than he could control, as even now it was hard to govern the knowledge, the *certainty*, that he was going to snare a dream-thing.

He knew it. He knew it. He knew it. With every wire-taut nerve in his body he knew it.

Here came one. Streaking through his mind, leaving a string of phosphorescent bubbles in its wake and the bubbles rose and burst and there were dark, bloody smears where they had been. Another—shooting itself along with its tail—its greasy sides ashine. Another—and another—and another—and then a seething whirlpool of them. There had never been so many. Spiny, pulpy, slick and eellike, some with feelers like catfish, some with white, gaping mouths and foreshortened embryo arms. Their contortions clogged his thoughts with weeping. But there was one down in the black, not-able-to-get-to part of his mind that watched him. It knew what he wanted. And it was blind. But it was watching him *through* its blindness. It was coming. Wriggling closer, bringing the black, not-able-to-get-to-part with it and where it passed the others sank away and his mind was wild with depraved weeping. Its nose holes went in and out, in and out, in and out, like something he had known long ago in some past, mysterious other life, and it whimpered as it came and whispered things to him. Disconnected things that swelled his heart and ran like juice along the cracks in his skull. In a moment it would be quite near, in a moment he would *know*.

"Pruitt. Pruitt." The words were drops of honey.

"Pruitt. Pruitt." Pollen words, nectareous, sprinkled with flower dust. The dream-thing waited. It did not—like the rest—dart away affrighted.

"Pruitt. Pruitt." The voice came from outside himself. From far away and down, from some incredible depth like the place in his mind where They had a nest—only it was distant—and deep. Quite deep. So hot and deep.

With an immense effort Pruitt blinked.

"Look at me." The voice was dulcet and alluring.

Again Pruitt blinked, and as his wits ebbed in like a sluggish tide bringing the watching dream-thing with it, he saw a man.

He stood tall and commanding and from chin to toe he was wrapped in a flowing cape and, in the flickering candlelight, the cape had the exact outlines of Pruitt's shadow, and in and about the cape swam the watching dream-thing, as if it were at home. Above the cloak the man's face was a grinning mask and through the mouth, the nostrils and the slits of eyes poured a reddish translucent light. A glow. Like that of a Halloween pumpkin head, only intensified a thousandfold.

"Pruitt. Look, Pruitt." The folds of the cloak lifted and fell as if an invisible arm had gestured. Pruitt followed the gesture hypnotically. His neck twisted round, slowly, slowly, until his gaze encompassed a rain of insects. A living curtain of them. A shimmering and noiseless cascade of colorless flies, gauzy winged long bodied.

"Flies, Pruitt. Millions of flies."

Pruitt once more rotated his neck until he confronted the stranger. The blind dream-thing giggled at him and swam into a pleat of darkness.

"Who—are—you?" The words were thick and sweet on Pruitt's tongue like other words he half remembered speaking a thousand years ago on some dim plane in some hazy twilight world.

"My name is Asmodeus, Pruitt. Asmodeus. Isn't it a beautiful name?"

"Yes."

"Say it, Pruitt."

"Asmodeus."

"Again."

"Asmodeus."

"Again, Pruitt."

"Asmodeus."

"What do you see in my cloak?"

"A dream-thought."

"And what is it doing?"

"It is gibbering at me."

"Why?"

"Because your cloak has the power of darkness and I may not enter until—"

"Until what, Pruitt?"

"Until I look into your eyes and see—"

"See what, Pruitt?"

"What is written therein."

"And what is written therein? Look into my eyes, Pruitt. Look long and well. What is written therein?"

"It is written what I wish to know. It is written—"

"What is written, Pruitt?"

"It is written of the limitless, the eternal, the foreverness, of the what is and was ordained to ever be, unceasingly, beyond the ends of Time for . . . for—"

"For whom, Pruitt?"

The boy wrenched his eyes away. "No," he said, and with rising crescendo, "no, no, no, no, no." He scooted backward across the floor, pushing with his hands, shoving with his heels, his face contorted with terror. "No," he babbled, "no, no, no, no, no, no, no, no, no, no."

"*Yes*, Pruitt. For whom?"

The boy reached the door and lurched to his feet, his jaw flaccid, his eyes starting in their sockets. He turned and fled up the path, heedless of the pelting flies that fastened themselves to his clothes and tangled in his hair, and touched his flesh like ghostly, clinging fingers, and scrunched beneath his feet as he ran on—his breath breaking from his lungs in sobbing gasps.

"Miss Bittner . . . help . . . Miss Bittner . . . Aunt . . . Harry . . . help—"

At the bend waiting for him stood the figure he had left behind in the bathhouse.

"For whom, Pruitt?"

"No, no, no."

"For whom, Pruitt?"

"No, oh no, *no!*"

"For whom, Pruitt?"

"For the DAMNED," the boy shrieked and, wheeling, he ran back the way he had come, the flies sticking to his skin, mashing as he tried frantically to rid himself of them as on he sped.

The man behind him began to chant. High, shrill, and mocking, and the dream-thought took it up, and the earth, and the trees, and the sky that dripped flies, and the pilings of the pier clustered with their pulsating bodies, and the water, patched as far as eye could see with clotted islands of flies, flies, flies. And from his own throat came laughter, crazed and wanton, unrestrained and terrible, peal upon peal of hellish laughter that would not stop. Even as his legs would not stop when they reached the end of the pier.

A red-breasted robin—a fly in its beak—watched the widening ripples. A garden lizard scampered over a tuft of grass and joined company with a toad at the water's edge, as if to lend their joint moral support to the turtle who slid off the bank and with jerky motions of its striped legs went down to investigate the thing that was entwined so securely in a fishing net there on the sandy bottom by the pier.

Miss Bittner idly flipped through a textbook on derivatives. The textbook was a relic of bygone days and the pages were studded with pressed wild flowers brittle with age. With a fingernail she loosened a tissue-thin four-leaf clover. It had left its yellow-green aura on the printed text.

"Beelzebub," Miss Bittner read absently, "stems from the Hebraic. Beel—meaning idol, zebub—meaning flies: Synonyms, lesser known, not in common usage, are: Appolyon, Abbadon, Asmodeus—" but Miss Bittner's attention flagged. She closed the book, yawned and wondered lazily where Pruitt was.

She went to the window and immediately drew back with revulsion. Green Bay flies. Heavens, they were all over everything.

The horrid creatures. Funny how they blew in off the water. She recalled last year, when she had been with the Braithwaites in Michigan, they had come—and in such multitudes—that the townspeople had had to shovel them up off the streets. Actually *shovel* them. She had been ill for three whole days thereafter.

She hoped Pruitt wouldn't be dismayed by them. She must guard against showing her own helpless panic as she had done at teatime. Children placed such implicit faith in the invincibility of their elders.

Dear Pruitt, he had been so charming to her today.

Dear, little Pruitt.

Judgement Day

FLANNERY O'CONNOR

This powerful, sad, and ultimately chilling account of an old man's translocation from his native Georgia to New York City is among Flannery O'Connor's most evocative stories. It also incorporates a religious dimension that may be found in all of her distinguished works: the novels Wise Blood *and* The Violent Bear It Away, *and the stories in her collections* A Good Man is Hard to Find *and the posthumously published* Everything That Rises Must Converge. *An imaginative and perceptive chronicler of life in the "new" American South, Ms. O'Connor died tragically young in 1964, at the age of thirty-nine.*

TANNER was conserving all his strength for the trip home. He meant to walk as far as he could get and trust to the Almighty to get him the rest of the way. That morning and the morning before, he had allowed his daughter to dress him and had conserved that much more energy. Now he sat in the chair by the window—his blue shirt buttoned at the collar, his coat on the back of the chair, and his hat on his head—waiting for her to leave. He couldn't escape until she got out of the way. The window looked out on a brick wall and down into an alley full of New York air, the kind fit for cats and garbage. A few snow flakes drifted past the window but they were too thin and scattered for his failing vision.

The daughter was in the kitchen washing dishes. She dawdled over everything, talking to herself. When he had first come, he had answered her, but that had not been wanted. She glowered at him as if, old fool that he was, he should still have sense enough not to answer a woman talking to herself. She questioned herself in one voice and answered herself in another. With the energy he had conserved yesterday letting her dress him, he had written a note and pinned it in his pocket. IF FOUND DEAD SHIP EXPRESS COLLECT TO COLEMAN PARRUM, CORINTH, GEORGIA. Under this he had continued: COLEMAN SELL MY BELONGINGS AND PAY THE FREIGHT ON ME & THE UNDERTAKER. ANYTHING LEFT OVER YOU CAN KEEP. YOURS TRULY T. C. TANNER. P.S. STAY WHERE YOU ARE. DON'T LET THEM TALK YOU INTO COMING UP HERE. IT'S NO KIND OF PLACE. It had taken him the better part of thirty minutes to write the paper; the script was wavery but decipherable with patience. He controlled one hand by holding the other on top of it. By the time he had got it written, she was back in the apartment from getting her groceries.

Today he was ready. All he had to do was push one foot in front of the other until he got to the door and down the steps. Once down the steps, he would get out of the neighborhood.

Once out of it, he would hail a taxi cab and go to the freight yards. Some bum would help him onto a car. Once he got in the freight car, he would lie down and rest. During the night the train would start South, and the next day or the morning after, dead or alive, he would be home. Dead or alive. It was being there that mattered; the dead or alive did not.

If he had had good sense he would have gone the day after he arrived; better sense and he would not have arrived. He had not got desperate until two days ago when he had heard his daughter and son-in-law taking leave of each other after breakfast. They were standing in the front door, she seeing him off for a three-day trip. He drove a long distance moving van. She must have handed him his leather head gear. "You ought to get you a hat," she said, "a real one."

"And sit all day in it," the son-in-law said, "like him in there. Yah! All he does is sit all day with that hat on. Sits all day with that damn black hat on his head. Inside!"

"Well you don't even have you a hat," she said. "Nothing but that leather cap with flaps. People that are somebody wear hats. Other kinds wear those leather caps like you got on."

"People that are somebody!" he cried. "People that are somebody! That kills me! That really kills me!" The son-in-law had a stupid muscular face and a yankee voice to go with it.

"My daddy is here to stay," his daughter said. "He ain't going to last long. He was somebody when he was somebody. He never worked for nobody in his life but himself and had people—other people—working for him."

"Yah? Niggers is what he had working for him," the son-in-law said. "That's all. I've worked a nigger or two myself."

"Those were just nawthun niggers you worked," she said, her voice suddenly going lower so that Tanner had to lean forward to catch the words. "It takes brains to work a real nigger. You got to know how to handle them."

"Yah so I don't have brains," the son-in-law said.

One of the sudden, very occasional, feelings of warmth for the daughter came over Tanner. Every now and then she said something that might make you think she had a little sense stored away somewhere for safe keeping.

"You got them," she said. "You don't always use them."

"He has a stroke when he sees a nigger in the building," the son-in-law said, "and she tells me . . ."

"Shut up talking so loud," she said. "That's not why he had the stroke."

There was a silence. "Where you going to bury him?" the son-in-law asked, taking a different tack.

"Bury who?"

"Him in there."

"Right here in New York," she said. "Where do you think? We got a lot. I'm not taking that trip down there again with nobody."

"Yah. Well I just wanted to make sure," he said.

When she returned to the room, Tanner had both hands gripped on the chair arms. His eyes were trained on her like the eyes of an angry corpse. "You promised you'd bury me there," he said. "Your promise ain't any good. Your promise ain't any good. Your promise ain't any good." His voice was so dry it was barely audible. He began to shake, his hands, his head, his feet. "Bury me here and burn in hell!" he cried and fell back into his chair.

The daughter shuddered to attention. "You ain't dead yet!" She threw out a ponderous sigh. "You got a long time to be worrying about that." She turned and began to pick up parts of the newspaper scattered on the floor. She had grey hair that hung to her shoulders and a round face, beginning to wear. "I do every last living thing for you," she muttered, "and this is the way you carry on." She stuck the papers under her arm and said, "And don't throw hell at me. I don't believe in it. That's a lot of hardshell Baptist hooey." Then she went into the kitchen.

He kept his mouth stretched taut, his top plate gripped between his tongue and the roof of his mouth. Still the tears flooded down his cheeks; he wiped each one furtively on his shoulder.

Her voice rose from the kitchen. "As bad as having a child. He wanted to come and now he's here, he don't like it."

He had not wanted to come.

"Pretended he didn't but I could tell. I said if you don't want to come I can't make you. If you don't want to live like decent people there's nothing I can do about it."

"As for me," her higher voice said, "when I die that ain't the time I'm going to start getting choosey. They can lay me in the nearest spot. When I pass from this world I'll be considerate of them that stay in it. I won't be thinking of just myself."

"Certainly not," the other voice said, "you never been that selfish. You're the kind that looks out for other people."

"Well I try," she said, "I try."

He laid his head on the back of his chair for a moment and the hat tilted down over his eyes. He had raised three boys and her. The three boys were gone, two in the war and one to the devil and there was nobody left who felt a duty toward him but her, married and childless, in New York City like Mrs. Big and ready when she came back and found him living the way he was to take him back with her. She had put her face in the door of the shack and had stared, expressionless, for a second. Then all at once she had screamed and jumped back.

"What's that on the floor?"

"Coleman," he said.

The old Negro was curled up on a pallet asleep at the foot of Tanner's bed, a stinking skin full of bones, arranged in what seemed vaguely human form. When Coleman was young, he had looked like a bear; now that he was old he looked like a monkey. With Tanner it was the opposite; when he was young he had looked like a monkey but when he got old, he looked like a bear.

The daughter stepped back onto the porch. There were the bottoms of two cane chairs tilted against the clapboard but she declined to take a seat. She stepped out about ten feet from the house as if it took that much space to clear the odor. Then she had spoken her piece.

"If you don't have any pride I have and I know my duty and I was raised to do it. My mother raised me to do it if you didn't. She was from plain people but not the kind that likes to settle in with niggers."

At that point the old Negro roused up and slid out the door, a doubled-up shadow which Tanner just caught sight of gliding away.

She had shamed him. He shouted so they both could hear. "Who you think cooks? Who you think cuts my firewood and empties my slops? He's paroled to me. That no-good scoundrel has been on my hands for thirty years. He ain't a bad nigger."

She was unimpressed. "Whose shack is this anyway?" she had asked. "Yours or his?"

"Him and me built it," he said. "You go on back up there. I wouldn't come with you for no million dollars or no sack of salt."

"It looks like him and you built it. Whose land is it on?"

"Some people that live in Florida," he said evasively. He had known then that it was land up for sale but he thought it was too sorry for anyone to buy. That same afternoon he had found out different. He had found out in time to go back with her. If he had found out a day later, he might still be there, squatting on the doctor's land.

When he saw the brown porpoise-shaped figure striding across the field that afternoon, he had known at once what had happened; no one had to tell him. If that nigger had owned the whole world except for one runty rutted peafield and he acquired it, he would walk across it that way, beating the weeds aside, his thick neck swelled, his stomach a throne for his gold watch and chain. Doctor Foley. He was only part black. The rest was Indian and white.

He was everything to the niggers—druggist and undertaker and general counsel and real estate man and sometimes he got the evil eye off them and sometimes he put it on. Be prepared, he said to himself, watching him approach, to take something off him, nigger though he be. Be prepared, because you ain't got a thing to hold up to him but the skin you came in, and that's no more use to you now than what a snake would shed. You don't have a chance with the government against you.

He was sitting on the porch in the piece of straight chair tilted against the shack. "Good evening, Foley," he said and nodded as the doctor came up and stopped short at the edge of the clearing, as if he had only just that minute seen him though it was plain he had sighted him as he crossed the field.

"I be out here to look at my property," the doctor said. "Good evening." His voice was quick and high.

Ain't been your property long, he said to himself. "I seen you coming," he said.

"I acquired this here recently," the doctor said and proceeded without looking at him again to walk around to one side of the shack. In a moment he came back and stopped in front of him. Then he stepped boldly to the door of the shack and put his head in. Coleman was in there that time too, asleep. He looked for a moment and then turned aside. "I know that nigger," he said. "Coleman Parrum—how long does it take him to sleep off that stump liquor you all make?"

Tanner took hold of the knobs on the chair bottom and held them hard. "This shack ain't in your property. Only on it, by my mistake," he said.

The doctor removed his cigar momentarily from his mouth. "It ain't my mis-take," he said and smiled.

He had only sat there, looking ahead.

"It don't pay to make this kind of mis-take," the doctor said.

"I never found anything that paid yet," he muttered.

"Everything pays," the Negro said, "if you knows how to make it," and he remained there smiling, looking the squatter up and down. Then he turned and went around the other side of the shack there was a silence. He was looking for the still.

Then would have been the time to kill him. There was a gun inside the shack and he could have done it as easy as not, but, from childhood, he had been weakened for that kind of violence by the fear of hell. He had never killed one, he had always handled them with his wits and with luck. He was known to have a way with niggers. There was an art to handling them. The secret of handling a nigger was to show him his brains didn't have a chance against yours; then he would jump on your back and know he had a good thing there for life. He had had Coleman on his back for thirty years.

Tanner had first seen Coleman when he was working six of them at a saw mill in the middle of a pine forest fifteen miles from nowhere. They were as sorry a crew as he had worked, the kind that on Monday they didn't show up. What was in the air had reached them. They thought there was a new Lincoln elected who was going to abolish work. He managed them with a very sharp penknife. He had had something wrong with his kidney then that made his hands shake and he had taken to whittling to force that waste motion out of sight. He did not intend them to see that his hands shook of their own accord and he did not intend to see it himself or to countenance it. The knife had moved constantly, violently, in his quaking hands and here and there small crude figures—that he never looked at again and could not have said what they were if he had—dropped to the ground. The Negroes picked them up and took them home; there was not much time between them and darkest Africa. The knife glittered constantly in his hands. More than once he had stopped short and said in an off-hand voice to some half-reclining, head-averted Negro, "Nigger, this knife is in my hand now but if you don't quit wasting my time and money, it'll be in your gut shortly." And the Negro would begin to rise—slowly, but he would be in the act—before the sentence was completed.

A large black loose-jointed Negro, twice his own size, had begun hanging around the edge of the saw mill, watching the others work and when he was not watching, sleeping, in full view of them, sprawled like a gigantic bear on his back. "Who is that?" he had asked. "If he wants to work, tell him to come here. If he don't, tell him to go. No idlers are going to hang around here."

None of them knew who he was. They knew he didn't want to

work. They knew nothing else, not where he had come from, nor why, though he was probably brother to one, cousin to all of them. He had ignored him for a day; against the six of them he was one yellow-faced scrawny white man with shaky hands. He was willing to wait for trouble, but not forever. The next day the stranger came again. After the six Tanner worked had seen the idler there for half the morning, they quit and began to eat, a full thirty minutes before noon. He had not risked ordering them up. He had gone to the source of the trouble.

The stranger was leaning against a tree on the edge of the clearing, watching with half-closed eyes. The insolence on his face barely covered the wariness behind it. His look said, this ain't much of a white man so why he come on so big, what he fixing to do?

He had meant to say, "Nigger, this knife is in my hand now but if you ain't out of my sight . . ." but as he drew closer he changed his mind. The Negro's eyes were small and bloodshot. Tanner supposed there was a knife on him somewhere that he would as soon use as not. His own penknife moved, directed solely by some intruding intelligence that worked in his hands. He had no idea what he was carving, but when he reached the Negro, he had already made two holes the size of half dollars in the piece of bark.

The Negro's gaze fell on his hands and was held. His jaw slackened. His eyes did not move from the knife tearing recklessly around the bark. He watched as if he saw an invisible power working on the wood.

He looked himself then and, astonished, saw the connected rims of a pair of spectacles.

He held them away from him and looked through the holes past a pile of shavings and on into the woods to the edge of the pen where they kept their mules.

"You can't see so good, can you boy?" he said and began scraping the ground with his foot to turn up a piece of wire. He picked up a small piece of haywire; in a minute he found another, shorter piece and picked that up. He began to attach these to the bark. He was in no hurry now that he knew what he was doing. When the spectacles were finished, he handed them to the Negro. "Put these on," he said. "I hate to see anybody can't see good."

There was an instant when the Negro might have done one thing or another, might have taken the glasses and crushed them in his hand or grabbed the knife and turned it on him. He saw the exact instant in the muddy liquor-swollen eyes when the pleasure of having a knife in this white man's gut was balanced against something else, he could not tell what.

The Negro reached for the glasses. He attached the bows carefully behind his ears and looked forth. He peered this way and that with exaggerated solemnity. And then he looked directly at Tanner and grinned, or grimaced, Tanner could not tell which, but he had an instant's sensation of seeing before him a negative image of himself, as if clownishness and captivity had been their common lot. The vision failed him before he could decipher it.

"Preacher," he said, "what you hanging around here for?" He picked up another piece of bark and began, without looking at it, to carve again. "This ain't Sunday."

"This here ain't Sunday?" the Negro said.

"This is Friday," he said. "That's the way it is with you preachers—drunk all week so you don't know when Sunday is. What you see through those glasses?"

"See a man."

"What kind of a man?"

"See the man make theseyer glasses."

"Is he white or black?"

"He white!" the Negro said as if only at that moment was his vision sufficiently improved to detect it. "Yessuh, he white!" he said.

"Well, you treat him like he was white," Tanner said. "What's your name?"

"Name Coleman," the Negro said.

And he had not got rid of Coleman since. You make a monkey out of one of them and he jumps on your back and stays there for life, but let one make a monkey out of you and all you can do is kill him or disappear. And he was not going to hell for killing a nigger. Behind the shack he heard the doctor kick over a bucket. He sat and waited.

In a moment the doctor appeared again, beating his way around the other side of the house, whacking at scattered clumps of Johnson grass with his cane. He stopped in the middle of the yard, about where that morning the daughter had delivered her ultimatum.

"You don't belong here," he began. "I could have you prosecuted."

Tanner remained there, dumb, staring across the field.

"Where's your still?" the doctor asked.

"If it's a still around here, it don't belong to me," he said and shut his mouth tight.

The Negro laughed softly. "Down on your luck, ain't you?" he murmured. "Didn't you used to own a little piece of land over acrost the river and lost it?"

He had continued to study the woods ahead.

"If you want to run the still for me, that's one thing," the doctor said. "If you don't, you might as well had be packing up."

"I don't have to work for you," he said. "The governmint ain't got around yet to forcing the white folks to work for the colored."

The doctor polished the stone in his ring with the ball of his thumb. "I don't like the governmint no bettern you," he said. "Where you going instead? You going to the city and get you a soot of rooms at the Biltmo' Hotel?"

Tanner said nothing.

"The day coming," the doctor said, "when the white folks IS going to be working for the colored and you mights well to git ahead of the crowd."

"That day ain't coming for me," Tanner said shortly.

"Done come for you," the doctor said. "Ain't come for the rest of them."

Tanner's gaze drove on past the farthest blue edge of the treeline into the pale empty afternoon sky. "I got a daughter in the north," he said. "I don't have to work for you."

The doctor took his watch from his watch pocket and looked at it and put it back. He gazed for a moment at the back of his hands. He appeared to have measured and to know secretly the time it would take everything to change finally upsidedown. "She don't want no old daddy like you," he said. "Maybe she say she do, but that ain't likely. Even if you rich," he said, "they don't want you. They got they own ideas. The black ones they rares and they pitches. I made mine," he said, "and I ain't done none of that." He looked again at Tanner. "I be back here next week," he said, "and if you still here, I know you going to work for me." He remained there a moment, rocking on his heels, waiting for some answer. Finally he turned and started beating his way back through the overgrown path.

Tanner had continued to look across the field as if his spirit had been sucked out of him into the woods and nothing was left on the chair but a shell. If he had known it was a question of this—sitting here looking out of this window all day in this no-place, or just running a still for a nigger, he would have run the still for the nigger. He would have been a nigger's white nigger any day. Behind him he heard the daughter come in from the kitchen. His heart accelerated but after a second he heard her plump herself down on the sofa. She was not yet ready to go. He did not turn and look at her.

She sat there silently a few moments. Then she began. "The trouble with you is," she said, "you sit in front of that window all the time where there's nothing to look out at. You need some inspiration and an out-let. If you would let me pull your chair around to look at the TV, you would quit thinking about morbid stuff, death and hell and judgement. My Lord."

"The Judgement is coming," he muttered. "The sheep'll be separated from the goats. Them that kept their promises from them that didn't. Them that did the best they could with what they had from them that didn't. Them that honored their father and their mother from them that cursed them. Them that . . ."

She heaved a mammoth sigh that all but drowned him out. "What's the use in me wasting my good breath?" she asked. She rose and went back in the kitchen and began knocking things about.

She was so high and mighty! At home he had been living in a shack but there was at least air around it. He could put his feet on the ground. Here she didn't even live in a house. She lived in a pigeon-hutch of a building, with all stripes of foreigner, all of them twisted in the tongue. It was no place for a sane man. The first morning here she had taken him sightseeing and he had seen in fifteen minutes exactly how it was. He had not been out of the apartment since. He never wanted to set foot again on the underground railroad or the steps that moved under you while you stood still or any elevator to the thirty-fourth floor. When he was safely back in the apartment again, he had imagined going over it with Coleman. He had to turn his head every few seconds to make sure Coleman was behind him. Keep to the inside or these people'll knock you down, keep right behind me or you'll get left, keep your hat on, you damn idiot, he had said, and Coleman had come on with his bent running shamble, panting and muttering, What we doing here? Where you get this fool idea coming here?

I come to show you it was no kind of place. Now you know you were well off where you were.

I knowed it before, Coleman said. Was you didn't know it.

When he had been here a week, he had got a postcard from Coleman that had been written for him by Hooten at the railroad station. It was written in green ink and said, "This is Coleman—X—howyou boss." Under it Hooten had written from himself, "Quit frequenting all those nitespots and come on home, you scoundrel, yours truly, W. P. Hooten." He had sent Coleman a card in return, care of Hooten, that said, "This place is alrite if you like it. Yours truly, W. T. Tanner." Since the daughter had to mail the card, he had not put on it that he was returning as soon as his pension check came. He had not intended to tell her but to leave her a note. When the check came, he would hire himself a taxi to the bus station and be on his way. And it would have made her as happy as it made him. She had found his company dour and her duty irksome. If he had sneaked out, she would have had the pleasure of having tried to do it and to top that off, the pleasure of his ingratitude.

As for him, he would have returned to squat on the doctor's land and to take his orders from a nigger who chewed ten-cent cigars. And to think less about it than formerly. Instead he had been done in by a nigger actor, or one who called himself an actor. He didn't believe the nigger was any actor.

There were two apartments on each floor of the building. He had been with the daughter three weeks when the people in the next hutch moved out. He had stood in the hall and watched the moving-out and the next day he had watched a moving-in. The hall was narrow and dark and he stood in the corner out of the way, offering only a suggestion every now and then to the movers that would have made their work easier for them if they had paid any attention. The furniture was new and cheap so he decided the people moving in might be a newly married couple and he would just wait around until they came and wish them well. After a while a large Negro in a light blue suit came lunging up the stairs, carrying two canvas suitcases, his head lowered against the strain. Behind him stepped a young tan-skinned woman with bright copper-colored hair. The Negro dropped the suitcases with a thud in front of the door of the next apartment.

"Be careful, Sweetie," the woman said. "My make-up is in there."

It broke upon him then just what was happening.

The Negro was grinning. He took a swipe at one of her hips.

"Quit it," she said, "there's an old guy watching."

They both turned and looked at him.

"Had-do," he said and nodded. Then he turned quickly into his own door.

His daughter was in the kitchen. "Who you think's rented that apartment over there?" he asked, his face alight.

She looked at him suspiciously. "Who?" she muttered.

"A nigger!" he said in a gleeful voice. "A South Alabama nigger if I ever saw one. And got him this high-yeller, high-stepping woman with red hair and they two are going to live next door to you!" He slapped his knee. "Yes siree!" he said. "Damn if they ain't!" It was the first time since coming up here that he had had occasion to laugh.

Her face squared up instantly. "All right now you listen to me," she said. "You keep away from them. Don't you go over there trying to get friendly with him. They ain't the same around here and I don't want any trouble with niggers, you hear me? If you have to live next to them, just mind your business and they'll mind theirs. That's the way people were meant to get along in this world. Everybody can get along if they just mind their business. Live and let live." She began to wrinkle her nose like a rabbit, a stupid way she had. "Up here everybody minds their own business and everybody gets along. That's all you have to do."

"I was getting along with niggers before you were born," he said. He went back out into the hall and waited. He was willing to bet the nigger would like to talk to someone who understood him. Twice while he waited, he forgot and in his excitement, spit his tobacco juice against the baseboard. In about twenty minutes, the door of the apartment opened again and the Negro came out. He had put on a tie and a pair of horn-rimmed spectacles and Tanner noticed for the first time that he had a small almost invisible goatee. A real swell. He came on without appearing to see there was anyone else in the hall.

"Haddy, John," Tanner said and nodded, but the Negro brushed past without hearing and went rattling rapidly down the stairs.

Could be deaf and dumb, Tanner thought. He went back into the apartment and sat down but each time he heard a noise in the hall, he got up and went to the door and stuck his head out to see if it might be the Negro. Once in the middle of the afternoon, he caught the Negro's eye just as he was rounding the bend of the stairs again but before he could get out a word, the man was in his own apartment and had slammed the door. He had never known one to move that fast unless the police were after him.

He was standing in the hall early the next morning when the woman came out of her door alone, walking on high gold-painted heels. He wished to bid her good morning or simply nod but instinct told him to beware. She didn't look like any kind of woman, black or white, he had ever seen before and he remained pressed against the wall, frightened more than anything else, and feigning invisibility.

The woman gave him a flat stare, then turned her head away and stepped wide of him as if she was skirting an open garbage can. He held his breath until she was out of sight. Then he waited patiently for the man.

The Negro came out about eight o'clock.

This time Tanner advanced squarely in his path. "Good morning, Preacher," he said. It had been his experience that if a Negro tended to be sullen, this title usually cleared up his expression.

The Negro stopped abruptly.

"I seen you move in," Tanner said. "I ain't been up here long myself. It ain't much of a place if you ask me. I reckon you wish you were back in South Alabama."

The Negro did not take a step or answer. His eyes began to move. They moved from the top of the black hat, down to the collarless blue shirt, neatly buttoned at the neck, down the faded galluses to the grey trousers and the hightop shoes and up again, very slowly, while some unfathomable dead-cold rage seemed to stiffen and shrink him.

"I thought you might know somewhere around here we could find us a pond, Preacher," Tanner said in a voice growing thinner but still with considerable hope in it.

A seething noise came out of the Negro before he spoke. 'I'm not from South Alabama," he said in a breathless wheezing voice. "I'm from New York City. And I'm not no preacher! I'm an actor."

Tanner chortled. "It's a little actor in most preachers, ain't it?" he said and winked. "I reckon you just preach on the side."

"I don't preach!" the Negro cried and rushed past him as if a swarm of bees had suddenly come down on him out of nowhere. He dashed down the stairs and was gone.

Tanner stood there for some time before he went back in the apartment. The rest of the day he sat in his chair and debated whether he would have one more try at making friends with him. Every time he heard a noise on the stairs he went to the door and looked out, but the Negro did not return until late in the afternoon. Tanner was standing in the hall waiting for him when he reached the top of the stairs. "Good evening, Preacher," he said, forgetting that the Negro called himself an actor.

The Negro stopped and gripped the banister rail. A tremor racked him from his head to his crotch. Then he began to come forward slowly. When he was close enough he lunged and grasped Tanner by both shoulders. "I don't take no crap," he whispered, "off no wool-hat red-neck son-of-a-bitch pecker-wood old bastard like you." He caught his breath. And then his voice came out in the sound of an exasperation so profound that it rocked on the verge of a laugh. It was high and piercing and weak. "And I'm not no preacher! I'm not even no Christian. I don't believe that crap. There ain't no Jesus and there ain't no God."

The old man felt his heart inside him hard and tough as an oak knot. "And you ain't black," he said. "And I ain't white!"

The Negro slammed him against the wall. He yanked the black hat down over his eyes. Then he grabbed his shirt front and shoved him backwards to his open door and knocked him through it. From the kitchen the daughter saw him blindly hit the edge of the inside door and fall reeling into the livingroom.

For days his tongue appeared to be frozen in his mouth. When it unthawed it was twice its normal size and he could not make her understand him. What he wanted to know was if the government check had come because he meant to buy a bus ticket with it and go home. After a few days, he made her understand. "It came,'' she said, ''and it'll just pay the first two weeks' doctor-bill and please tell me how you're going home when you can't talk or walk or think straight and you got one eye crossed yet? Just please tell me that?''

It had come to him then slowly just what his present situation was. At least he would have to make her understand that he must be sent home to be buried. They could have him shipped back in a refrigerated car so that he would keep for the trip. He didn't want any undertaker up here messing with him. Let them get him off at once and he would come in on the early morning train and they could wire Hooten to get Coleman and Coleman would do the rest; she would not even have to go herself. After a lot of argument, he wrung the promise from her. She would ship him back.

After that he slept peacefully and improved a little. In his dreams he could feel the cold early morning air of home coming in through the cracks of the pine box. He could see Coleman waiting, red-eyed, on the station platform and Hooten standing there with his green eyeshade and black alpaca sleeves. If the old fool had stayed at home where he belonged, Hooten would be thinking, he wouldn't be arriving on the 6:30 in no box. Coleman had turned the borrowed mule and cart so that they could slide the box off the platform onto the open end of the wagon. Everything was ready and the two of them, shut-mouthed, inched the loaded coffin toward the wagon. From inside he began to scratch on the wood. They let go as if it had caught fire.

They stood looking at each other, then at the box.

''That him,'' Coleman said. ''He in there his self.''

''Naw,'' Hooten said, ''must be a rat got in there with him.''

''That him. This here one of his tricks.''

''If it's a rat he might as well stay.''

''That him. Git a crowbar.''

Hooten went grumbling off and got the crowbar and came back and began to pry open the lid. Even before he had the upper end pried open, Coleman was jumping up and down, wheezing and panting from excitement. Tanner gave a thrust upward with both hands and sprang up in the box. "Judgement Day! Judgement Day!" he cried. "Don't you two fools know it's Judgement Day?"

Now he knew exactly what her promises were worth. He would do as well to trust to the note pinned in his coat and to any stranger who found him dead in the street or in the boxcar or wherever. There was nothing to be looked for from her except that she would do things her way. She came out of the kitchen again, holding her hat and coat and rubber boots.

"Now listen," she said, "I have to go to the store. Don't you try to get up and walk around while I'm gone. You've been to the bathroom and you shouldn't have to go again. I don't want to find you on the floor when I get back."

You won't find me atall when you get back, he said to himself. This was the last time he would see her flat dumb face. He felt guilty. She had been good to him and he had been nothing but a nuisance to her.

"Do you want a glass of milk before I go?" she asked.

"No," he said. Then he drew breath and said, "You got a nice place here. It's a nice part of the country. I'm sorry if I've give you a lot of trouble getting sick. It was my fault trying to be friendly with that nigger." And I'm a damned liar besides, he said to himself to kill the outrageous taste such a statement made in his mouth.

For a moment she stared as if he were losing his mind. Then she seemed to think better of it. "Now don't saying something pleasant like that once in a while make you feel better?" she asked and sat down on the sofa.

His knees itched to unbend. Git on, git on, he fumed silently. Make haste and go.

"It's great to have you here," she said. "I wouldn't have you any other place. My own daddy." She gave him a big smile and hoisted her right leg up and began to pull on her boot. "I wouldn't wish a dog out on a day like this," she said, "but I got to go. You can sit here and hope I don't slip and break my neck."

She stamped the booted foot on the floor and then began to tackle the other one.

He turned his eyes to the window. The snow was beginning to stick and freeze to the outside pane. When he looked at her again, she was standing there like a big doll stuffed into its hat and coat. She drew on a pair of green knitted gloves. "Okay," she said, "I'm gone. You sure you don't want anything?"

"No," he said, "go ahead on."

"Well so long then," she said.

He raised the hat enough to reveal a bald palely speckled head. The hall door closed behind her. He began to tremble with excitement. He reached behind him and drew the coat into his lap. When he got it on, he waited until he had stopped panting, then he gripped the arms of the chair and pulled himself up. His body felt like a great heavy bell whose clapper swung from side to side but made no noise. Once up, he remained standing a moment, swaying until he got his balance. A sensation of terror and defeat swept over him. He would never make it. He would never get there dead or alive. He pushed one foot forward and did not fall and his confidence returned. "The Lord is my shepherd," he muttered, "I shall not want." He began moving toward the sofa where he would have support. He reached it. He was on his way.

By the time he got to the door, she would be down the four flights of steps and out of the building. He got past the sofa and crept along by the wall, keeping his hand on it for support. Nobody was going to bury him here. He was as confident as if the woods of home lay at the bottom of the stairs. He reached the front door of the apartment and opened it and peered into the hall. This was the first time he had looked into it since the actor had knocked him down. It was dank-smelling and empty. The thin piece of linoleum stretched its moldy length to the door of the other apartment, which was closed. "Nigger actor," he said.

The head of the stairs was ten or twelve feet from where he stood and he bent his attention to getting there without creeping around the long way with a hand on the wall. He held his arms a little way out from his sides and pushed forward directly. He was half way there when all at once his legs disappeared, or felt as if they had. He looked down, bewildered, for they were still there. He fell forward and grasped the banister post with both hands. Hanging there, he gazed for what seemed the longest time he had ever looked at anything down the steep unlighted steps; then he closed his eyes and pitched forward. He landed upsidedown in the middle of the flight.

He felt presently the tilt of the box as they took it off the train and got it on the baggage wagon. He made no noise yet. The train jarred and slid away. In a moment the baggage wagon was rumbling under him, carrying him back to the station side. He heard footsteps rattling closer and closer to him and he supposed that a crowd was gathering. Wait until they see this, he thought.

"That him," Coleman said, "one of his tricks."

"It's a damn rat in there," Hooten said.

"It's him. Git the crowbar."

In a moment a shaft of greenish light fell on him. He pushed through it and cried in a weak voice, "Judgement Day! Judgement Day! You idiots didn't know it was Judgement Day, did you?

"Coleman?" he murmured.

The Negro bending over him had a large surly mouth and sullen eyes.

"Ain't any coal man, either," he said. This must be the wrong station, Tanner thought. Those fools put me off too soon. Who is this nigger? It ain't even daylight here.

At the Negro's side was another face, a woman's—pale, topped with a pile of copper-glinting hair and twisted as if she had just stepped in a pile of dung.

"Oh," Tanner said, "it's you."

The actor leaned closer and grasped him by the front of his shirt. "Judgement day," he said in a mocking voice. "Ain't no judgement day, old man. Cept this. Maybe this here judgement day for you."

Tanner tried to catch hold of a banister-spoke to raise himself but his hand grasped air. The two faces, the black one and the pale one, appeared to be wavering. By an effort of will he kept them focussed before him while he lifted his hand, as light as a breath, and said in his jauntiest voice, "Hep me up, Preacher. I'm on my way home!"

His daughter found him when she came in from the grocery store. His hat had been pulled down over his face and his head and arms thrust between the spokes of the banister, his feet dangled over the stairwell like those of a man in stocks. She tugged at him frantically and then flew for the police. They cut him out with a saw and said he had been dead about an hour.

She buried him in New York City, but after she had done it she could not sleep at night. Night after night she turned and tossed and very definite lines began to appear in her face, so she had him dug up and shipped the body to Corinth. Now she rests well at night and her good looks have mostly returned.

The Birds

DAPHNE DU MAURIER

Daphne du Maurier's Rebecca *(1938) is perhaps the most famous Gothic suspense novel ever published, but it is representative of only one facet of Ms. du Maurier's considerable talents. She has also published mainstream novels* (The Loving Spirit, I'll Never Be Young Again), *historical thrillers* (Jamaica Inn, Frenchman's Creek), *plays* (The Years Between, September Tide), *travel books* (Vanishing Cornwall), *biographies* (Golden Lads, The Winding Stair), *and collections of short stories* (Not After Midnight; Kiss Me Again, Stranger). *"The Birds" is certainly the best known of her short fiction, after having been brought to the screen by Alfred Hitchcock in 1963; in our opinion (and we think you'll agree), it is far superior to the film, both in content and in the raising of goosebumps.*

ON December the third the wind changed overnight and it was winter. Until then the autumn had been mellow, soft. The earth was rich where the plow had turned it.

Nat Hocken, because of a wartime disability, had a pension and did not work full time at the farm. He worked three days a week, and they gave him the lighter jobs. Although he was married, with children, his was a solitary disposition; he liked best to work alone.

It pleased him when he was given a bank to build up, or a gate to mend, at the far end of the peninsula, where the sea surrounded the farmland on either side. Then, at midday, he would pause and eat the meat pie his wife had baked for him and, sitting on the cliff's edge, watch the birds.

In autumn great flocks of them came to the peninsula, restless, uneasy, spending themselves in motion; now wheeling, circling in the sky; now settling to feed on the rich, new-turned soil; but even when they fed, it was as though they did so without hunger, without desire.

Restlessness drove them to the skies again. Crying, whistling, calling, they skimmed the placid sea and left the shore.

Make haste, make speed, hurry and begone; yet where, and to what purpose? The restless urge of autumn, unsatisfying, sad, had put a spell upon them, and they must spill themselves of motion before winter came.

Perhaps, thought Nat, a message comes to the birds in autumn, like a warning. Winter is coming. Many of them will perish. And like people who, apprehensive of death before their time, drive themselves to work or folly, the birds do likewise; tomorrow we shall die.

The birds had been more restless than ever this fall of the year. Their agitation more remarked because the days were still.

As Mr. Trigg's tractor traced its path up and down the western hills, and Nat, hedging, saw it dip and turn, the whole machine and the man upon it were momentarily lost in the great cloud of wheeling, crying birds.

Nat remarked upon them to Mr. Trigg when the work was finished for the day.

"Yes," said the farmer, "there are more birds about than usual. I have a notion the weather will change. It will be a hard winter. That's why the birds are restless."

The farmer was right. That night the weather turned.

The bedroom in the cottage faced east. Nat woke just after two and heard the east wind, cold and dry. It sounded hollow in the chimney, and a loose slate rattled on the roof. Nat listened, and he could hear the sea roaring in the bay. He drew the blanket round him, leaned closer to the back of his wife, deep in sleep. Then he heard the tapping on the windowpane. It continued until, irritated by the sound, Nat got out of bed and went to the window. He opened it; and as he did so something brushed his hand, jabbing at his knuckles, grazing the skin. Then he saw the flutter of wings and the thing was gone again, over the roof, behind the cottage.

It was a bird. What kind of bird he could not tell. The wind must have driven it to shelter on the sill.

He shut the window and went back to bed, but feeling his knuckles wet, put his mouth to the scratch. The bird had drawn blood.

Frightened, he supposed, bewildered, seeking shelter, the bird had stabbed at him in the darkness. Once more he settled himself to sleep.

Presently the tapping came again—this time more forceful, more insistent. And now his wife woke at the sound, and turning in the bed, said to him, "See to the window, Nat; it's rattling."

"I've already been to it," he told her. "There's some bird there, trying to get in."

"Send it away," she said. "I can't sleep with that noise."

He went to the window for the second time, and now when he

opened it, there was not one bird on the sill but half a dozen; they flew straight into his face.

He shouted, striking out at them with his arms, scattering them; like the first one, they flew over the roof and disappeared.

He let the window fall and latched it.

Suddenly a frightened cry came from the room across the passage where the children slept.

"It's Jill," said his wife, roused at the sound.

There came a second cry, this time from both children. Stumbling into their room, Nat felt the beating of wings about him in the darkness. The window was wide open. Through it came the birds, hitting first the ceiling and the walls, then swerving in midflight and turning to the children in their beds.

"It's all right. I'm here," shouted Nat, and the children flung themselves, screaming, upon him, while in the darkness the birds rose, and dived, and came for him again.

"What is it, Nat? What's happened?" his wife called. Swiftly he pushed the children through the door to the passage and shut it upon them, so that he was alone in their bedroom with the birds.

He seized a blanket from the nearest bed, and using it as a weapon, flung it to right and left about him.

He felt the thud of bodies, heard the fluttering of wings; but the birds were not yet defeated, for again and again they returned to the assault, jabbing his hands, his head, their little stabbing beaks sharp as pointed forks.

The blanket became a weapon of defense. He wound it about his head, and then in greater darkness, beat at the birds with his bare hands. He dared not stumble to the door and open it lest the birds follow him.

How long he fought with them in the darkness he could not tell; but at last the beating of the wings about him lessened, withdrew; and through the dense blanket he was aware of light.

He waited, listened; there was no sound except the fretful crying of one of the children from the bedroom beyond.

He took the blanket from his head and stared about him. The cold gray morning light exposed the room.

Dawn and the open window had called the living birds; the dead lay on the floor.

Sickened, Nat went to the window and stared out across his patch of garden to the fields.

It was bitter cold, and the ground had all the hard, black look of the frost that the east wind brings. The sea, fiercer now with turning tide, whitecapped and steep, broke harshly in the bay. Of the birds there was no sign.

Nat shut the window and the door of the small bedroom and went back across the passage to his own room.

His wife sat up in bed, one child asleep beside her; the smaller one in her arms, his face bandaged.

"He's sleeping now," she whispered. "Something must have cut him; there was blood at the corners of his eyes. Jill said it was the birds. She said she woke up and the birds were in the room."

His wife looked up at Nat, searching his face for confirmation. She looked terrified, bewildered. He did not want her to know that he also was shaken, dazed almost, by the events of the past few hours.

"There are birds in there," he said. "Dead birds, nearly fifty of them."

He sat down on the bed beside his wife.

"It's the hard weather," he said. "It must be that; it's the hard weather. They aren't the birds, maybe, from around here. They've been driven down from upcountry."

"But Nat," whispered his wife, "it's only this night that the weather turned. They can't be hungry yet. There's food for them out there in the fields."

"It's the weather," repeated Nat. "I tell you, it's the weather."

His face, too, was drawn and tired, like hers. They stared at one another for a while without speaking.

Nat went to the window and looked out. The sky was hard and leaden, and the brown hills that had gleamed in the sun the day before looked dark and bare. Black winter had descended in a single night.

The children were awake now. Jill was chattering, and young Johnny was crying once again. Nat heard his wife's voice, soothing, comforting them as he went downstairs.

Presently they came down. He had breakfast ready for them.

"Did you drive away the birds?" asked Jill.

"Yes, they've all gone now," Nat said. "It was the east wind brought them in."

"I hope they won't come again," said Jill.

"I'll walk with you to the bus," Nat said to her.

Jill seemed to have forgotten her experience of the night before. She danced ahead of him, chasing the leaves, her face rosy under her pixy hood.

All the while Nat searched the hedgerows for the birds, glanced over them to the fields beyond, looked to the small wood above the farm where the rooks and jackdaws gathered; he saw none. Soon the bus came ambling up the hill.

Nat saw Jill onto the bus, then turned and walked back toward the farm. It was not his day for work, but he wanted to satisfy himself that all was well. He went to the back door of the farmhouse; he heard Mrs. Trigg singing, the wireless making a background for her song.

"Are you there, missus?" Nat called.

She came to the door, beaming, broad, a good-tempered woman.

"Hullo, Mr. Hocken," she said. "Can you tell me where this cold is coming from? Is it Russia? I've never seen such a change. And it's going on, the wireless says. Something to do with the Arctic Circle."

"We didn't turn on the wireless this morning," said Nat. "Fact is, we had trouble in the night."

"Kiddies poorly?"

"No." He hardly knew how to explain. Now, in daylight, the battle of the birds would sound absurd.

He tried to tell Mrs. Trigg what had happened, but he could see from her eyes that she thought his story was the result of a nightmare following a heavy meal.

"Sure they were real birds?" she said, smiling.

"Mrs. Trigg," he said, "there are fifty dead birds—robins, wrens, and such, lying low on the floor of the children's bedroom. They went for me; they tried to go for young Johnny's eyes."

Mrs. Trigg stared at him doubtfully.

"Well, there now," she answered, "I suppose the weather brought them; once in the bedroom they wouldn't know where they were. Foreign birds maybe, from that Arctic Circle."

"No," said Nat. "They were the birds you see about here every day."

"Funny thing," said Mrs. Trigg. "No explaining it, really. You ought to write up and ask the *Guardian*. They'd have some answer for it. Well, I must be getting on."

Nat walked back along the lane to his cottage. He found his wife in the kitchen with young Johnny.

"See anyone?" she asked.

"Mrs. Trigg," he answered. "I don't think she believed me. Anyway, nothing wrong up there."

"You might take the birds away," she said. "I daren't go into the room to make the beds until you do. I'm scared."

"Nothing to scare you now," said Nat. "They're dead, aren't they?"

He went up with a sack and dropped the stiff bodies into it, one by one. Yes, there were fifty of them all told. Just the ordinary, common birds of the hedgerow; nothing as large even as a thrush. It must have been fright that made them act the way they did.

He took the sack out into the garden and was faced with a fresh problem. The ground was frozen solid, yet no snow had fallen; nothing had happened in the past hours but the coming of the east wind. It was unnatural, queer. He could see the white-capped seas breaking in the bay. He decided to take the birds to the shore and bury them.

When he reached the beach below the headland, he could scarcely stand, the force of the east wind was so strong. It was low tide; he crunched his way over the shingle to the softer sand and then, his back to the wind, opened up his sack.

He ground a pit in the sand with his heel, meaning to drop the birds into it; but as he did so, the force of the wind lifted them as though in flight again, and they were blown away from him along the beach, tossed like feathers, spread and scattered.

The tide will take them when it turns, he said to himself.

He looked out to sea and watched the crested breakers, combing green. They rose stiffly, curled, and broke again; and because it was ebb tide, the roar was distant, more remote, lacking the sound and thunder of the flood.

Then he saw them. The gulls. Out there, riding the seas.

What he had thought at first were the whitecaps of the waves were gulls. Hundreds, thousands, tens of thousands.

They rose and fell in the troughs of the seas, heads to the wind, like a mighty fleet at anchor, waiting on the tide.

Nat turned; leaving the beach, he climbed the steep path home.

Someone should know of this. Someone should be told. Something was happening, because of the east wind and the weather, that he did not understand.

As he drew near the cottage, his wife came to meet him at the door. She called to him, excited. "Nat," she said, "it's on the wireless. They've just read out a special news bulletin. It's not only here, it's everywhere. In London, all over the country. Something has happened to the birds. Come listen; they're repeating it."

Together they went into the kitchen to listen to the announcement.

"Statement from the Home Office, at eleven A.M. this morning. Reports from all over the country are coming in hourly about the vast quantity of birds flocking above towns, villages, and outlying districts, causing obstruction and damage and even attacking individuals. It is thought that the Arctic air stream at present covering the British Isles is causing birds to migrate south in immense numbers, and that intense hunger may drive these birds to attack human beings. Householders are warned to see to their windows, doors, and chimneys, and to take reasonable precautions for the safety of their children. A further statement will be issued later.''

A kind of excitement seized Nat. He looked at his wife in triumph. ''There you are,'' he said. ''I've been telling myself all morning there's something wrong. And just now, down on the beach, I looked out to sea and there were gulls, thousands of them, riding on the sea, waiting.''

''What are they waiting for, Nat?'' she asked.

He stared at her. ''I don't know,'' he said slowly.

He went over to the drawer where he kept his hammer and other tools.

''What are you going to do, Nat?''

''See to the windows and the chimneys, like they tell you to.''

''You think they would break in with the windows shut? Those wrens and robins and such? Why, how could they?''

He did not answer. He was not thinking of the robins and the wrens. He was thinking of the gulls.

He went upstairs and worked there the rest of the morning, boarding the windows of the bedrooms, filling up the chimney bases.

''Dinner's ready.'' His wife called him from the kitchen.

''All right. Coming down.''

When dinner was over and his wife was washing up, Nat switched on the one o'clock news. The same announcement was repeated, but the news bulletin enlarged upon it. ''The flocks of birds have caused dislocation in all areas,'' said the announcer, ''and in London the mass was so dense at ten o'clock this morning that it seemed like a vast black cloud. The birds settled on rooftops, on window ledges, and on chimneys. The species included blackbird, thrush, the common house sparrow, and as might be expected in the metropolis, a vast quantity of pigeons, starlings, and that frequenter of the London river, the black-headed gull. The sight was so unusual that traffic came to a standstill in many thoroughfares, work was abandoned in shops and offices, and the streets and pavements were crowded with people standing about to watch the birds."

The announcer's voice was smooth and suave; Nat had the impression that he treated the whole business as he would an elaborate joke. There would be others like him, hundreds of them, who did not know what it was to struggle in darkness with a flock of birds.

Nat switched off the wireless. He got up and started work on the kitchen windows. His wife watched him, young Johnny at her heels.

"What they ought to do," she said, "is to call the Army out and shoot the birds."

"Let them try," said Nat. "How'd they set about it?"

"I don't know. But something should be done. They ought to do something."

Nat thought to himself that "they" were no doubt considering the problem at that very moment, but whatever "they" decided to do in London and the big cities would not help them here, nearly three hundred miles away.

"How are we off for food?" he asked.

"It's shopping day tomorrow, you know that. I don't keep uncooked food about. Butcher doesn't call till the day after. But I can bring back something when I go in tomorrow."

Nat did not want to scare her. He looked in the larder for himself and in the cupboard where she kept her tins.

They could hold out for a couple of days.

He went on hammering the boards across the kitchen windows. Candles. They were low on candles. That must be another thing she meant to buy tomorrow. Well, they must go early to bed tonight. That was, if—

He got up and went out the back door and stood in the garden, looking down toward the sea.

There had been no sun all day, and now, at barely three o'clock, a kind of darkness had already come; the sky was sullen, heavy, colorless like salt. He could hear the vicious sea drumming on the rocks.

He walked down the path halfway to the beach. And then he stopped. He could see the tide had turned. The gulls had risen. They were circling, hundreds of them, thousands of them, lifting their wings against the wind.

It was the gulls that made the darkening of the sky.

And they were silent. They just went on soaring and circling, rising, falling, trying their strength against the wind. Nat turned. He ran up the path back to the cottage.

"I'm going for Jill," he said to his wife.

"What's the matter?" she asked. "You've gone quite white."

"Keep Johnny inside," he said. "Keep the door shut. Light up now and draw the curtains."

"It's only gone three," she said.

"Never mind. Do what I tell you."

He looked inside the tool shed and took the hoe.

He started walking up the lane to the bus stop. Now and again he glanced back over his shoulder; and he could see the gulls had risen higher now, their circles were broader, they were spreading out in huge formation across the sky.

He hurried on. Although he knew the bus would not come before four o'clock, he had to hurry.

He waited at the top of the hill. There was half an hour still to go.

The east wind came whipping across the fields from the higher ground. In the distance he could see the clay hills, white and clean against the heavy pallor of the sky.

Something black rose from behind them, like a smudge at first, then widening, becoming deeper. The smudge became a cloud; and the cloud divided again into five other clouds, spreading north, east, south, and west; and then they were not clouds at all but birds.

He watched them travel across the sky, within two or three hundred feet of him. He knew, from their speed, that they were bound inland; they had no business with the people here on the peninsula. They were rocks, crows, jackdaws, magpies, jays, all birds that usually preyed upon the smaller species, but bound this afternoon on some other mission.

He went to the telephone call box, stepped inside, lifted the receiver. The exchange would pass the message on. "I'm speaking from the highway," he said, "by the bus stop. I want to report large formations of birds traveling upcountry. The gulls are also forming in the bay."

"All right," answered the voice, laconic, weary.

"You'll be sure and pass this message on to the proper quarter?"

"Yes, Yes." Impatient now, fed up. The buzzing note resumed.

She's another, thought Nat. She doesn't care.

The bus came lumbering up the hill. Jill climbed out.

"What's the hoe for, Dad?"

"I just brought it along," he said. "Come on now, let's get home. It's cold; no hanging about. See how fast you can run."

He could see the gulls now, still silent, circling the fields, coming in toward the land.

"Look, Dad; look over there. Look at all the gulls."

"Yes. Hurry now."

"Where are they flying to? Where are they going?"

"Upcountry, I dare say. Where it's warmer."

He seized her hand and dragged her after him along the lane.

"Don't go so fast. I can't keep up."

The gulls were copying the rooks and the crows. They were spreading out, in formation, across the sky. They headed, in bands of thousands, to the four compass points.

"Dad, what is it? What are the gulls doing?"

They were not intent upon their flight, as the crows, as the jackdaws, had been. They still circled overhead. Nor did they fly so high. It was as though they waited upon some signal; as though some decision had yet to be given.

"I wish the gulls would go away." Jill was crying. "I don't like them. They're coming closer to the lane."

He started running, swinging Jill after him. As they went past the farm turning, he saw the farmer backing his car into the garage. Nat called to him.

"Can you give us a lift?" he said.

Mr. Trigg turned in the driver's seat and stared at them. Then a smile came to his cheerful, rubicund face. "It looks as though we're in for some fun," he said. "Have you seen the gulls? Jim and I are going to take a crack at them. Everyone's gone bird crazy, talking of nothing else. I hear you were troubled in the night. Want a gun?"

Nat shook his head.

The small car was packed, but there was room for Jill on the back seat.

"I don't want a gun," said Nat, "but I'd be obliged if you'd run Jill home. She's scared of the birds."

"Okay," said the farmer. "I'll take her home. Why don't you stop behind and join the shooting match? We'll make the feathers fly."

Jill climbed in, and turning the car, the driver sped up the lane. Nat followed after. Trigg must be crazy. What use was a gun against a sky of birds?

They were coming in now toward the farm, circling lower in the sky. The farm, then, was their target. Nat increased his pace toward his own cottage. He saw the farmer's car turn and come back along the lane. It drew up beside him with a jerk.

"The kid has run inside," said the farmer. "Your wife was watching for her. Well, what do you make of it? They're saying in town the Russians have done it. The Russians have poisoned the birds."

"How could they do that?" asked Nat.

"Don't ask me. You know how stories get around."

"Have you boarded your windows?" asked Nat.

"No. Lot of nonsense. I've had more to do today than to go round boarding up my windows."

"I'd board them now if I were you."

"Garn. You're windy. Like to come to our place to sleep?"

"No, thanks all the same."

"All right. See you in the morning. Give you a gull breakfast."

The farmer grinned and turned his car to the farm entrance. Nat hurried on. Past the little wood, past the old barn, and then across the stile to the remaining field. As he jumped the stile, he heard the whir of wings. A black-backed gull dived down at him from the sky. It missed, swerved in flight, and rose to dive again. In a moment it was joined by others—six, seven, a dozen.

Nat dropped his hoe. The hoe was useless. Covering his head with his arms, he ran toward the cottage.

They kept coming at him from the air—noiseless, silent, save for the beating wings. The terrible, fluttering wings. He could feel the blood on his hands, his wrists, upon his neck. If only he could keep them from his eyes. Nothing else mattered.

With each dive, with each attack, they became bolder. And they had no thought for themselves. When they dived low and missed, they crashed, bruised and broken, on the ground.

As Nat ran he stumbled, kicking their spent bodies in front of him.

He found the door and hammered upon it with his bleeding hands. "Let me in," he shouted. "It's Nat. Let me in."

Then he saw the gannet, poised for the dive, above him in the sky.

The gulls circled, retired, soared, one with another, against the wind.

Only the gannet remained. One single gannet, above him in the sky. Its wings folded suddenly to its body. It dropped like a stone.

Nat screamed; and the door opened.

He stumbled across the threshold, and his wife threw her weight against the door.

They heard the thud of the gannet as it fell.

His wife dressed his wounds. They were not deep. The backs of his hands had suffered most, and his wrists. Had he not worn a cap, the birds would have reached his head. As for the gannet—the gannet could have split his skull.

The children were crying, of course. They had seen the blood on their father's hands.

"It's all right now," he told them. "I'm not hurt."

His wife was ashen. "I saw them overhead," she whispered. "They began collecting just as Jill ran in with Mr. Trigg. I shut the door fast, and it jammed. That's why I couldn't open it at once when you came."

"Thank God the birds waited for me," he said. "Jill would have fallen at once. They're flying inland, thousands of them. Rooks, crows, all the bigger birds. I saw them from the bus stop. They're making for the towns."

"But what can they do, Nat?"

"They'll attack. Go for everyone out in the streets. Then they'll try the windows, the chimneys."

"Why don't the authorities do something? Why don't they get the Army, get machine guns?"

"There's been no time. Nobody's prepared. We'll hear what they have to say on the six o'clock news."

"I can hear the birds," Jill said. "Listen, Dad."

Nat listened. Muffled sounds came from the windows, from the door. Wings brushing the surface, sliding, scraping, seeking a way of entry. The sound of many bodies pressed together, shuffling on the sills. Now and again came a thud, a crash, as some bird dived and fell.

Some of them will kill themselves that way, he thought, but not enough. Never enough.

"All right," he said aloud. "I've got boards over the windows, Jill. The birds can't get in."

He went and examined all the windows. He found wedges—pieces of old tin, strips of wood and metal—and fastened them at the sides of the windows to reinforce the boards.

His hammering helped to deafen the sound of the birds, the shuffling, the tapping, and—more ominous—the splinter of breaking glass.

"Turn on the wireless," he said.

He went upstairs to the bedrooms and reinforced the windows there. Now he could hear the birds on the roof—the scraping of claws, a sliding, jostling sound.

He decided the whole family must sleep in the kitchen and keep up the fire. He was afraid of the bedroom chimneys. The boards he had placed at their bases might give way. In the kitchen they would be safe because of the fire.

He would have to make a joke of it. Pretend to the children they were playing camp. If the worst happened and the birds forced an entry by way of the bedroom chimneys, it would be hours, days perhaps, before they could break down the doors. The birds would be imprisoned in the bedrooms. They could do no harm there. Crowded together, they would stifle and die. He began to bring the mattresses downstairs.

At sight of them, his wife's eyes widened in apprehension.

"All right," he said cheerfully. "We'll all sleep together in the kitchen tonight. More cozy, here by the fire. Then we won't be worried by those silly old birds tapping at the windows."

He made the children help him rearrange the furniture, and he took the precaution of moving the dresser against the windows.

We're safe enough now, he thought. We're snug and tight. We can hold out. It's just the food that worries me. Food and coal for the fire. We've enough for two or three days, not more. By that time—

No use thinking ahead as far as that. And they'd be given directions on the wireless.

And now, in the midst of many problems, he realized that only dance music was coming over the air. He knew the reason. The usual programs had been abandoned; this only happened at exceptional times.

At six o'clock the records ceased. The time signal was given. There was a pause, and then the announcer spoke. His voice was solemn, grave. Quite different from midday.

"This is London," he said. "A national emergency was proclaimed at four o'clock this afternoon. Measures are being taken to safeguard the lives and property of the population, but it must be understood that these are not easy to effect immediately, owing to the unforeseen and unparalleled nature of the present crisis. Every householder must take precautions about his own building. Where several people live together, as in flats and hotels, they must unite to do the utmost that they can to prevent entry. It is absolutely imperative that every individual stay indoors tonight.

"The birds, in vast numbers, are attacking anyone on sight, and have already begun an assault upon buildings; but these, with due care, should be impenetrable.

"The population is asked to remain calm.

"Owing to the exceptional nature of the emergency, there will be no further transmission from any broadcasting station until seven A.M. tomorrow."

They played "God Save the Queen." Nothing more happened.

Nat switched off the set. He looked at his wife. She stared back at him.

"We'll have supper early," suggested Nat. "Something for a treat—toasted cheese, eh? Something we all like."

He winked and nodded at his wife. He wanted the look of dread, of apprehension, to leave her face.

He helped with the supper, whistling, singing, making as much clatter as he could. It seemed to him that the shuffling and the tapping were not so intense as they had been at first, and presently he went up to the bedrooms and listened. He no longer heard the jostling for place upon the roof.

They've got reasoning powers, he thought. They know it's hard to break in here. They'll try elsewhere.

Supper passed without incident. Then, when they were clearing away, they heard a new sound, a familiar droning.

His wife looked up at him, her face alight.

"It's planes," she said. "They're sending out planes after the birds. That will get them. Isn't that gunfire? Can't you hear guns?"

It might be gunfire, out at sea. Nat could not tell. Big naval guns might have some effect upon the gulls out at sea, but the gulls were inland now. The guns couldn't shell the shore because of the population.

"It's good, isn't it," said his wife, "to hear the planes?"

Catching her enthusiasm, Jill jumped up and down with Johnny. "The planes will get the birds."

Just then they heard a crash about two miles distant. Followed by a second, then a third. The droning became more distant, passed away out to sea.

"What was that?" asked his wife.

"I don't know," answered Nat. He did not want to tell her that the sound they had heard was the crashing of aircraft.

It was, he had no doubt, a gamble on the part of the authorities to send out reconnaissance forces, but they might have known the gamble was suicidal. What could aircraft do against birds that flung themselves to death against propeller and fuselage but hurtle to the ground themselves?

"Where have the planes gone, Dad?" asked Jill.

"Back to base," he said. "Come on now, time to tuck down for bed."

There was no further drone of aircraft, and the naval guns had ceased. Waste of life and effort, Nat said to himself. We can't destroy enough of them that way. Cost too heavy. There's always gas. Maybe they'll try spraying with gas, mustard gas. We'll be warned first, of course, if they do. There's one thing, the best brains of the country will be on it tonight.

Upstairs in the bedrooms all was quiet. No more scraping and stabbing at the windows. A lull in battle. The wind hadn't dropped, though. Nat could still hear it roaring in the chimneys. And the sea breaking down on the shore.

Then he remembered the tide. The tide would be on the turn. Maybe the lull in battle was because of the tide. There was some law the birds obeyed, and it had to do with the east wind and the tide.

He glanced at his watch. Nearly eight o'clock. It must have gone high water an hour ago. That explained the lull. The birds attacked with the flood tide.

He reckoned the time limit in his head. They had six hours to go without attack. When the tide turned again, around 1:20 in the morning, the birds would come back.

He called softly to his wife and whispered to her that he would go out and see how they were faring at the farm, see if the telephone was still working there so that they might get news from the exchange.

"You're not to go," she said at once, "and leave me alone with the children. I can't stand it."

"All right," he said, "all right. I'll wait till morning. And we can get the wireless bulletin then, too, at seven. But when the tide ebbs again, I'll try for the farm; they may let us have bread and potatoes."

His mind was busy again, planning against emergency. They would not have milked, of course, this evening. The cows would be standing by the gate, waiting; the household would be inside, battened behind boards as they were here at the cottage.

That is, if they had had time to take precautions.

Softly, stealthily, he opened the back door and looked outside.

It was pitch-dark. The wind was blowing harder than ever, coming in steady gusts, icy, from the sea.

He kicked at the step. It was heaped with birds. These were the suicides, the divers, the ones with broken necks. Wherever he looked, he saw dead birds. The living had flown seaward with the turn of the tide. The gulls would be riding the seas now, as they had done in the forenoon.

In the far distance on the hill, something was burning. One of the aircraft that had crashed; the fire, fanned by the wind, had set light to a stack.

He looked at the bodies of the birds. He had a notion that if he stacked them, one upon the other, on the window sills, they would be added protection against the next attack.

Not much, perhaps, but something. The bodies would have to

be clawed at, pecked and dragged aside before the living birds gained purchase on the sills and attacked the panes.

He set to work in the darkness. It was queer. He hated touching the dead birds, but he went on with his work. He noticed grimly that every windowpane was shattered. Only the boards had kept the birds from breaking in.

He stuffed the cracked panes with the bleeding bodies of the birds and felt his stomach turn. When he had finished, he went back into the cottage and barricaded the kitchen door, making it doubly secure.

His wife had made him cocoa; he drank it thirstily. He was very tired. "All right," he said, smiling, "don't worry. We'll get through."

He lay down on his mattress and closed his eyes.

He dreamed uneasily because, through his dreams, ran the dread of something forgotten. Some piece of work that he should have done. It was connected, in some way, with the burning aircraft.

It was his wife, shaking his shoulder, who awoke him finally.

"They've begun," she sobbed. "They've started this last hour. I can't listen to it any longer alone. There's something smells bad too, something burning."

Then he remembered. He had forgotten to make up the fire.

The fire was smoldering, nearly out. He got up swiftly and lighted the lamp.

The hammering had started at the windows and the door, but it was not that he minded now. It was the smell of singed feathers.

The smell filled the kitchen. He knew what it was at once. The birds were coming down the chimney, squeezing their way down to the kitchen range.

He got sticks and paper and put them on the embers, then reached for the can of kerosene.

"Stand back," he shouted to his wife. He threw some of the kerosene onto the fire.

The flame roared up the pipe, and down into the fire fell the scorched, blackened bodies of the birds.

The children waked, crying. "What is it?" asked Jill. "What's happened?"

Nat had no time to answer her. He was raking the bodies from the chimney, clawing them out onto the floor.

The flames would drive away the living birds from the chimney top. The lower joint was the difficulty though. It was choked with the smoldering, helpless bodies of the birds caught by fire.

He scarcely heeded the attack on the windows and the door. Let them beat their wings, break their backs, lose their lives, in the desperate attempt to force an entry into his home. They would not break in.

"Stop crying," he called to the children. "There's nothing to be afraid of. Stop crying."

He went on raking out the burning, smoldering bodies as they fell into the fire.

This'll fetch them, he said to himself. The draft and the flames together. We're all right as long as the chimney doesn't catch.

Amid the tearing at the window boards came the sudden homely striking of the kitchen clock. Three o'clock.

A little more than four hours to go. He could not be sure of the exact time of high water. He reckoned the tide would not turn much before half past seven.

He waited by the range. The flames were dying. But no more blackened bodies fell from the chimney. He thrust his poker up as far as it could go and found nothing.

The danger of the chimney's being choked up was over. It could not happen again, not if the fire was kept burning day and night.

I'll have to get more fuel from the farm tomorrow, he thought. I can do all that with the ebb tide. It can be worked; we can fetch what we need when the tide's turned. We've just got to adapt ourselves, that's all.

They drank tea and cocoa, ate slices of bread. Only half a loaf left, Nat noticed. Never mind, though; they'd get by.

If they could hang on like this until seven, when the first news bulletin came through, they would not have done too badly.

"Give us a smoke," he said to his wife. "It will clear away the smell of the scorched feathers."

"There's only two left in the packet," she said. "I was going to buy you some."

"I'll have one," he said.

He sat with one arm around his wife and one around Jill, with Johnny on his lap, the blankets heaped about them on the mattress.

"You can't help admiring the beggars," he said. "They've got persistency. You'd think they'd tire of the game, but not a bit of it."

Admiration was hard to sustain. The tapping went on and on; and a new, rasping note struck Nat's ear, as though a sharper beak than any hitherto had come to take over from its fellows.

He tried to remember the names of birds; he tried to think which species would go for this particular job.

It was not the tap of the woodpecker. That would be light and frequent. This was more serious; if it continued long, the wood would splinter as the glass had done.

Then he remembered the hawks. Could the hawks have taken over from the gulls? Were there buzzards now upon the sills, using talons as well as beaks? Hawks, buzzards, kestrels, falcons; he had forgotten the birds of prey. He had forgotten the gripping power of the birds of prey. Three hours to go; and while they waited, the sound of the splintering wood, the talons tearing at the wood.

Nat looked about him, seeing what furniture he could destroy to fortify the door.

The windows were safe because of the dresser. He was not certain of the door. He went upstairs; but when he reached the landing, he paused and listened.

There was a soft patter on the floor of the children's bedroom. The birds had broken through.

The other bedroom was still clear. He brought out the furniture to pile at the head of the stairs should the door of the children's bedroom go.

"Come down, Nat. What are you doing?" called his wife.

"I won't be long," he shouted. "I'm just making everything shipshape up here."

He did not want her to come. He did not want her to hear the pattering in the children's bedroom, the brushing of those wings against the door.

After he suggested breakfast, he found himself watching the clock, gazing at the hands that went so slowly around the dial. If his theory was not correct, if the attack did not cease with the turn of the tide, he knew they were beaten. They could not continue through the long day without air, without rest, without fuel.

A crackling in his ears drove away the sudden, desperate desire for sleep.

"What is it? What now?" he said sharply.

"The wireless," said his wife. "I've been watching the clock. It's nearly seven."

The comfortable crackling of the wireless brought new life.

They waited. The kitchen clock struck seven.

The crackling continued. Nothing else. No chimes. No music.

They waited until a quarter past. No news bulletin came through.

"We heard wrong," he said. "They won't be broadcasting until eight o'clock."

They left the wireless switched on. Nat thought of the battery, wondered how much power was left in the battery. If it failed, they would not hear the instructions.

"It's getting light," whispered his wife. "I can't see it but I can feel it. And listen! The birds aren't hammering so loud now."

She was right. The rasping, tearing sound grew fainter every moment. So did the shuffling, the jostling for place upon the step, upon the sills. The tide was on the turn.

By eight there was no sound at all. Only the wind. And the crackling of the wireless. The children, lulled at last by the stillness, fell asleep.

At half past eight Nat switched the wireless off.

"We'll miss the news," said his wife.

"There isn't going to be any news," said Nat. "We've got to depend upon ourselves."

He went to the door and slowly pulled away the barricades. He drew the bolts, and kicking the broken bodies from the step outside the door, breathed the cold air.

He had six working hours before him, and he knew he must reserve his strength to the utmost, not waste it in any way.

Food and light and fuel; these were the most necessary things. If he could get them, they could endure another night.

He stepped into the garden; and as he did so, he saw the living birds. The gulls had gone to ride the sea, as they had done before. They sought sea food and the buoyancy of the tide before they returned to the attack.

Not so the land birds. They waited, and watched.

Nat saw them on the hedgerows, on the soil, crowded in the trees, outside in the field—line upon line of birds, still, doing nothing. He went to the end of his small garden.

The birds did not move. They merely watched him.

I've got to get food, Nat said to himself. I've got to go to the farm to get food.

He went back to the cottage. He saw to the windows and the door.

"I'm going to the farm," he said.

His wife clung to him. She had seen the living birds from the open door.

"Take us with you," she begged. "We can't stay here alone I'd rather die than stay here alone."

"Come on, then," he said. "Bring baskets and Johnny's pram. We can load up the pram."

They dressed against the biting wind. His wife put Johnny in the pram, and Nat took Jill's hand.

"The birds," Jill whimpered. "They're all out there in the fields."

"They won't hurt us," he said. "Not in the light."

They started walking across the field toward the stile, and the birds did not move. They waited, their heads turned to the wind.

When they reached the turning to the farm, Nat stopped and told his wife to wait in the shelter of the hedge with the two children. "But I want to see Mrs. Trigg," she protested. "There are lots of things we can borrow if they went to market yesterday, and—"

"Wait here," Nat interrupted. "I'll be back in a moment."

The cows were lowing, moving restlessly in the yard, and he could see a gap in the fence where the sheep had knocked their way through to roam unchecked in the front garden before the farmhouse.

No smoke came from the chimneys. Nat was filled with misgiving. He did not want his wife or the children to go down to the farm.

He went down alone, pushing his way through the herd of lowing cows, who turned this way and that, distressed, their udders full.

He saw the car standing by the gate. Not put away in the garage.

All the windows of the farmhouse were smashed. There were many dead gulls lying in the yard and around the house.

The living birds perched on the group of trees behind the farm and on the roof of the house. They were quite still. They watched him. Jim's body lay in the yard. What was left of it. His gun was beside him.

The door of the house was shut and bolted, but it was easy to push up a smashed window and climb through.

Trigg's body was close to the telephone. He must have been trying to get through to the exchange when the birds got him. The receiver was off the hook, and the instrument was torn from the wall.

No sign of Mrs. Trigg. She would be upstairs. Was it any use going up? Sickened, Nat knew what he would find there.

Thank God, he said to himself, there were no children.

He forced himself to climb the stairs, but halfway up he turned and descended again. He could see Mrs. Trigg's legs protruding from the open bedroom door. Beside her were the bodies of black-backed gulls and an umbrella, broken. It's no use doing anything, Nat thought. I've only got five hours; less than that. The Triggs would understand. I must load up with what I can find.

He tramped back to his wife and children.

"I'm going to fill up the car with stuff," he said. "We'll take it home and return for a fresh load."

"What about the Triggs?" asked his wife.

"They must have gone to friends," he said.

"Shall I come and help you then?"

"No, there's a mess down there. Cows and sheep all over the place. Wait; I'll get the car. You can sit in the car."

Her eyes watched his all the time he was talking. He believed she understood. Otherwise she certainly would have insisted on helping him find the bread and groceries.

They made three journeys altogether, to and from the farm, before he was satisfied they had everything they needed. It was surprising, once he started thinking, how many things were necessary. Almost the most important of all was planking for the windows. He had to go around searching for timber. He wanted to renew the boards on all the windows at the cottage.

On the final journey he drove the car to the bus stop and got out and went to the telephone box.

He waited a few minutes, jangling the hook. No good, though. The line was dead. He climbed onto a bank and looked over the countryside, but there was no sign of life at all, nothing in the fields but the waiting, watching birds.

Some of them slept; he could see their beaks tucked into their feathers.

You'd think they'd be feeding, he said to himself, not just standing that way.

Then he remembered. They were gorged with food. They had eaten their fill during the night. That was why they did not move this morning.

He lifted his face to the sky. It was colorless, gray. The bare trees looked bent and blackened by the east wind.

The cold did not affect the living birds, waiting out there in the fields.

This is the time they ought to get them, Nat said to himself. They're a sitting target now. They must be doing this all over the country. Why don't our aircraft take off now and spray them with mustard gas? What are all our chaps doing? They must know; they must see for themselves.

He went back to the car and got into the driver's seat.

"Go quickly past that second gate," whispered his wife. "The postman's lying there. I don't want Jill to see."

It was a quarter to one by the time they reached the cottage. Only an hour to go.

"Better have dinner," said Nat. "Hot up something for yourself and the children, some of that soup. I've no time to eat now. I've got to unload all this stuff from the car."

He got everything inside the cottage. It could be sorted later. Give them all something to do during the long hours ahead.

First he must see to the windows and the door.

He went around the cottage methodically, testing every window and the door. He climbed onto the roof also, and fixed boards across every chimney except the kitchen's.

The cold was so intense he could hardly bear it, but the job had to be done. Now and again he looked up, searching the sky for aircraft. None came. As he worked, he cursed the inefficiency of the authorities.

He paused, his work on the bedroom chimney finished, and looked out to sea. Something was moving out there. Something gray and white among the breakers.

"Good old Navy," he said. "They never let us down. They're coming down channel; they're turning into the bay."

He waited, straining his eyes toward the sea. He was wrong,

though. The Navy was not there. It was the gulls rising from the sea. And the massed flocks in the fields, with ruffled feathers, rose in formation from the ground and, wing to wing, soared upward to the sky.

The tide had turned again.

Nat climbed down the ladder and went inside the cottage. The family were at dinner. It was a little after two.

He bolted the door, put up the barricade, and lighted the lamp.

"It's nighttime," said young Johnny.

His wife had switched on the wireless once again. The crackling sound came, but nothing else.

"I've been all round the dial," she said, "foreign stations and all. I can't get anything but the crackling."

"Maybe they have the same trouble," he said. "Maybe it's the same right through Europe."

They ate in silence.

The tapping began at the windows, at the door, the rustling, the jostling, the pushing for position on the sills. The first thud of the suicide gulls upon the step.

When he had finished dinner, Nat planned, he would put the supplies away, stack them neatly, get everything shipshape. The boards were strong against the windows and across the chimneys. The cottage was filled with stores, with fuel, with all they needed for the next few days.

His wife could help him, and the children too. They'd tire themselves out between now and a quarter to nine, when the tide would ebb; then he'd tuck them down on their mattresses, see that they slept good and sound until three in the morning.

He had a new scheme for the windows, which was to fix barbed wire in front of the boards. He had brought a great roll of it from the farm. The nuisance was, he'd have to work at this in the dark, when the lull came between nine and three. Pity he had not thought of it before. Still, as long as the wife and kids slept—that was the main thing.

The smaller birds were at the windows now. He recognized

the light tap-tapping of their beaks and the soft brush of their wings.

The hawks ignored the windows. They concentrated their attack upon the door.

Nat listened to the tearing sound of splintering wood, and wondered how many million years of memory were stored in those little brains, behind the stabbing beaks, the piercing eyes, now giving them this instinct to destroy mankind with all the deft precision of machines.

"I'll smoke that last cigarette," he said to his wife. "Stupid of me. It was the one thing I forgot to bring back from the farm."

He reached for it, switched on the crackling wireless.

He threw the empty packet onto the fire and watched it burn.

Night Court

MARY ELIZABETH COUNSELMAN

A native of Alabama, Mary Elizabeth Counselman is a well-known and respected writer of macabre fiction who regularly contributed to the pulp magazine Weird Tales *in the forties and fifties, as well as to such "slicks" as the* Saturday Evening Post, Good Housekeeping, *and* Ladies' Home Journal. *The best of her fantasy and horror fiction may be found in her 1978 Arkham House collection,* Half in Shadow. *"Night Court," which first appeared in* Weird Tales *in 1953, is one of her finest stories and should be read by anyone who has ever been guilty of "criminal behavior in the driver's seat of a motor vehicle . . . ."*

BOB WAITED, humming to himself in the stifling telephone booth, his collar and tie loosened for comfort in the late August heat, his Panama tilted rakishly over one ear to make room for the instrument. Through it he could hear a succession of female voices: "Gareyville calling Oak Grove thuh-ree, tew, niyun, six . . . collect. . . ." "Oak Grove. What was that number . . .?" "Thuh-ree, tew. . . ."

He stiffened as a low, sweetly familiar voice joined the chorus: "Yes, yes! I—I accept the charges . . . Hello? Bob . . .?"

Instinctively he pressed the phone closer to his mouth, the touch of it conjuring up the feel of cool lips, soft blonde hair, and eyes that could melt a steel girder.

"Marian? Sure it's me! . . . Jail? No! No, honey, that's all over. I'm free! Free as a bird, yeah! The judge said it was unavoidable. Told you, didn't I?" He mugged into the phone as though somehow, in this age of speed, she could see as well as hear him across the twenty-odd miles that separated them. "It was the postponement that did it. Then they got this new judge—and guess what? He used to go to school with Dad and Uncle Harry! It was a cinch after that . . . Huh?"

He frowned slightly, listening to the soft voice coming over the wire; the voice he could not wait to hear congratulating him. Only, she wasn't. She was talking to him—he grinned sheepishly—the way Mom talked to Dad sometimes, when he came swooping into the driveway. One drink too many at the country club after his Saturday golf. . . .

"Say!" he snorted. "Aren't you *glad* I don't have to serve ten to twenty years for manslaughter . . . ?"

"Oh, Bob." There was a sadness in his financée's voice, a troubled note. "I . . . I'm glad. Of course I'm glad about it. But . . . it's just that you sound so smug, so. . . . That poor old Negro. . . ."

"Smug!" He stiffened, holding the phone away slightly as if it had stung him. "Honey . . . how can you say a thing like that! Why, I've done everything I could for his family. Paid his mortgage on that little farm! Carted one of his kids to the hospital every week for two months, like. . . ." His voice wavered, laden with a genuine regret. "Like the old guy would do himself, I guess, if he was still . . . *Marian!* You think I'm not *sorry* enough; is that it?" he demanded.

There was a little silence over the wire. He could picture her, sitting there quietly in the Marshalls' cheery-chintz living room. Maybe she had her hair pinned back in one of those ridiculous, but oddly attractive, "pony-tails" the teen-agers were wearing this year. Her little cat-face would be tiled up to the lamp, eyes closed, the long fringe of lashes curling up over shadowy lids. Bob fidgeted, wanting miserably to see her expression at that moment.

"Well? Say something?"

The silence was broken by a faint sigh.

"Darling . . . what is there to say? You're so thoughtless! Not callous; I don't mean that. Just . . . *careless!* Bob, you've got to unlearn what they taught you in Korea. You're . . . you're home again, and this is what you've been fighting for, isn't it? For . . . for the people around us to be safe? For life not to be cheap, something to be thrown away just to save a little *time*. . . ."

"Say, listen!" He was scowling now, anger hardening his mouth into ugly lines. "I've had enough lectures these past two months—from Dad, from the sheriff, from Uncle Harry. You'd think a guy twenty-two years old, in combat three years and got his feet almost frozen off, didn't know the score! What's the matter with everybody?" Bob's anger was mounting. "Listen! I got a medal last year for killing fourteen North Koreans. For gunning 'em down! Deliberately! But now, just because I'm driving a little too fast and some old creep can't get his wagon across the highway. . . ."

"Bob!"

". . . now, all at once, I'm not a hero, I'm a murderer! I don't know the value of human life! I don't give a hoot how many people I. . . ."

"Darling!"

A strangled sob came over the long miles. That stopped him. He gripped the phone, uncertainty in his oddly tip-tilted eyes that had earned him, in service, the nickname of "Gook."

"Darling, you're all mixed up. Bob . . .? Bob dear, are you listening? If I could just *talk* to you tonight . . . ! What time is it? Oh, it's after *six!* I . . . I don't suppose you could drive over here tonight. . . ."

The hard line of his mouth wavered, broke. He grinned.

"No? Who says I can't?" His laughter, young, winged and exultant, floated up. "Baby, I'll burn the road . . . Oops! I mean. . . ." He broke off, sheepishly. "No, no; I'll keep 'er under fifty. Honest!" Laughing, he crossed his heart—knowing Marian so well that he knew she would sense the gesture left over from their school days. "There's so much to talk over now," he added eagerly. "Uncle Harry's taking me into the firm. I start peddling real estate for him next week. No kiddin'! And . . . and that little house we looked at. . . . It's for sale, all right! Nine hundred down, and. . . ."

"Bob . . . Hurry! Please!" The voice over the wire held, again, the tone he loved, laughing and tender. "But drive carefully. Promise!"

"Sure, sure! Twenty miles, twenty minutes!"

He hung up, chuckling, and strode out into the street. Dusk was falling, the slow Southern dusk that takes its time about folding its dark quilt over the Blue Ridge foothills. With a light, springy step Bob walked to where his blue convertible was parked outside the drugstore, sandwiched between a pickup truck and a sedan full of people. As he climbed under the steering wheel, he heard a boy's piping voice, followed by the shushing monotone of an elder:

"Look! That's Bob Trask! He killed that old Negro last Fourth-o-July. . . ."

"Danny, hush! Don't talk so loud! He can hear. . . ."

"Benny Olsen told me it's his second bad wreck. . . ."

"Danny!"

". . . and that's the third car he's tore up in two years. Boy, you oughta seen that roadster he had! Sideswiped a truck and tore off the whole. . . ."

"Hmph! License was never revoked, either! Politics! If his uncle wasn't city commissioner. . . ."

Bob's scowl returned, cloudy with anger. People! They made up their own version of how an accident happened. That business with the truck, for instance. Swinging out into the highway just as he had tried to pass! Who could blame him for *that?* Or the fact that, weeks later, the burly driver had happened to die? From a ruptured appendix! The damage suit had been thrown out of court, because nobody could prove the collision had been what caused it to burst.

Backing out of the parking space in a bitter rush, Bob drove the convertible south, out of Gareyville on 31, headed for Oak Grove. Accidents! Anybody could be involved in an accident! Was a guy supposed to be lucky all the time? Or a mind-reader, always clairvoyant about the other driver?

As the white ribbon of highway unreeled before him, Bob's anger cooled. He smiled a little, settling behind the steering wheel and switching on the radio. Music poured out softly. He leaned back, soothed by its sound and the rush of wind tousling his dark hair.

The law had cleared him of reckless driving; and that was all that counted. The landscape blurred as the sun sank. Bob switched on his headlights, dimmed. There was, at this hour, not much traffic on Chattanooga Road.

Glancing at his watch, Bob pressed his foot more heavily on the accelerator. Six-fifteen already? Better get to Marian's before that parent of hers insisted on dragging her off to a movie. He chuckled. His only real problem now was to win over Marian's mother, who made no bones of her disapproval of him, ever since his second wreck. "*Show me the way a man drives a car, and I'll tell you what he's like inside. . . .*" Bob had laughed when Marian had repeated those words. A man could drive, he had pointed out, like an old-maid schoolteacher and still be involved in an accident that was not legally his fault. All right, *two* accidents! A guy could have lousy luck twice, couldn't he? Look at the statistics! Fatal accidents happened every day . . .

Yawning, at peace with himself and the lazy countryside sliding past his car window, Bob let the speedometer climb another ten miles an hour. Sixty-five? He smiled, amused. Marian was such an old grandma about driving fast! After they were married, he would have to teach her, show her. Why, he had had this old boat up to ninety on this same tree-shaded stretch of highway! A driver like himself, a good driver with a good car, had perfect control over his vehicle at any. . . .

The child seemed to appear out of nowhere, standing in the center of the road. A little girl in a frilly pink dress, her white face turned up in sudden horror, picked out by the headlights' glare.

Bob's cry was instinctive as he stamped on the brakes, and wrenched at the steering wheel. The car careened wildly, skidding sidewise and striking the child broadside. Then, in a tangle of wheels and canvas top, it rolled into a shallow ditch, miraculously right side up. Bob felt his head strike something hard—the windshield. It starred out with tiny shimmering cracks, but did not shatter. Darkness rushed over him; the sick black darkness of the unconscious; but through it, sharp as a knife thrust, bringing him back to hazy awareness, was the sound of a child screaming.

"*Oh, no ohmygodohgod. . . .*" Someone was sobbing, whimpering the words aloud. Himself.

Shaking his head blurrily, Bob stumbled from the tilted vehicle and looked about. Blood was running from a cut on his forehead, and his head throbbed with a surging nausea. But, ignoring the pain, he sank to his knee and peered under the car.

She was there. A little girl perhaps five years old. Ditch water matted the soft blonde hair and trickled into the half-closed eyes, tip-tilted at a pixie-like angle and fringed with long silky lashes. Bob groaned aloud, cramming his knuckles into his squared mouth to check the sob that burst out of him like a gust of desperate wind. She was pinned under a front wheel. Such a lovely little girl, appearing out here, miles from town, dressed as for a party. A sudden thought struck him that he knew this child, that he had seen her somewhere, sometime. On a bus? In a movie lobby . . .? Where?

He crawled under the car afraid to touch her, afraid not to. She did not stir. Was she dead? Weren't those frilly little organdy ruffles on her small chest moving, ever so faintly . . .? If he could only get her out from under that wheel! Get the car moving, rush her to a hospital . . . ! Surely, surely there was some spark of life left in that small body . . . !

Bob stood up, reeling, rubbing his eyes furiously as unconsciousness threatened to engulf him again. It was at that moment that he heard the muffled roar of a motorcycle. He whirled. Half in eagerness, half in dread, he saw a shadowy figure approaching him down the twilight-misted highway.

The figure on the motorcycle, goggled and uniformed as a state highway patrolman, braked slowly a few feet away. With maddening deliberateness of movement, he dismounted, flipped out a small report-pad, and peered at the convertible, jotting down its license number. Bob beckoned frantically, pointing at the child pinned under the car. But the officer made no move to help him free her; took no notice of her beyond a cursory glance and a curt nod.

Instead, tipping back his cap from an oddly pale face, he rested one booted foot on the rear bumper and beckoned Bob to his side.

''All right, buddy. . . .'' His voice, Bob noted crazily, was so low that he could scarcely hear it; a whisper, a lip-movement pronouncing sounds that might have been part of the wind soughing in the roadside trees. ''Name: Robert Trask? I had orders to be on the lookout for you. . . .''

''Orders?'' Bob bristled abruptly, caught between anxiety for the child under his car and an instinct for self-preservation. "Now, wait! I've got no record of reckless driving. I . . . I was involved in a couple of accidents; but the charges were dropped. . . . Look!" he burst out. "While you're standing here yapping, this child may be. . . . Get on that scooter of yours and go phone an ambulance, you! I'll report you for dereliction of duty! . . . Say!" he yelled, as the officer did not move, but went on scribbling in his book. "What kind of a man *are* you, anyway? Wasting time booking me, when there still may be time to save this . . . this poor little . . .!"

The white, goggle-obscured face lifted briefly, expressionless as a mask. Bob squirmed under the scrutiny of eyes hidden behind the green glass; saw the lips move . . . and noticed, for the first time, how queerly the traffic officer held his head. His pointed chin was twisted sidewise, almost meeting the left shoulder. When he looked up, his whole body turned, like a man with a crick in his neck . . .

"What kind of man are *you?*" said the whispering lips. "That's what we have to find out. . . . And that's why I got orders to bring you in. *Now!*"

"Bring me in . . . ?" Bob nodded dully. "Oh, you mean I'm under arrest? Sure, sure . . . but the little girl!" He glared, suddenly enraged by the officer's stolid indifference to the crushed form under the car. "Listen, if you don't get on that motorbike and go for help, I . . . I'll knock you out and go myself! Resisting arrest; leaving the scene of an accident. . . . Charge me with anything you like! But if there's still time to save her. . . ."

The goggled eyes regarded him steadily for a moment. Then, nodding, the officer scribbled something else in his book.

"Time?" the windy whisper said, edged with irony. "Don't waste time, eh? . . . Why don't you speed-demons think about other people's time before you cut it off? Why? *Why?* That's what we want to find out, what we *have* to find out . . . *Come on!*" The whisper lashed out, sibilant as a striking snake. "Let's go, buddy! *Walk!*"

Bob blinked, swayed. The highway patrolman, completely ignoring the small body pinned under the convertible, had strode across the paved road with a peremptory beckoning gesture. He seemed headed for a little byroad that branched off the highway, losing itself among a thick grove of pine trees. It must, Bob decided eagerly, lead to some farmhouse where the officer meant to phone for an ambulance. Staggering, he followed, with a last anxious glance at the tiny form spread-eagled under his car wheel. Where had he seen that little face? *Where* . . . ? Some neighbor's child, visiting out here in the country. . . . ?

"You . . . you think she's . . . dead?" he blurted, stumbling after the shadowy figure ahead of him. "Is it too late . . . ?"

The officer with the twisted neck half turned, swiveling his whole body to look back at him.

"That," the whispering voice said, "all depends. Come on, you—snap it up! We got all night, but there's no sense wastin' time! Eh, buddy?" The thin lips curled ironically. "Time! That's the most important thing in the world . . . to them as still have it!"

Swaying dizzily, Bob hurried after him up the winding little byroad. It led, he saw with a growing sense of unease, through a country cemetery. . . . Abruptly, he brought up short, peering ahead at a gray gleam through the pines. Why, there was no farmhouse ahead! A fieldstone chapel with a high peaked roof loomed against the dusk, its arched windows gleaming redly in the last glow of sunset.

"Hey!" he snapped. "What *is* this? Where the hell are you taking me?"

The highway patrolman turned again, swiveling his body instead of his stiff, twisted neck.

"Night court," his whisper trailed back on a thread of wind.

"*Night* court!" Bob halted completely, anger stiffening his resolve not to be railroaded into anything, no matter what he had done to that lovely little girl back there in the ditch. "Say! Is this some kind of a gag? A kangaroo court, is it? You figure on lynching me after you've . . . ?"

He glanced about the lonely graveyard in swift panic, wondering if he could make a dash for it. This was no orderly minion of the law, this crazy deformed figure stalking ahead of him! A crank, maybe? Some joker dressed up as a highway patrolman . . . ? Bob backed away a few steps, glancing left and right. A mental case, a crackpot . . . ?

He froze. The officer held a gun leveled at his heart.

"Don't try it!" The whisper cracked like a whiplash. "Come on, bud. You'll get a fair trial in this court—fairer than the likes of you deserve!"

Bob moved forward, helpless to resist. The officer turned his back, almost insolently, and stalked on up the narrow road. At the steps of the chapel he stood aside, however, waving his gun for Bob to open the heavy doors. Swallowing on a dry throat, he obeyed—and started violently as the rusty hinges made a sound like a hollow groan.

Then, hesitantly, his heart beginning to hammer with apprehension, Bob stepped inside. Groping his way into the darker interior of the chapel, he paused for a moment to let his eyes become accustomed to the gloom. Row on row of hardwood benches faced a raised dais, on which was a pulpit. Here, Bob realized with a chill coursing down his spine, local funeral services were held for those to be buried in the churchyard outside. As he moved forward, his footsteps echoed eerily among the beamed rafters overhead. . . .

Then he saw them. People in those long rows of benches! There seemed to be over a hundred of them, seated in silent groups of twos and threes, facing the pulpit. In a little alcove, set aside for the choir, Bob saw another, smaller group—and found himself suddenly counting them with a surge of panic. There were twelve in the choir box. Twelve, the number of a jury! Dimly he could see their white faces, with dark hollows for eyes, turning to follow his halting progress down the aisle.

Then, like an echo of a voice, deep and reverberating, someone called his name.

"The defendant will please take the stand . . . !"

Bob stumbled forward, his scalp prickling at the ghostly resemblance of this mock-trial to the one in which he had been acquitted only that morning. As though propelled by unseen hands, he found himself hurrying to a seat beside the pulpit, obviously reserved for one of the elders, but now serving as a witness-stand. He sank into the big chair, peering through the half-darkness in an effort to make out some of the faces around him. . . .

Then, abruptly, as the "bailiff" stepped forward to "swear him in," he stifled a cry of horror.

The man had no face. Where his features had been there was a raw, reddish mass. From this horror, somehow, a nightmare slit of mouth formed the words: ". . . to tell the truth, the whole truth, and nothing but the truth, so help you God?"

"I . . . I do," Bob murmured; and compared to the whispered tones of the bailiff, his own voice shocked him with its loudness.

"State your name."

"R-robert Trask. . . ."

"Your third offense, isn't it, Mr. Trask?" the judge whispered dryly. "A habitual reckless driver. . . ."

Bob was shaking now, caught in the grip of a nameless terror. What was this? Who were all these people, and why had they had him brought here by a motorcycle cop with a twisted . . . ?

He caught his breath again sharply, stifling another cry as the figure of a dignified elderly man became visible behind the pulpit, where he had been half-shrouded in shadow. Bob blinked at him, sure that his stern white face was familiar—very familiar, not in the haunting way in which that child had seemed known to him, lying there crushed under his car. This man. . . .

His head reeled all at once. Of course! Judge Abernathy! Humorous, lenient old Judge Ab, his father's friend, who had served in the Gareyville circuit court . . . Bob gulped. In 1932! Why, he had been only a youngster then! Twenty years would make this man all of ninety-eight years old, if. . . . And it was suddenly that "*if*" which made Bob's scalp prickle with uneasiness. *If he were alive.* Judge Ab was *dead!* Wasn't he? Hadn't he heard his mother and dad talking about the old man, years ago;

talking in hushed, sorrowful tones about the way he had been killed by a hit-and-run driver who had never been caught?

Bob shook his head, fighting off the wave of dizziness and nausea that was creeping over him again. It was crazy, the way his imagination was running away with him! Either this was not Judge Ab, but some old fellow who vaguely resembled him in this half-light. . . . Or it *was* Judge Ab, alive, looking no older than he had twenty-odd years ago, at which time he was supposed to have been killed.

Squinting out across the rows of onlookers, Bob felt a growing sense of unreality. He could just make out, dimly, the features of the people seated in the first two rows of benches. Other faces, pale blurs against the blackness, moved restlessly as he peered at them . . . Bob gasped. His eyes made out things in the semi-gloom that he wished he had not seen. Faces mashed and cut beyond the semblance of a face! Bodies without arms! One girl. . . . He swayed in his chair sickly; her shapely form was without a head!

He got a grip on his nerves with a tremendous effort. Of course! It wasn't real; it was all a horrible, perverted sort of practical joke! All these people were tricked up like corpses in a Chamber-of-Commerce "horror" parade. He tried to laugh, but his lips jerked with the effort. . . . Then they quivered, sucking in breath.

The "prosecuting attorney" had stepped forward to question him—as, hours ago, he had been questioned by the attorney for Limestone County. Only . . . Bob shut his eyes quickly. It couldn't be! They wouldn't, whoever these people in this lonely chapel might be, they *wouldn't* make up some old Negro to look like the one whose wagon he had . . . had. . . .

The figure moved forward, soundlessly. Only someone who had seen him on the morgue slab, where they had taken him after the accident, could have dreamed up that woolly white wig, that wrinkled old black face, and . . . and that gash at his temple, on which now the blood seemed to have dried forever. . . .

"Hidy, Cap'm," the figure said in a different whisper. "I got to ast you a few questions. Don't lie, now! Dat's de *wust* thing you could do—tell a lie in dis-*yeah* court! . . . 'Bout how fast you figger you was goin' when you run over de girl-baby?"

"I. . . . Pretty fast," he blurted. "Sixty-five, maybe seventy an hour."

The man he had killed nodded, frowning. "Yassuh, Dat's about right, sixty-five accordin' to de officer here." He glanced at the patrolman with the twisted neck, who gave a brief, grotesque nod of agreement.

Bob waited sickly. The old Negro—or whoever was dressed up as a dead man—moved toward him, resting his hand on the ornate rail of the chapel pulpit.

"Cap'm. . . ." His soft whisper seemed to come from everywhere, rather than from the moving lips in that black face. "Cap'm . . . *why*? How come you was drivin' fifteen miles over the speed-limit on this-yeah road? Same road where you run into my wagon. . . ."

The listeners in the tiers of pews began to sway all at once, like reeds in the wind. "*Why?*" someone in the rear took up the word, and then another echoed it, until a faint rhythmic chant rose and fell all over the crowded chapel:

"*Why? Why? Why? . . . Why? Why? Why?*"

"*Order!*" The "judge," the man who looked like the judge long dead, banged softly with his gavel; or it could have been a shutter banging at one of those arched chapel windows, Bob thought strangely.

The chanting died away. Bob swallowed nervously. For the old Negro was looking up at him expectantly, waiting for an answer to his simple question—the question echoed by those looking and listening from that eerie "courtroom." *Why*? Why was he driving so fast? If he could only make up something, some good reason. . . .

"I . . . I had a date with my girl," Bob heard his own voice, startling in its volume compared to the whispers around him.

"Yassuh?" The black prosecutor nodded gently. "She was

gwine off someplace, so's you had to hurry to catch up wid her? Or else, was she bad-off sick and callin' for you . . . ?"

"I . . . No," Bob said, miserably honest. "No. There wasn't any hurry. I just . . . didn't want to. . . ." He gestured futilely. "I wanted to be with her as quick as I could! Be-because I love her. . . ." He paused, waiting to hear a titter of mirth ripple over the listeners.

There was no laughter. Only silence, somber and accusing.

"Yassuh." Again the old Negro nodded his graying head, the head with the gashed temple. "All of us wants to be wid the ones we love. We don't want to waste no time doin' it. . . . Only, you got to remember de Lawd give each of us a certain po'tion of time to use. And he don't aim for us to cut off de supply dat belong to somebody else. They got a right to live and love and be happy, too!"

The grave words hit Bob like a hammer blow—or like, he thought oddly, words he had been forming in his own mind, but holding off, not letting himself think because they might hurt. He fidgeted in the massive chair, twisting his hands together in sudden grim realization. Remorse had not, up to this moment, touched him deeply. But it now brought tears welling up, acid-like, to burn his eyes.

"Oh . . . please!" he burst out. "Can't we get this over with, this . . . this crazy mock-trial? I don't know who you are, all you people here. But I know you've . . . you've been incensed because my . . . my folks pulled some wires and got me out of two traffic accidents that I . . . I should have been punished for! Now I've . . . I've run over a little girl, and you're afraid if I go to regular court-trial, my uncle will get me free again; is that it? That's it, isn't it . . . ?" he lashed out, half rising. "All this . . . this masquerade! Getting yourselves up like . . . like people who are dead . . . ! You're doing it to scare me!" He laughed harshly. "But it doesn't scare me, kid tricks like . . . like. . . ."

He broke off, aware of another figure that had moved forward, rising from one of the forward benches. A burly man in overalls, wearing a trucker's cap. . . . One big square hand was pressed to his side, and he walked as though in pain. Bob recognized those rugged features with a new shock.

"Kid . . . listen!" His rasping whisper sounded patient, tired. "We ain't here to scare nobody. . . . Hell, that's for Hallowe'en parties! The reason we hold court here, night after night, tryin' some thick-skinned jerk who thinks he owns the road. . . . Look, we just want t' know *why;* see? Why we had to be killed. Why some nice joe like you, with a girl and a happy future ahead of 'im, can't understand that . . . that *we* had a right to live, too! Me! Just a dumb-lug of a truck jockey, maybe. . . . But I was doin' all right. I was gettin' by, raisin' my kids right. . . ." The square hand moved from the man's side, gestured briefly, and pressed back again.

"I figured to have my fool appendix out, soon as I made my run and got back home that Sunday. Only, you. . . . Couldn't you have spared me ten seconds, mac?" the hoarse whisper accused. "Wouldn't you loan me that much of your . . . your precious time, instead of takin' away all of mine? Mine, and this ole darkey's? And tonight. . . ."

An angry murmur swept over the onlookers, like a rising wind.

"Order!" The gavel banged again, like a muffled heartbeat. "The accused is not on trial for previous offenses. Remarks of the defense attorney—who is distinctly out of order—will be stricken from the record. Does the prosecution wish to ask the defendant any more questions to determine the *reason* for the accident?"

The old Negro shook his head, shrugging. "Nawsuh, Jedge. Reckon not."

Bob glanced sidewise at the old man who looked so like Judge Ab. He sucked in a quick breath as the white head turned, revealing a hideously crushed skull matted with some dark brown substance. Hadn't his father said something, years ago, about that hit-and-run driver running a wheel over his old friend's head? Were those . . . where those tire-tread marks on this man's white collar . . . ? Bob ground his teeth. How far would these

Hallowe'en mummers go to make their macabre little show realistic . . . ?

But now, to his amazement, the burly man in trucker's garb moved forward, shrugging.

"Okay, your Honor," his hoarse whisper apologized. "I . . . I know it's too late for justice, not for us here. And if the court appoints me to defend this guy, I'll try. . . . Look buddy," his whisper softened. "You have reason to believe your girl was steppin' out on you? That why you was hurryin', jumpin' the speed-limit, to get there before she . . . ? You were out of your head, crazy-jealous?"

Bob glared, "Say!" he snapped. "This is going too far, dragging my fiancée's name into this . . . this fake trial. . . . Go ahead! I'm guilty of reckless driving—three times! I admit it! There was no reason on this earth for me to be speeding, no excuse for running over that . . . that poor little kid! It's . . . it's just that I. . . ." His voice broke, "I didn't *see* her! Out here in the middle of nowhere—a child! How was I to know? The highway was clear, and then all at once, there she was right in front of my car. . . . But . . . but I *was* going too fast. I deserve to be lynched! Nothing you do to me would be enough. . . ."

He crumpled in the chair, stricken with dry sobs of remorse. But fear, terror of this weirdly made-up congregation, left him slowly, as, looking from the judge to the highway patrolman, from the old Negro to the trucker, he saw only pity in their faces, and a kind of sad bewilderment.

"But—why? Why need it happen?" the elderly judge asked softly, in a stern voice Bob thought he could remember from childhood. "Why does it go on and on? This senseless slaughter! If we could only *understand* . . . ! If we could only make the living understand, and stop and think, before it's too late for . . . another such as we. There is no such thing as an accidental death! Accidents are murders—because someone could have prevented them!"

The white-haired man sighed, like a soft wind blowing

through the chapel. The sigh was caught up by others, until it rose and fell like a wailing gust echoing among the rafters.

Bob shivered, hunched in his chair. The hollow eyes of the judge fixed themselves on him, stern but pitying. He hung his head, and buried his face in his hands, smearing blood from the cut on his forehead.

"I . . . I . . . Please! Please don't say any more!" he sobbed. "I guess I just didn't realize, I was too wrapped up in my own selfish. . . ." His voice broke. "And now it's too late. . . ."

Silently, the shadowy figures of the old Negro and the burly truck driver moved together in a kind of grim comradeship. They looked at the judge mutely as though awaiting his decision. The gaunt figure with the crushed skull cleared his throat in a way Bob thought he remembered. . . .

"Too late? Yes . . . for these two standing before you. But the dead," his somber whisper rose like a gust of wind in the dark chapel, "the dead cannot punish the living. They are part of the past, and have no control over the present . . . or the future."

"Yet, sometimes," the dark holes of eyes bored into Bob's head sternly, "the dead can guide the living, by giving them a glimpse into the future. The future as it will be . . . unless the living use their power to change it! Do you understand, Robert Trask? Do you understand that you are on trial in this night court, not for the past but for the future . . . ?"

Bob shook his head, bewildered. "The . . . future? I don't understand. I. . . ." He glanced up eagerly. "The little girl! You . . . you mean, she's all right? She isn't dead . . . ?" he pressed, hardly daring to hope.

"She is not yet born," the old man whispered quietly. "But one day you will see her, just as you saw her tonight, lying crushed under your careless wheels . . . unless. . . ." The whisper changed abruptly; became the dry official voice of a magistrate addressing his prisoner. "It is therefore the judgment of this court that, in view of the defendant's plea of guilty and in view of his extreme youth and of his war-record, sentence shall be suspended pending new evidence of criminal behavior in the driver's seat of a motor vehicle. If such new evidence should be brought to the attention of this court, sentence shall be pronounced and the extreme penalty carried out. . . . Do you understand, Mr. Trask?'' the grave voice repeated. ''*The extreme penalty!* . . . Case dismissed.''

The gavel banged. Bob nodded dazedly, again burying his face in his hands and shaking with dry sobs. A wave of dizziness swept over him. He felt the big chair tilt, it seemed, and suddenly he was falling, falling forward into a great black vortex that swirled and eddied. . . .

Light snatched him back to consciousness, a bright dazzling light that pierced his eyeballs and made him gag with nausea. Hands were pulling at him, lifting him. Then, slowly, he became aware of two figures bending over him: a gnome-like little man with a lantern, and a tall, sunburned young man in the uniform of a highway patrolman. It was not, Bob noted blurrily, the same one, the one with the twisted neck. . . . He sat up, blinking.

''My, my, young feller!'' The gnome with the lantern was trying to help him up from where he lay on the chapel floor in front of the pulpit. ''Nasty lump on your head there! I'm the sexton: live up the road a piece. I heard your car hit the ditch a while ago, and called the Highway Patrol. Figgered you was drunk. . . .'' He sniffed suspiciously, then shrugged. ''Don't smell drunk. What happened? You fall asleep at the wheel?''

Bob shut his eyes, groaning. He let himself be helped to one of the front pews and leaned back against it heavily before answering. Better tell the truth now. Get it over with. . . .

''The . . . little girl. Pinned under my car—you found her?'' He forced out the words sickly. ''I . . . didn't see her, but. . . . It was my fault. I was . . . driving too fast. Too fast to stop when she stepped out right in front of my. . . .''

He broke off, aware that the tall tanned officer was regarding him with marked suspicion.

"What little girl?" he snapped. "There's nobody pinned under your car, buddy! I looked. Your footprints were the only ones leading away from the accident . . . and I traced them here! Besides, you were dripping blood from that cut on you. . . . Say! You trying to kid somebody?"

"No, no!" Bob gestured wildly. "Who'd kid about a thing like . . . ? Maybe the other highway patrolman took her away on his motorcycle! He. . . . All of them. . . . There didn't seem any doubt that she'd been killed instantly. But then, the judge said she . . . she wasn't even born yet! They made me come here, to . . . try me! In . . . night court, they called it! All of them pretending to be . . . dead people, accident victims. Blood all over them! Mangled. . . ." He checked himself, realizing how irrational he sounded. "I fainted," his voice trailed uncertainly. "I guess when they . . . they heard you coming, they all ran away. . . ."

"*Night* court?" The officer arched one eyebrow, tipped back his cap, and eyed Bob dubiously. "Say, you *sure* you're sober, buddy? Or maybe you got a concussion. . . . There's been nobody here. Not a soul; has there, Pop?"

"Nope." The sexton lifted his lamp positively, causing shadows to dance weirdly over the otherwise empty chapel. A film of dust covered the pews, undisturbed save where Bob himself now sat. "Ain't been nary a soul here since the Wilkins funeral; that was Monday three weeks ago. My, you never saw the like o' flowers. . . ."

The highway patrolman gestured him to silence, peering at Bob once more. "What was that you said about another speed cop? There was no report tonight. What was his badge number? You happen to notice?"

Bob shook his head vaguely; then dimly recalled numbers he had seen on a tarnished shield pinned to that shadowy uniform.

"Eight something . . . 84! That was it! And . . . and he had a kind of twisted set to his head. . . ."

The officer scowled suddenly, hands on hips. "Sa-ay!" he said in a cold voice. "What're you tryin' to pull? Nobody's worn

Badge No. 84 since Sam Lacy got killed two years ago. Chasin' a speed-crazy high school kid, who swerved and made him fall off his motor. Broke his neck!'' He compressed his lips grimly. ''You're tryin' to pull some kind of gag about *that?*''

''No! No-no. . . . !'' Bob rose shakily to his feet. ''I . . . I . . . Maybe I just dreamed it all! That clonk on the head. . . .'' He laughed all at once, a wild sound, full of hysterical relief. ''You're positive there was no little girl pinned under my wheel? No . . . no signs of . . . ?''

He started toward the wide-flung doors of the chapel, reeling with laughter. But it had all seemed so real! Those nightmare faces, the whispering voices: that macabre trial for a traffic fatality that had never happened anywhere but in his own overwrought imagination . . . !

Still laughing, he climbed into his convertible; found it undamaged by its dive into the ditch, and backed out onto the road again. He waved. Shrugging, grinning, the highway officer and the old sexton waved back, visible in a yellow circle of lantern light.

Bob gunned his motor and roared away. A lone tourist, rounding a curve, swung sharply off the pavement to give him room as he swooped over the wrong side of the yellow line. Bob blew his horn mockingly, and trod impatiently on the accelerator. Marian must be tired of waiting! And the thought of holding her in his arms, laughing with her, telling her about that crazy, dream-trial. . . . Dead men! Trying him, the living, for the traffic death of a child yet to be born! ''The extreme penalty!'' If not lynching, what would that be? He smiled, amused. Was anything that could happen to a man really ''a fate worse than death . . .''?

Bob's smile froze.

Quite suddenly his foot eased up on the accelerator. His eyes widened, staring ahead at the dark highway illuminated by the twin glare of his headlights. Sweat popped out on his cool forehead all at once. Jerkily his hands yanked at the smooth plastic of the steering wheel, pulling the convertible well over to the right side of the highway. . . .

In that instant, Bob thought he knew where he had seen the hauntingly familiar features of that lovely little girl lying dead, crushed, under the wheel of his car. "The extreme penalty?" He shuddered, and slowed down, driving more carefully into the darkness ahead. The darkness of the future. . . .

For, the child's blonde hair and long lashes, he knew with a swift chill of dread, had been a tiny replica of Marian's . . . and the tip-tilted pixy eyes, closed in violent death, had borne a startling resemblance to his own.

The Lovely House

SHIRLEY JACKSON

"The Lovely House" is a haunting tale, crafted with the steadily rising suspense that is a trademark of its author, and the seemingly ordinary events of the story lead to a most extraordinary conclusion. Shirley Jackson (1919–1965) was one of the foremost modern writers of horror fiction; her 1949 collection, The Lottery, *and 1959 novel,* The Haunting of Hill House, *are considered classics of the genre. In addition, Ms. Jackson wrote a superb murder novel,* We Have Always Lived in the Castle *(1962), as well as nonfiction books, juveniles, and plays. Her last short story,* "The Possibility of Evil," *published posthumously in 1965, was awarded the Mystery Writers of America Edgar for best short story of that year.*

I

THE HOUSE in itself was, even before anything had happened there, as lovely a thing as she had ever seen. Set among its lavish grounds, with a park and a river and a wooded hill surrounding it, and carefully planned and tended gardens close upon all sides, it lay upon the hills as though it were something too precious to be seen by everyone; Margaret's very coming there had been a product of such elaborate arrangement, and such letters to and fro, and such meetings and hopings and wishings, that when she alighted with Carla Montague at the doorway of Carla's home, she felt that she too had come home, to a place striven for and earned. Carla stopped before the doorway and stood for a minute, looking first behind her, at the vast reaching gardens and the green lawn going down to the river, and the soft hills beyond, and then at the perfect grace of the house, showing so clearly the long-boned structure within, the curving staircases and the arched doorways and the tall thin lines of steadying beams, all of it resting back against the hills, and up, past rows of windows and the flying lines of the roof, on, to the tower—Carla stopped, and looked, and smiled, and then turned and said, "Welcome, Margaret."

"It's a lovely house," Margaret said, and felt that she had much better have said nothing.

The doors were opened and Margaret, touching as she went the warm head of a stone faun beside her, passed inside. Carla, following, greeted the servants by name, and was welcomed with reserved pleasure; they stood for a minute on the rose and white tiled floor. "Again, welcome, Margaret," Carla said.

Far ahead of them the great stairway soared upward, held to the hall where they stood by only the slimmest of carved balustrades; on Margaret's left hand a tapestry moved softly as the door behind was closed. She could see the fine threads of the weave, and the light colors, but she could not have told the picture unless she went far away, perhaps as far away as the staircase, and looked at it from there; perhaps, she thought, from halfway up the stairway this great hall, and perhaps the whole house, is visible, as a complete body of story together, all joined and in sequence. Or perhaps I shall be allowed to move slowly from one thing to another, observing each, or would that take all the time of my visit?

"I never saw anything so lovely," she said to Carla, and Carla smiled.

"Come and meet my mama," Carla said.

They went through doors at the right, and Margaret, before she could see the light room she went into, was stricken with fear at meeting the owners of the house and the park and the river, and as she went beside Carla she kept her eyes down.

"Mama," said Carla, "this is Margaret, from school."

"Margaret," said Carla's mother, and smiled at Margaret kindly. "We are very glad you were able to come."

She was a tall lady wearing pale green and pale blue, and Margaret said as gracefully as she could, "Thank you, Mrs. Montague; I am very grateful for having been invited."

"Surely," said Mrs. Montague softly, "surely my daughter's friend Margaret from school should be welcome here; surely we should be grateful that she has come."

"Thank you, Mrs. Montague," Margaret said, not knowing how she was answering, but knowing that she was grateful.

When Mrs. Montague turned her kind eyes on her daughter, Margaret was at last able to look at the room where she stood next to her friend; it was a pale green and a pale blue long room with tall windows that looked out onto the lawn and the sky, and thin colored china ornaments on the mantel. Mrs. Montague had left her needlepoint when they came in and from where Margaret stood she could see the pale sweet pattern from the underside; all soft colors it was, melting into one another endlessly, and not finished. On the table nearby were books, and one large book of sketches that were most certainly Carla's;

Carla's harp stood next to the windows, and beyond one window were marble steps outside, going shallowly down to a fountain, where water moved in the sunlight. Margaret thought of her own embroidery—a pair of slippers she was working for her friend—and knew that she should never be able to bring it into this room, where Mrs. Montague's long white hands rested on the needlepoint frame, soft as dust on the pale colors.

"Come," said Carla, taking Margaret's hand in her own. "Mama has said that I might show you some of the house."

They went out again into the hall, across the rose and white tiles which made a pattern too large to be seen from the floor, and through a doorway where tiny bronze fauns grinned at them from the carving. The first room that they went into was all gold, with gilt on the window frames and on the legs of the chairs and tables, and the small chairs standing on the yellow carpet were made of gold brocade with small gilded backs, and on the wall were more tapestries showing the house as it looked in the sunlight with even the trees around it shining, and these tapestries were let into the wall and edged with thin gilded frames.

"There is so much tapestry," Margaret said.

"In every room," Carla agreed. "Mama has embroidered all the hangings for her own room, the room where she writes her letters. The other tapestries were done by my grandmamas and my great-grandmamas and my great-great-grandmamas."

The next room was silver, and the small chairs were of silver brocade with narrow silvered backs, and the tapestries on the walls of this room were edged with silver frames and showed the house in moonlight, with the white light shining on the stones and the windows glittering.

"Who uses these rooms?" Margaret asked.

"No one," Carla said.

They passed then into a room where everything grew smaller as they looked at it: the mirrors on both sides of the room showed the door opening and Margaret and Carla coming through, and then, reflected, a smaller door opening and a small Margaret and a smaller Carla coming through, and then, reflected again, a still smaller door and Margaret and Carla, and so on, endlessly, Margaret and Carla diminishing and reflecting. There was a table here and nesting under it another lesser table, and under that another one, and another under that one, and on the greatest table lay a carved wooden bowl holding within it another carved wooden bowl, and another within that, and another within that one. The tapestries in this room were of the house reflected in the lake, and the tapestries themselves were reflected, in and out, among the mirrors on the wall, with the house in the tapestries reflected in the lake.

This room frightened Margaret rather, because it was so difficult for her to tell what was in it and what was not, and how far in any direction she might easily move, and she backed out hastily, pushing Carla behind her. They turned from here into another doorway which led them out again into the great hall under the soaring staircase, and Carla said, "We had better go upstairs and see your room; we can see more of the house another time. We have *plenty* of time, after all," and she squeezed Margaret's hand joyfully.

They climbed the great staircase, and passed, in the hall upstairs, Carla's room, which was like the inside of a shell in pale colors, with lilacs on the table, and the fragrance of the lilacs followed them as they went down the halls.

The sound of their shoes on the polished floor was like rain, but the sun came in on them wherever they went. "Here," Carla said, opening a door, "is where we have breakfast when it is warm; here," opening another door, "is the passage to the room where Mama does her letters. And that—" nodding, "—is the stairway to the tower, and *here* is where we shall have dances when my brother comes home."

"A real tower?" Margaret said.

"And *here*," Carla said, "is the old schoolroom, and my brother and I studied here before he went away, and I stayed on alone studying here until it was time for me to come to school and meet *you*."

"Can we go up into the tower?" Margaret asked.

"Down here, at the end of the hall," Carla said, "is where all my grandpapas and my grandmamas and my great-great-grandpapas and grandmamas live." She opened the door to the long gallery, where pictures of tall old people in lace and pale waistcoats leaned down to stare at Margaret and Carla. And then, to a walk at the top of the house, where they leaned over and looked at the ground below and the tower above, and Margaret looked at the gray stone of the tower and wondered who lived there, and Carla pointed out where the river ran far below, far away, and said they should walk there tomorrow.

"When my brother comes," she said, "he will take us boating on the river."

In her room, unpacking her clothes, Margaret realized that her white dress was the only one possible for dinner, and thought that she would have to send home for more things; she had intended to wear her ordinary gray downstairs most evenings before Carla's brother came, but knew she could not when she saw Carla in light blue, with pearls around her neck. When Margaret and Carla came into the drawing room before dinner Mrs. Montague greeted them very kindly, and asked had Margaret seen the painted room, or the room with the tiles?

"We had no time to go near that part of the house at all," Carla said.

"After dinner, then," Mrs. Montague said, putting her arm affectionately around Margaret's shoulders, "we will go and see the painted room and the room with the tiles, because they are particular favorites of mine."

"Come and meet my papa," Carla said.

The door was just opening for Mr. Montague, and Margaret, who felt almost at ease now with Mrs. Montague, was frightened again of Mr. Montague, who spoke loudly and said, "So this is m'girl's friend from school? Lift up your head, girl, and let's have a look at you." When Margaret looked up blindly, and smiled weakly, he patted her cheek and said, "We shall have to make you look bolder before you leave us,'' and then he tapped his daughter on the shoulder and said she had grown to a monstrous fine girl.

They went in to dinner, and on the walls of the dining room were tapestries of the house in the seasons of the year, and the dinner service was white china with veins of gold running through it, as though it had been mined and not molded. The fish was one Margaret did not recognize, and Mr. Montague very generously insisted upon serving her himself without smiling at her ignorance. Carla and Margaret were each given a glassful of pale spicy wine.

''When my brother comes,'' Carla said to Margaret, ''we will not dare be so quiet at table.'' She looked across the white cloth to Margaret, and then to her father at the head, to her mother at the foot, with the long table between them, and said, ''My brother can make us laugh all the time.''

''Your mother will not miss you for these summer months?'' Mrs. Montague said to Margaret.

''She has my sisters, ma'am,'' Margaret said, ''and I have been away at school for so long that she has learned to do without me.''

''We mothers never learn to do without our daughters,'' Mrs. Montague said, and looked fondly at Carla. ''Or our sons,'' she added with a sigh.

''When my brother comes,'' Carla said, ''you will see what this house can be like with life in it.''

''When does he come?'' Margaret asked.

''One week,'' Mr. Montague said, ''three days, and four hours.''

When Mrs. Montague rose, Margaret and Carla followed her, and Mr. Montague rose gallantly to hold the door for them all.

That evening Carla and Margaret played and sang duets, although Carla said that their voices together were too thin to be appealing without a deeper voice accompanying, and that when her brother came they should have some splendid trios. Mrs.

Montague complimented their singing, and Mr. Montague fell asleep in his chair.

Before they went upstairs Mrs. Montague reminded herself of her promise to show Margaret the painted room and the room with the tiles, and so she and Margaret and Carla, holding their long dresses up away from the floor in front so that their skirts whispered behind them, went down a hall and through a passage and down another hall, and through a room filled with books and then through a painted door into a tiny octagonal room where each of the sides were paneled and painted, with pink and blue and green and gold small pictures of shepherds and nymphs, lambs and fauns, playing on the broad green lawns by the river, with the house standing lovely behind them. There was nothing else in the little room, because seemingly the paintings were furniture enough for one room, and Margaret felt surely that she could stay happily and watch the small painted people playing, without ever seeing anything more of the house. But Mrs. Montague led her on, into the room of the tiles, which was not exactly a room at all, but had one side all glass window looking out onto the same lawn of the pictures in the octagonal room. The tiles were set into the floor of this room, in tiny bright spots of color which showed, when you stood back and looked at them, that they were again a picture of the house, only now the same materials that made the house made the tiles, so that the tiny windows were tiles of glass, and the stones of the tower were chips of gray stone, and the bricks of the chimneys were chips of brick.

Beyond the tiles of the house Margaret, lifting her long skirt as she walked, so that she should not brush a chip of the tower out of place, stopped and said, "What is *this?*" And stood back to see, and then knelt down and said, "*What* is this?"

"Isn't she enchanting?" said Mrs. Montague, smiling at Margaret, "I've always loved her."

"I was wondering what Margaret would say when she saw it," said Carla, smiling also.

It was a curiously made picture of a girl's face, with blue chip eyes and a red chip mouth, staring blindly from the floor, with long light braids made of yellow stone chips going down evenly on either side of her round cheeks.

"She is pretty," said Margaret, stepping back to see her better. "What does it say underneath?"

She stepped back again, holding her head up and back to read the letters, pieced together with stone chips and set unevenly in the floor. "Here was Margaret," it said, "who died for love."

II

There was, of course, not time to do everything. Before Margaret had seen half the house, Carla's brother came home. Carla came running up the great staircase one afternoon calling, "Margaret, Margaret, he's come," and Margaret, running down to meet her, hugged her and said, "I'm so glad."

He had certainly come, and Margaret, entering the drawing room shyly behind Carla, saw Mrs. Montague with tears in her eyes and Mr. Montague standing straighter and prouder than before, and Carla said, "Brother, here is Margaret."

He was tall and haughty in uniform, and Margaret wished she had met him a little later, when she had perhaps been to her room again, and perhaps tucked up her hair. Next to him stood his friend, a captain, small and dark and bitter, and smiling bleakly upon the family assembled. Margaret smiled back timidly at them both, and stood behind Carla.

Everyone then spoke at once. Mrs. Montague said, "We've missed you so," and Mr. Montague said, "Glad to have you back, m'boy," and Carla said, "We shall have such times—I've promised Margaret—" and Carla's brother said, "So this is Margaret?" and the dark captain said, "I've been wanting to come."

It seemed that they all spoke at once, every time; there would be a long waiting silence while all of them looked around with joy at being together, and then suddenly everyone would have found something to say. It was so at dinner. Mrs. Montague said,

"You're not eating enough," and "You used to be more fond of pomegranates," and Carla said, "We're to go boating," and "We'll have a dance, won't we?" and "Margaret and I insist upon a picnic," and "I saved the river for my brother to show to Margaret." Mr. Montague puffed and laughed and passed the wine, and Margaret hardly dared lift her eyes. The black captain said, "Never realized what an attractive old place it could be, after all," and Carla's brother said, "There's much about the house I'd like to show Margaret."

After dinner they played charades, and even Mrs. Montague did Achilles with Mr. Montague, holding his heel and both of them laughing and glancing at Carla and Margaret and the captain. Carla's brother leaned on the back of Margaret's chair and once she looked up at him and said, "No one ever calls you by name. Do you actually have a name?"

"Paul," he said.

The next morning they walked on the lawn, Carla with the captain and Margaret with Paul. They stood by the lake, and Margaret looked at the pure reflection of the house and said, "It almost seems as though we could open a door and go in."

"There," said Paul, and he pointed with his stick at the front entrance, "there is where we shall enter, and it will swing open for us with an underwater crash."

"Margaret," said Carla, laughing, "you say odd things, sometimes. If you tried to go into *that* house, you'd be in the lake."

"Indeed, and not like it much, at all," the captain added.

"Or would you have the side door?" asked Paul, pointing with his stick.

"I think I prefer the front door," said Margaret.

"But you'd be drowned," Carla said. She took Margaret's arm as they started back toward the house, and said, "We'd make a scene for a tapestry right now, on the lawn before the house."

"Another tapestry?" said the captain, and grimaced.

They played croquet, and Paul hit Margaret's ball toward a wicket, and the captain accused her of cheating prettily. And they played word games in the evening, and Margaret and Paul won, and everyone said Margaret was so clever. And they walked endlessly on the lawns before the house, and looked into the still lake, and watched the reflection of the house in the water, and Margaret chose a room in the reflected house for her own, and Paul said she should have it.

"That's the room where Mama writes her letters," said Carla, looking strangely at Margaret.

"Not in our house in the lake," said Paul.

"And I suppose if you like it she would lend it to you while you stay," Carla said.

"Not at all," said Margaret amiably. "I think I should prefer the tower anyway."

"Have you seen the rose garden?" Carla asked.

"Let me take you there," said Paul.

Margaret started across the lawn with him, and Carla called to her, "Where are you off to now, Margaret?"

"Why, to the rose garden," Margaret called back, and Carla said, staring, "You are really very odd, sometimes, Margaret. And it's growing colder, far too cold to linger among the roses," and so Margaret and Paul turned back.

Mrs. Montague's needlepoint was coming on well. She had filled in most of the outlines of the house, and was setting in the windows. After the first small shock of surprise, Margaret no longer wondered that Mrs. Montague was able to set out the house so well without a pattern or a plan; she did it from memory and Margaret, realizing this for the first time, thought "How amazing," and then "But of course how else *would* she do it?"

To see a picture of the house, Mrs. Montague needed only to lift her eyes in any direction, but, more than that, she had of course never used any other model for her embroidery; she had of course learned the faces of the house better than the faces of her children. The dreamy life of the Montagues in the house was most clearly shown Margaret as she watched Mrs. Montague surely and capably building doors and windows, carvings and cornices, in her embroidered house, smiling tenderly across the room to where Carla and the captain bent over a book together, while her fingers almost of themselves turned the edge of a carving Margaret had forgotten or never known about until, leaning over the back of Mrs. Montague's chair, she saw it form itself under Mrs. Montague's hands.

The small thread of days and sunlight, then, that bound Margaret to the house, was woven here as she watched. And Carla, lifting her head to look over, might say, "Margaret, do come and look, here. Mother is always at her work, but my brother is rarely home."

They went for a picnic, Carla and the captain and Paul and Margaret, and Mrs. Montague waved to them from the doorway as they left, and Mr. Montague came to his study window and lifted his hand to them. They chose to go to the wooded hill beyond the house, although Carla was timid about going too far away—"I always like to be where I can see the roofs, at least," she said—and sat among the trees, on moss greener than Margaret had ever seen before, and spread out a white cloth and drank red wine.

It was a very proper forest, with neat trees and the green moss, and an occasional purple or yellow flower growing discreetly away from the path. There was no sense of brooding silence, as there sometimes is with trees about, and Margaret realized, looking up to see the sky clearly between the branches, that she had seen this forest in the tapestries in the breakfast room, with the house shining in the sunlight beyond.

"Doesn't the river come through here somewhere?" she asked, hearing, she thought, the sound of it through the trees. "I feel so comfortable here among these trees, so at home."

"It is possible," said Paul, "to take a boat from the lawn in front of the house and move without sound down the river, through the trees, past the fields and then, for some reason, around past the house again. The river, you see, goes almost around the house in a great circle. We are are very proud of that."

"The river *is* nearby," said Carla. "It goes almost completely around the house."

"Margaret," said the captain. "You must not look rapt on a picnic unless you are contemplating nature."

"I was, as a matter of fact," said Margaret. "I was contemplating a caterpillar approaching Carla's foot."

"Will you come and look at the river?" said Paul, rising and holding his hand out to Margaret. "I think we can see much of its great circle from near here."

"Margaret," said Carla as Margaret stood up, "you are *always* wandering off."

"I'm coming right back," Margaret said, with a laugh. "It's only to look at the river."

"Don't be away long," Carla said. "We must be getting back before dark."

The river as it went through the trees was shadowed and cool, broadening out into pools where only the barest movement disturbed the ferns along its edge, and where small stones made it possible to step out and see the water all around, from a precarious island, and where without sound a leaf might be carried from the limits of sight to the limits of sight, moving swiftly but imperceptibly and turning a little as it went.

"Who lives in the tower, Paul?" asked Margaret, holding a fern and running it softly over the back of her hand. "I know someone lives there, because I saw someone moving at the window once."

"Not *lives* there," said Paul, amused. "Did you think we kept a political prisoner locked away?"

"I thought it might be the birds, at first," Margaret said, glad to be describing this to someone.

"No," said Paul, still amused. "There's an aunt, or a great-aunt, or perhaps even a great-great-great-aunt. She doesn't live there, at all, but goes there because she says she cannot *endure* the sight of tapestry." He laughed. "She has filled the tower with books, and a huge old cat, and she may practice alchemy there, for all anyone knows. The reason you've never seen her would be that she has one of her spells of hiding away. Sometimes she is downstairs daily."

"Will I ever meet her?" Margaret asked wonderingly.

"Perhaps," Paul said. "She might take it into her head to come down formally one night to dinner. Or she might wander carelessly up to you where you sat on the lawn, and introduce herself. Or you might never see her, at that."

"Suppose I went up to the tower?"

Paul glanced at her strangely. "I suppose you could, if you wanted to," he said. "*I've* been there."

"Margaret," Carla called through the woods. "Margaret, we shall be late if you do not give up brooding by the river."

All this time, almost daily, Margaret was seeing new places in the house: the fan room, where the most delicate filigree fans had been set into the walls with their fine ivory sticks painted in exquisite miniature; the small room where incredibly perfect wooden and glass and metal fruits and flowers and trees stood on glittering glass shelves, lined up against the windows. And daily she passed and repassed the door behind which lay the stairway to the tower, and almost daily she stepped carefully around the tiles on the floor which read "Here was Margaret, who died for love."

It was no longer possible, however, to put off going to the tower. It was no longer possible to pass the doorway several times a day and do no more than touch her hand secretly to the panels, or perhaps set her head against them and listen, to hear if there were footsteps up or down, or a voice calling her. It was not possible to pass the doorway once more, and so in the early morning Margaret set her hand firmly to the door and pulled it open, and it came easily, as though relieved that at last, after so many hints and insinuations, and so much waiting and such helpless despair, Margaret had finally come to open it.

The stairs beyond, gray stone and rough, were, Margaret thought, steep for an old lady's feet, but Margaret went up effortlessly, though timidly. The stairway turned around and around, going up to the tower, and Margaret followed, setting her feet carefully upon one step after another, and holding her hands against the warm stone wall on either side, looking forward and up, expecting to be seen or spoken to before she reached the top; perhaps, she thought once, the walls of the tower were transparent and she was clearly, ridiculously visible from the outside, and Mrs. Montague and Carla, on the lawn—if indeed they ever looked upward to the tower—might watch her and turn to one another with smiles, saying, "There is Margaret, going up to the tower at last," and, smiling, nod to one another.

The stairway ended, as she had not expected it would, in a heavy wooden door, which made Margaret, standing on the step below to find room to raise her hand and knock, seem smaller, and even standing at the top of the tower she felt that she was not really tall.

"Come in," said the great-aunt's voice, when Margaret had knocked twice; the first knock had been received with an expectant silence, as though inside someone had said inaudibly, "Is that someone knocking at *this* door?" and then waited to be convinced by a second knock; and Margaret's knuckles hurt from the effort of knocking to be heard through a heavy wooden door. She opened the door awkwardly from below—how much easier this all would be, she thought, if I knew the way—went in, and said politely, before she looked around, "I'm Carla's friend. They said I might come up to the tower to see it, but of course if you would rather I went away I shall." She had planned to say this more gracefully, without such an implication that invitations to the tower were issued by the downstairs Montagues, but the long climb and her being out of breath forced her to say everything at once, and she had really no time for the sounding periods she had composed.

In any case the great-aunt said politely—she was sitting at the other side of the round room, against the window, and she was not very clearly visible—"I am amazed that they told you about me at all. However, since you are here I cannot pretend that I really object to having you; you may come in and sit down."

Margaret came obediently into the room and sat down on the stone bench which ran all the way around the tower room, under the windows which of course were on all sides and open to the winds, so that the movement of the air through the tower room was insistent and constant, making talk difficult and even distinguishing objects a matter of some effort.

As though it were necessary to establish her position in the house emphatically and immediately, the old lady said, with a gesture and a grin, "My tapestries," and waved at the windows. She seemed to be not older than a great-aunt, although perhaps too old for a mere aunt, but her voice was clearly able to carry through the sound of the wind in the tower room and she seemed compact and strong beside the window, not at all as though she might be dizzy from looking out, or tired from the stairs.

"May I look out the window?" Margaret asked, almost of the cat, which sat next to her and regarded her without friendship, but without, as yet, dislike.

"Certainly," said the great-aunt. "Look out the windows, by all means."

Margaret turned on the bench and leaned her arms on the wide stone ledge of the window, but she was disappointed. Although the tops of the trees did not reach halfway up the tower, she could see only branches and leaves below and no sign of the wide lawns or the roofs of the house or the curve of the river.

"I hoped I could see the way the river went, from here."

"The river doesn't go from here," said the old lady, and laughed.

"I mean," Margaret said, "they told me that the river went around in a curve, almost surrounding the house."

"Who told you?" said the old lady.

"Paul."

"I see," said the old lady. "*He's* back, is he?"

"He's been here for several days, but he's going away again soon."

"And what's *your* name?" asked the old lady, leaning forward.

"Margaret."

"I see," said the old lady again. "That's my name, too," she said.

Margaret thought that "How nice" would be an inappropriate reply to this, and something like "Is it?" or "Just imagine" or "What a coincidence" would certainly make her feel more foolish than she believed she really was, so she smiled uncertainly at the old lady and dismissed the notion of saying "What a lovely name."

"He should have come and gone sooner," the old lady went on, as though to herself. "Then we'd have it all behind us."

"Have all *what* behind us?" Margaret asked, although she felt that she was not really being included in the old lady's conversation with herself, a conversation that seemed—and probably was—part of a larger conversation which the old lady had with herself constantly and on larger subjects than the matter of Margaret's name, and which even Margaret, intruder as she was, and young, could not be allowed to interrupt for very long. "Have all *what* behind us?" Margaret asked insistently.

"I say," said the old lady, turning to look at Margaret, "he should have come and gone already, and we'd all be well out of it by now."

"I see," said Margaret. "Well, I don't think he's going to be here much longer. He's talking of going." In spite of herself, her voice trembled a little. In order to prove to the old lady that the trembling in her voice was imaginary, Margaret said almost defiantly, "It will be very lonely here after he has gone."

"We'll be well out of it, Margaret, you and I," the old lady said. "Stand away from the window, child, you'll be wet."

Margaret realized with this that the storm, which had—she knew now—been hanging over the house for long sunny days had broken, suddenly, and that the wind had grown louder and was bringing with it through the windows of the tower long stinging rain. There were drops on the cat's black fur, and Margaret felt the side of her face wet. "Do your windows close?" she asked. "If I could help you—?"

"I don't mind the rain," the old lady said. "It wouldn't be the first time it's rained around the tower."

"I don't mind it," Margaret said hastily, drawing away from

the window. She realized that she was staring back at the cat, and added nervously, "Although, of course, getting wet is—" She hesitated and the cat stared back at her without expression. "I mean," she said apologetically, "some people don't *like* getting wet."

The cat deliberately turned its back on her and put its face closer to the window.

"What were you saying about Paul?" Margaret asked the old lady, feeling somehow that there might be a thin thread of reason tangling the old lady and the cat and the tower and the rain, and even, with abrupt clarity, defining Margaret herself and the strange hesitation which had caught at her here in the tower. "He's going away soon, you know."

"It would have been better if it were over with by now," the old lady said. "These things don't take really long, you know, and the sooner the better, I say."

"I suppose *that's* true," Margaret said intelligently.

"After all," said the old lady dreamily, with raindrops in her hair, "we don't always see ahead, into things that are going to happen."

Margaret was wondering how soon she might politely go back downstairs and dry herself off, and she meant to stay politely only so long as the old lady seemed to be talking, however remotely, about Paul. Also, the rain and the wind were coming through the window onto Margaret in great driving gusts, as though Margaret and the old lady and the books and the cat would be washed away, and the top of the tower cleaned of them.

"I *would* help you if I could," the old lady said earnestly to Margaret, raising her voice almost to a scream to be heard over the wind and the rain. She stood up to approach Margaret, and Margaret, thinking she was about to fall, reached out a hand to catch her. The cat stood up and spat, the rain came through the window in a great sweep, and Margaret, holding the old lady's hands, heard through the sounds of the wind the equal sounds of all the voices in the world, and they called to her saying, "Goodbye, goodbye," and "All is lost" and another voice saying, "I will always remember you," and still another called, "It is so dark." And, far away from the others, she could hear a voice calling, "Come back, come back." Then the old lady pulled her hands away from Margaret and the voices were gone. The cat shrank back and the old lady looked coldly at Margaret and said, "As I was saying, I would help you if I *could*."

"I'm so sorry," Margaret said weakly. "I thought you were going to fall."

"Goodbye," said the old lady.

III

At the ball Margaret wore a gown of thin blue lace that belonged to Carla, and yellow roses in her hair, and she carried one of the fans from the fan room, a daintily painted ivory thing which seemed indestructible, since she dropped it twice, and which had a tiny picture of the house painted on its ivory sticks, so that when the fan was closed the house was gone. Mrs. Montague had given it to her to carry, and had given Carla another, so that when Margaret and Carla passed one another dancing, or met by the punch bowl or in the halls, they said happily to one another, "Have you still got your fan? I gave mine to someone to hold for a minute; I showed mine to everyone. Are you still carrying your fan? I've got *mine*."

Margaret danced with strangers and with Paul, and when she danced with Paul they danced away from the others, up and down the long gallery hung with pictures, in and out between the pillars which led to the great hall opening into the room of the tiles. Near them danced ladies in scarlet silk, and green satin, and white velvet, and Mrs. Montague, in black with diamonds at her throat and on her hands, stood at the top of the room and smiled at the dancers, or went on Mr. Montague's arm to greet guests who came laughingly in between the pillars looking eagerly and already moving in time to the music as they walked. One lady wore white feathers in her hair, curling down against her shoulder; another had a pink scarf over her arms, and it floated behind her as she danced. Paul was in his haughty uniform, and Carla wore red roses in her hair and danced with the captain.

"Are you really going tomorrow?" Margaret asked Paul once during the evening; she knew that he was, but somehow asking the question—which she had done several times before—established a communication between them, of his right to go and her right to wonder, which was sadly sweet to her.

"I *said* you might meet the great-aunt," said Paul, as though in answer; Margaret followed his glance, and saw the old lady of the tower. She was dressed in yellow satin, and looked very regal and proud as she moved through the crowd of dancers, drawing her skirt aside if any of them came too close to her. She was coming toward Margaret and Paul where they sat on small chairs against the wall, and when she came close enough she smiled, looking at Paul, and said to him, holding out her hands, "I am very glad to see you, my dear."

Then she smiled at Margaret and Margaret smiled back, thankful that the old lady held out no hands to her.

"Margaret told me you were here," the old lady said to Paul, "and I came down to see you once more."

"I'm happy that you did," Paul said. "I wanted to see you so much that I almost came to the tower."

They both laughed and Margaret, looking from one to the other of them, wondered at the strong resemblance between them. Margaret sat very straight and stiff on her narrow chair, with her blue lace skirt falling charmingly around her and her hands folded neatly in her lap, and listened to their talk. Paul had found the old lady a chair and they sat with their heads near together, looking at one another as they talked, and smiling.

"You look very fit," the old lady said. "Very fit indeed." She sighed.

"You look wonderfully well," Paul said.

"Oh, well," said the old lady. "I've aged. I've aged, I know it."

"So have I," said Paul.

"Not noticeably," said the old lady, shaking her head and regarding him soberly for a minute. "*You* never will, I suppose."

At that moment the captain came up and bowed in front of Margaret, and Margaret, hoping that Paul might notice, got up to dance with him.

"I saw you sitting there alone," said the captain, "and I seized the precise opportunity I have been awaiting all evening."

"Excellent military tactics," said Margaret, wondering if these remarks had not been made a thousand times before, at a thousand different balls.

"I could be a splendid tactician," said the captain gallantly, as though carrying on his share of the echoing conversation, the words spoken under so many glittering chandeliers, "if my objective were always so agreeable to me."

"I saw you dancing with Carla," said Margaret.

"Carla," he said, and made a small gesture that somehow showed Carla as infinitely less than Margaret. Margaret knew that she had seen him make the same gesture to Carla, probably with reference to Margaret. She laughed.

"I forget what I'm supposed to say now," she told him.

"You're supposed to say," he told her seriously, " 'And do you really leave us so soon?' "

"And do you really leave us so soon?" said Margaret obediently.

"The sooner to return," he said, and tightened his arm around her waist. Margaret said, it being her turn, "We shall miss you very much."

"*I* shall miss *you*," he said, with a manly air of resignation.

They danced two waltzes, after which the captain escorted her handsomely back to the chair from which he had taken her, next to which Paul and the old lady continued in conversation, laughing and gesturing. The captain bowed to Margaret deeply, clicking his heels.

"May I leave you alone for a minute or so?" he asked. "I believe Carla is looking for me."

"I'm perfectly all right here," Margaret said. As the captain hurried away she turned to hear what Paul and the old lady were saying.

"I remember, I remember," said the old lady laughing, and she tapped Paul on the wrist with her fan. "I never imagined there would be a time when I should find it funny."

"But it *was* funny," said Paul.

"We were so young," the old lady said. "I can hardly remember."

She stood up abruptly, bowed to Margaret, and started back across the room among the dancers. Paul followed her as far as the doorway and then left her to come back to Margaret. When he sat down next to her he said, "So you met the old lady?"

"I went to the tower," Margaret said.

"She told me," he said absently, looking down at his gloves. "Well," he said finally, looking up with an air of cheerfulness. "Are they *never* going to play a waltz?"

Shortly before the sun came up over the river the next morning they sat at breakfast, Mr. and Mrs. Montague at the ends of the table, Carla and the captain, Margaret and Paul. The red roses in Carla's hair had faded and been thrown away, as had Margaret's yellow roses, but both Carla and Margaret still wore their ball gowns, which they had been wearing for so long that the soft richness of them seemed natural, as though they were to wear nothing else for an eternity in the house, and the gay confusion of helping one another dress, and admiring one another, and straightening the last folds to hang more gracefully, seemed all to have happened longer ago than memory, to be perhaps a dream that might never have happened at all, as perhaps the figures in the tapestries on the walls of the dining room might remember, secretly, an imagined process of dressing themselves and coming with laughter and light voices to sit on the lawn where they were woven. Margaret, looking at Carla, thought that she had never seen Carla so familiarly as in this soft white gown, with her hair dressed high on her head—had it really been curled and pinned that way? Or had it always, forever, been so?—and the fan in her hand—had she not always had that fan, held just so?—and when Carla turned her head slightly on her long neck she captured the air of one of the portraits in the long gallery. Paul and the captain were still somehow trim in their uniforms; they were leaving at sunrise.

"Must you really leave this morning?" Margaret whispered to Paul.

"You are all kind to stay up and say goodbye," said the captain, and he leaned forward to look down the table at Margaret, as though it were particularly kind of her.

"Every time my son leaves me," said Mrs. Montague, "it is as though it were the first time."

Abruptly, the captain turned to Mrs. Montague and said, "I noticed this morning that there was a bare patch on the grass before the door. Can it be restored?"

"I had not known," Mrs. Montague said, and she looked nervously at Mr. Montague, who put his hand quietly on the table and said, "We hope to keep the house in good repair so long as we are able."

"But the broken statue by the lake?" said the captain. "And the tear in the tapestry behind your head?"

"It is wrong of you to notice these things," Mrs. Montague said, gently.

"What can I do?" he said to her. "It is impossible not to notice these things. The fish are dying, for instance. There are no grapes in the arbor this year. The carpet is worn to thread near your embroidery frame," he bowed to Mrs. Montague, "and in the house itself—" bowing to Mr. Montague, "—there is a noticeable crack over the window of the conservatory, a crack in the solid stone. Can you repair that?"

Mr. Montague said weakly, "It is very wrong of you to notice these things. Have you neglected the sun, and the bright perfection of the drawing room? Have you been recently to the gallery of portraits? Have you walked on the green portions of the lawn, or only watched for the bare places?"

"The drawing room is shabby," said the captain softly. "The

green brocade sofa is torn a little near the arm. The carpet has lost its luster. The gilt is chipped on four of the small chairs in the gold room, the silver paint scratched in the silver room. A tile is missing from the face of Margaret, who died for love, and in the great gallery the paint has faded slightly on the portrait of—" bowing to Mr. Montague, "—your great-great-great-grandfather, sir."

Mr. Montague and Mrs. Montague looked at one another, and then Mrs. Montague said, "Surely it is not necessary to reproach *us* for these things?"

The captain reddened and shook his head.

"My embroidery is very nearly finished," Mrs. Montague said. "I have only to put the figures into the foreground."

"*I* shall mend the brocade sofa," said Carla.

The captain glanced once around the table, and sighed. "I must pack," he said. "We cannot delay our duties even though we have offended lovely women." Mrs. Montague, turning coldly away from him, rose and left the table, with Carla and Margaret following.

Margaret went quickly to the tile room, where the white face of Margaret who died for love stared eternally into the sky beyond the broad window. There was indeed a tile missing from the wide white cheek, and the broken spot looked like a tear, Margaret thought; she kneeled down and touched the tile face quickly to be sure that it was not a tear.

Then she went slowly back through the lovely rooms, across the broad rose and white tiled hall, and into the drawing room, and stopped to close the tall doors behind her.

"There really is a tile missing," she said.

Paul turned and frowned; he was standing alone in the drawing room, tall and bright in his uniform, ready to leave. "You are mistaken," he said. "It is not possible that anything should be missing."

"I saw it."

"It is not *true*, you know," he said. He was walking quickly up and down the room, slapping his gloves on his wrist, glancing nervously, now and then, at the door, at the tall windows opening out onto the marble stairway. "The house is the same as ever," he said. "It does not change."

"But the worn carpet . . ." It was under his feet as he walked.

"Nonsense," he said violently. "Don't you think I'd know my own house? I care for it constantly, even when *they* forget; without this house I could not exist; do you think it would begin to crack while I am here?"

"How can you keep it from aging? Carpets *will* wear, you know, and unless they are replaced. . ."

"Replaced?" he stared as though she had said something evil. "What could replace anything in this house?" He touched Mrs. Montague's embroidery frame, softly. "All we can do is add to it."

There was a sound outside; it was the family coming down the great stairway to say goodbye. He turned quickly and listened, and it seemed to be the sound he had been expecting. "I will always remember you," he said to Margaret, hastily, and turned again toward the tall windows. "Goodbye."

"It is so dark," Margaret said, going beside him. "You will come back?"

"I will come back," he said sharply. "Goodbye." He stepped across the sill of the window onto the marble stairway outside; he was black for a moment against the white marble, and Margaret stood still at the window watching him go down the steps and away through the gardens. "Lost, lost," she heard faintly, and, from far away, "all is lost."

She turned back to the room, and, avoiding the worn spot in the carpet and moving widely around Mrs. Montague's embroidery frame, she went to the great doors and opened them. Outside, in the hall with the rose and white tiled floor, Mr. and Mrs. Montague and Carla were standing with the captain.

"Son," Mrs. Montague was saying. "When will you be back?"

"Don't *fuss* at me," the captain said. "I'll be back when I can."

Carla stood silently, a little away. "Please be careful," she said, and, "Here's Margaret, come to say goodbye to you, brother."

"Don't linger, m'boy," said Mr. Montague. "Hard on the women."

"There are so many things Margaret and I planned for you while you were here," Carla said to her brother. "The time has been so short."

Margaret, standing beside Mrs. Montague, turned to Carla's brother *(and Paul; who was Paul?)* and said "Goodbye." He bowed to her and moved to go to the door with his father.

"It is hard to see him go," Mrs. Montague said. "And we do not know when he will come back." She put her hand gently on Margaret's shoulder. "We must show you more of the house," she said. "I saw you one day try the door of the ruined tower; have you seen the hall of flowers? Or the fountain room?"

"When my brother comes again," Carla said, "we shall have a musical evening, and perhaps he will take us boating on the river."

"And my visit?" said Margaret smiling. "Surely there will be an end to my visit?"

Mrs. Montague, with one last look at the door from which Mr. Montague and the captain had gone, dropped her hand from Margaret's shoulder and said, "I must go to my embroidery. I have neglected it while my son was with us."

"You will not leave us before my brother comes again?" Carla asked Margaret.

"I have only to put the figures into the foreground," Mrs. Montague said, hesitating on her way to the drawing room. "I shall have you exactly if you sit on the lawn near the river."

"We shall be models of stillness," said Carla, laughing. "Margaret, will you come and sit beside me on the lawn?"

Kindling Point

MARCIA MULLER

Old Victorian houses, Ouija boards, and forces beyond human ken are familiar devices in macabre fiction; but the use Marcia Muller makes of them in this contemporary tale is unusual, surprising, and disquieting in its ambiguousness. Ms. Muller has published other horror fiction (and coedited several other anthologies with Bill Pronzini), but she is best known for her excellent detective novels featuring San Francisco private eye Sharon McCone (Edwin of the Iron Shoes, Ask the Cards a Question, Games to Keep the Dark Away), *and Santa Barbara museum curator Elena Oliverez* (The Tree of Death, Fiesta of the Slain Soldiers). *(B.P.)*

"SO HOW are the ghosts today?" I asked.

The two nine-year-olds started and looked up at me. My daughter Carolyn and Alison, the little girl from across the street, sat cross-legged on the dining room's Oriental carpet. On either side of them, long white tapers burned in my silver candelabra, and the heavy red drapes were pulled shut. The girls had been leaning forward, their eyes closed, fingers on the heart-shaped pointer of a Ouija board.

I stood in the doorway, my arms folded across my breasts, trying to look severe. Did they realize that those tapers had cost three dollars each? Had they noticed wax was dripping onto the—mercifully—as yet unfinished floor? I maintained my stern stance for about fifteen seconds, then started to laugh.

The girls relaxed and exchanged relieved smiles. I went in and dropped to the floor beside them, wiping wax from the base of one candlestick.

"That's what you were doing, wasn't it?" I said. "Contacting ghosts?"

"Yes," Carolyn said.

"What do they have to say?"

"Oh, lots of things." She bent her head and traced her index finger around the outside of the Ouija pointer.

Ever since my husband and I had bought the Victorian house in San Francisco's Noe Valley District, our daughter had been preoccupied with the idea of ghosts. And I had to admit it was the perfect place for a haunting, with its huge, gloomy rooms and corner turret. Alison and her parents lived across the street in a house that had been restored before she was born, and now that the two girls had become friends, Carolyn had managed to infect her with the same fantasy. Alison—unlike me—probably enjoyed the novelty of crumbling plaster, peeling wallpaper, and dark corners where heaven-knows-what might lurk.

But I had my doubts about the diversion they'd picked for this

Sunday afternoon. It was one of those beautiful, fog-free days that happen all too seldom during the San Francisco summer. The girls should have been at the park, or at least out in the big weed-choked yard. Instead, they sat in the dining room—easily the gloomiest place in the house—raising ghosts.

Still, I couldn't complain. For various private reasons, I'd been distracted and hadn't been paying much attention to them.

"How many ghosts are there?" I asked.

Carolyn's face, framed by her wings of smooth dark hair, was flushed. "Three. Three and a half."

"A half?"

"Well, there's a dog. He doesn't speak, of course."

"What kind of dog?"

"Afghan."

It would be, in a house like this.

"The others are called Nathan, Paul, and Elizabeth."

"And the dog's name is Prince," Alison added.

I studied my neighbor's child. She was a beauty, the image of her mother, except her red hair was short and curly, while Lydia's was long and straight. Alison was with us for the week because her parents were away on one of those last-ditch jaunts to try to save their marriage, and the child seemed to know something important was afoot. Maybe I was sensitive to it because of my own situation, but since they'd deposited her late Friday afternoon, her normally laughing face had looked pinched and her blue eyes were often distant. If it took calling forth make-believe spirits to cheer her, then the girls were welcome to do so all afternoon.

"When did these ghosts live?" I asked.

"Around nineteen hundred," Alison said.

"Did they live here in this house?"

"Yes. And they died here. *Horribly.*"

The way she said it made my unease return. "How did they die?"

"They wouldn't say," Carolyn said. "I mean, Elizabeth

wanted to tell us, but Nathan interrupted her. Nathan hates Elizabeth, and Paul too."

"I didn't know ghosts hated."

"Nathan does. Paul was his friend once; he feels awfully bad that Nathan hates him. So does Elizabeth; she cries."

Mentally I reversed my stance on the spirit-raising; it was not healthy for them to be dwelling on such things. I blew out the candles, got up, and set them on the table. "Well, frankly, I think it's too nice a day to stay inside like this. How would you like to run over to Bud's for an ice cream cone?"

"Yes!" they said in unison.

"Good. Pack up the Ouija board, Carolyn, and I'll see if your dad wants to go with us." I went through the parlor to the hall and hurried up to the second story, calling out to Ted.

He was where I'd known he would be, in the little tower room, beer in hand, staring moodily out the curved window at the row of brightly painted Victorian houses across the street. He wore faded Levi's, with a tool belt around his slim waist, and a workman's cap covered his fine blond hair. In spite of the utilitarian costume, he hadn't done a thing all day.

We'd moved into the house in March and, from the first, things had gone wrong. The new plumbing had cost much more than our original estimate, and the contractor we'd hired had proved incompetent and quit when the job was half finished. The electrician had likewise failed us. After that—since we had a good bit of money saved and my decorating firm was doing well—Ted had decided to quit his job in computer sales and do the work himself.

After an initial flurry of activity, however, less and less seemed to get done. Often Ted would be gone when I came home from work at six, or only coming through the door, offering half-hearted excuses. Finally I'd persuaded him to hire a carpenter to help him frame in the upstairs bathrooms, but I'd recently noticed the man was doing all the work himself, unsupervised. When I questioned Ted about what he was doing with his time, he mumbled something unsatisfactory about investigating the price of supplies at the lumberyards. I privately thought he'd been hanging out in one of the neighborhood bars. After that, there was little conversation between us, and he spent most of the evenings and weekends sulking in the tower room.

I thought I knew what was going through his mind as he stared out the window—he was looking at those pretty restored houses and doubting ours would ever be like them. Too much time had gone by, and the money we'd put aside for the renovation was running out. I had feared this would happen, had not wanted to buy the house, had actively fought against it—but so far I'd not stooped to saying, "I told you so." Still, Ted must have known the words were on the tip of my tongue, and he'd also sensed another, deeper change in me. So he escaped from the chaos of our lives to this little room and watched the pretty buildings across the street—and drank.

It wasn't so bad during the week, because my job as a decorator kept me busy, and when I was home there were meals to get and Carolyn to attend to. But on the weekends, I had no work to occupy my mind, and I couldn't even phone Mike for comfort . . .

At the sound of my footsteps, Ted turned.

"Hi," I said, trying to sound cheerful, "do you want to take a break? I promised the girls a trip to Bud's."

He shook his head and took a sip of beer. "I wouldn't be very good company, Emily."

"Shall I bring you back something?"

"No." He turned back to the brightly painted panorama outside. "You just go ahead. Have a good time." He sounded very tired, as if the last polite words had cost him a great deal.

That night we ate in the big, drafty dining room. The candles flickered eerily on the high coved ceiling and, as usual, I toyed with my food, shivering. Ted, on the other hand, seemed more cheerful than he had that afternoon, and he quizzed the girls about the ghosts.

"This Nathan—who is he?"

"The owner of the house," Carolyn said. "Elizabeth is his wife. The dog, Prince, belongs to her."

"And who's Paul?"

Carolyn looked down at her plate. "He's their friend, Nathan's friend, from back in New York. He was staying with them."

"Was?"

"Well, he was but then he left."

"What Carolyn means," Alison said, "is that Nathan threw him out. You see, Paul fell in love with Elizabeth, and she fell in love with him. Nathan found out and made Paul leave."

I felt a distinct chill on my shoulder blades. When I glanced at Ted, he was watching me carefully.

"Nathan found some jewelry Paul had given Elizabeth," Alison went on, "and he tried to make her throw it away. But she hid it in a hole in the wall at the back of her closet. Because she really loved Paul and couldn't bear to part with it."

Tension stretched down the table between Ted and me. I said, "It's awfully cold in here." My voice was louder than it should have been. "Isn't anybody else cold? Can't you turn up that heater, Ted?" There was a gas heater that had been installed in the fireplace behind him.

He dropped his eyes from mine, turned his chair, and fiddled with the heater. "For a while we can, but not long. I think this thing's sprung a leak; it could be dangerous."

But not so dangerous, I thought, as this conversation about betrayal and infidelity.

I was not cut out to have an affair—and indeed I wasn't having one. What I had was a friendship with an old college friend of Ted's—but it was a friendship I'd come to depend upon more and more in the last couple of months. Ted and I had grown apart long before his insistence on buying this albatross of a house; Mike, whose photography studio was a few doors down from my decorating shop on Union Street, saw the world the way I did. But it was just a friendship, and the only reason I didn't tell Ted I was seeing Mike was that it might upset him at a time when he didn't need further upheaval. That was what I told myself.

But when I told it to Mike—as I often did, and as I did at lunch the following day, Monday—he merely fixed me with his clear photographer's eye and shook his head. "If we were just friends, you'd be able to phone me from home on the weekends. And it wouldn't have taken me a month to get you out of dark restaurants into the sunshine." He motioned around the little courtyard café down the street from our offices. "If we were just friends, you wouldn't be so insistent that that's all we are."

"Well, then, what *are* we?"

"Confused. You are, that is. I'm not." He covered my hand with his.

"What a mess. You're Ted's friend too. Like Paul was Nathan's friend."

"Who?"

"Oh, right. You don't know about Paul and Elizabeth and Nathan. And Prince, the Afghan . . ."

Retelling the ghost story to Mike was the reason it was very much on my mind when I climbed the steps of the Victorian and turned my key in the lock that evening. And stepped into the hall to find Carolyn, Alison, Ted, and the carpenter we'd hired to frame in the bathrooms. They were kneeling on the floor, staring down at an open box lined with yellowed satin. A box containing an old-fashioned necklace set with deep red stones.

An eerie sense of dread descended on me. "What's that?"

Ted was the first to look up, eyes full of wonder. "It appears we've found Elizabeth's jewels. The ones she couldn't bear to part with."

I shut the door and went over to take a closer look. The necklace was obviously old, very beautiful, and I'd never seen it before in my life. "Where did that come from?"

The carpenter spoke. "The back of the closet in the middle

bedroom. I had to rip out that wall to put in the door to the new bathroom, and Ted had asked me to look for anything that might be hidden there."

The girls were both silent, staring up at me. Carolyn had her hand to her mouth.

I whirled on Ted. "I suppose this is your idea of a joke?"

"Emily . . ." He paused, shaken. "It's no joke. Oh, it was at first when I had him look. But they were there, like the girls said."

"Like Elizabeth said," Carolyn reminded him.

"That's silly." I shook my head. "There's no such thing as ghosts. The Ouija board is just a toy; for God's sake, it's put out by the same people who make Monopoly. . ."

"Then where did this necklace come from?" Ted said quietly.

It was a good question, and I couldn't answer it.

That night I broke my rule and called Mike from the phone extension in the kitchen. The girls were upstairs in Carolyn's room and Ted was again in his tower, where he couldn't hear me. Quickly I told Mike about the garnet necklace. "Do you think Ted could have planted it there, to make me feel guilty?" I asked.

"Why would he?"

"If he suspected about us . . ."

"Emily, Ted's not that subtle. If he suspected he'd come out and ask you."

"Maybe once he would have, but now I don't know. He's been so strange lately."

"Believe me, I've known him for twenty years. That's too complicated a ploy for Ted."

"But then where *did* it come from?" My voice was shrill, trembly.

"I don't know, but you've got to get hold of yourself. Do you want to meet someplace for a drink and talk about this?"

"I do, but I can't."

"All right. But listen—I didn't know this when we had lunch, but I'm going to have to go to Los Angeles on a shoot for a couple of days. A new commercial that the client is in a hurry for. Will you be okay?''

''Oh, Mike, I . . .''

''Will you?''

''I guess.''

''It's only Los Angeles, and I'll give you the number where I can be reached, in case you need me.''

I copied it down and said good night, feeling strangely abandoned. Was this how Elizabeth had felt when Nathan made Paul leave the house?

The next morning I was so distracted that I left at home three fabric sample books I'd promised to show a client. At noon I went back to fetch them and found the carpenter in the kitchen, getting a drink of water. He was a gentle young man, sort of a throwback to the hippie days, and I'd felt confident about leaving the girls alone in the house with him.

''Have you seen Carolyn and Alison?'' I asked, looking into the refrigerator to see if there was any tuna salad left.

''Uh, yes.'' He sounded distinctly uncomfortable.

I straightened and looked at him. His face matched his voice. ''Well, where are they?''

''In the yard. Emily, I think you should know about this. They were playing with the Ouija board again.''

''Dammit, I'm going to throw that thing in the trash—''

''Afterwards they came upstairs where I was working and told me this story about those . . . people they claim used to live here.''

''Now what?''

''It seems that after Nathan booted Paul out, Elizabeth kept on seeing him. Nathan found out, and he . . . uh, he shot her dog. It's supposed to be buried in the back yard, under that rose arbor.''

''And they're. . .''

"Out there digging for the bones."

I was through the door and down the stone path in an instant. The arbor, a tumbledown structure overgrown with wild roses and weeds, stood at the rear of the lot. I hurried back there, then stopped some distance away.

The girls knelt on the ground, in front of a shallow hole. A shovel lay between them.

I began walking over to them, slowly. Came up behind them. Peered over their shoulders into the grave.

Bones lay there. Old bones grimed with dirt. Bones that were about the right size for an Afghan. . .

That night Ted laid down the law—no more Ouija board, no more digging in the garden. The girls didn't protest; they were strangely subdued, and seemed relieved at his exercise of parental authority. Immediately after they'd cleared the table they went to Carolyn's room. Tonight Ted took an entire fifth of Scotch to the tower.

I went into the kitchen, turned on all the lights, then switched on the radio to a country-and-western station. The down-home music did nothing to dispel the shadows of the past—or the uncertainties of the future. Finally I called Mike at the number he'd given me in Los Angeles.

"Can bones really last all those years in a shallow grave?" I asked after I'd told him the events of the day.

"I don't know." His voice lacked its usual assurance.

"Could Ted have put them there? Would he do a grisly thing like that?"

"I just don't think so."

"Then who did it? *When?*"

"Emily, I think I should come home."

"But your commercial—"

"I don't like the way you sound. I can be there in—"

"No," I said firmly. "I can deal with this. Finish your work there and then come."

But as I hung up, I thought again of Elizabeth, all alone here after Paul left, without even her dog for comfort. . .

The next morning the woman in the San Francisco History Room at the public library took down the information I was seeking and went back into the archives. She returned about ten minutes later.

"We have nothing on the house at that address, ma'am, " she said. "Perhaps if you could be more specific about the date."

"I'm interested in anything around the turn of the century. Who lived there, anything unusual that might have happened."

"Do you mean before 1906?"

"Why does that matter?"

"The earthquake and fire in that year destroyed a great many city records, as well as newspaper files. Events prior to that date are hard to trace."

"Oh. I see."

"I can refer you to the California Historical Society."

"Oh, yes. Please."

She wrote an address on a slip of paper and handed it to me. "Good luck."

The elegant mansion on Jackson Street that housed the Historical Society contained many records of San Francisco's past—but none that mentioned my house.

"If it had been one of the grand mansions, perhaps there would be some mention of it," the woman said regretfully. "But frankly, there are so many fine homes in the city whose past simply cannot be documented . . ."

"What if there were some scandal connected with it?"

"A scandal?" Her eyes, behind wire-rimmed glasses, grew sharp. "What sort of scandal?"

I paused. Was it a scandal for a man to shoot his wife's dog? Suddenly I realized how foolish I would look if I were to spill out a tale of old bones and jewelry hidden within the walls.

"Oh, it was just a rhetorical question." I turned away. "Thank you for trying to help me."

That evening, while getting out a fresh tablecloth before dinner, I noticed the Ouija board had been removed from the drawer in the sideboard where Ted had put it. I considered mentioning it to him, but decided to let the matter lie. He had received an estimate from the man who was supposed to refinish the floors today, and he had seemed upset about it. There was no need to disturb him further.

So I set the table, called the girls, and was about to take the roast out of the oven when the phone rang. It was Lydia, Alison's mother. They were coming home tonight and would pick up their daughter in about two hours. I watched Alison carrying the potatoes to the table, then said, "Is everything okay?"

"Yes, we seem to have worked our problems out."

"Well, I'm glad for you." But I hung up feeling pensive. Lydia had sounded so light and happy. Would I feel like that if I were ever able to coax Ted out of his self-imposed isolation? Or did I even want to try?

Shrugging off the thought, I finished putting dinner on the table and sent Carolyn to find Ted. As we passed the plates around, I told Alison she would be going home tonight. She smiled, then looked at Carolyn, and they nodded to one another. I remembered those secret looks of childhood and wished I knew what this one meant.

Ted said, "They patch it up?"

I glanced at Alison, but she was intent on her plate. "Yes, it sounds that way."

He grunted, then switched the subject. "Emily, we need to talk about the floor situation."

Whenever Ted used the term "situation," something was amiss. "The man came out today and gave you an estimate?"

"Yes." Mottled spots of red appeared on his cheeks. "It's outrageous, twice what it should be."

"For heaven's sake, why?"

"Those dark marks—the ones we thought were water stains? They're not; they're deep burns. And the parquetry—they don't do that kind of work any more."

"Burns? There's no evidence of a fire in here."

Carolyn and Alison looked up from their plates.

"There is if you know what to look for." Ted got up and opened the draperies that covered the windows on either side of the fireplace. "Compare these two windows. You see the difference?"

Now that he pointed it out, I did. One window was a standard sash type like all the others in the house. The other was of a different style, with a crossbar bisecting the panes.

"This one," Ted said, motioning at it, "has been replaced. And it's on the side of the room where the burns are most severe. After the floor guy left I went upstairs and talked with the carpenter. He said he's found a lot of charred wood up there, wood that was covered over with lath and plaster."

I sighed. "So now what?"

"We put off the refinishing. It's just too much money."

I set down my fork, silent, picturing many more months of ugly, stained floors. But it wasn't really the floors, it was everything else—the disorder of our lives. A chill stole over me and I said, "Ted, will you turn up the heater?"

He did so and returned to his place.

"Ted," I finally said, "it's time we rethink this whole project."

His mouth twisted bitterly. "I knew you'd say that."

"It's eating up every cent we have saved. We're not even living decently. I'm not sure it's worth it—"

"You've never been sure it was worth it! Your whole attitude has been wrong from the day we moved in here. Before we moved in."

"I admit I made it clear from the beginning that I didn't want—"

"You certainly did! You've made a lot of things clear." He

threw his napkin on the table and stood up. "Maybe if you'd had a more positive outlook, none of this would have happened."

Stunned, I watched him go to the sideboard and take out another bottle of Scotch. Then he left the room, undoubtedly heading for his tower.

I looked at Carolyn. She was wide-eyed and a little afraid. Alison, on the other hand, was nonchalantly cleaning her plate. Such scenes were probably common at her house. I said, "Daddy's just upset about the floors."

In a small voice, Carolyn said, "May we be excused?"

I nodded and they left.

Not wanting to sit there amid the wreckage of dinner, I took the dishes to the kitchen, shutting the swinging door against the gloom of the dining room. Tonight the country-and-western music on the radio only grated on my nerves. I turned it off, put the food away, loaded the dishwasher, and began to pace. After several passes by the phone, I picked up the receiver and dialed Mike's hotel in Los Angeles. He had checked out, the clerk said, and had taken the limousine to the airport.

Good, I thought, he'll be home tonight. I would be able to talk to someone who understood, explain this hopelessness I felt. Something had to be done; I couldn't go on like this.

I heard a rustling sound from the far side of the room. Mice, probably. On top of everything else, now we were going to have mice.

Aloud I said, "I can't go on like this any longer."

The rustling stopped. At least the creatures were afraid of humans. Unlike the ghosts, who seemed determined to invade our lives.

Ghosts, Emily? Come on. They don't exist. It's some monstrous plot Ted has cooked up to make you feel guilty.

Sure it is.

The girls, then. They suspect what's going on and they're playing games with you.

But they're only nine!

Never mind that. Think what goes on at Alison's house . . .

I pictured the look they had exchanged at the table. What kind of guile was behind it?

The rustling sound began again. It came from the dining room. I went over to the swinging door, moving softly. Pushed it open. Peered into the gloom.

The girls were on either side of the table, kneeling on their chairs, fingertips pressed to the Ouija board pointer. They had relit the candles, and the flickering flames made weird patterns on the walls and ceiling. I was about to step in and demand to know how they could disobey, but something stopped me. There was a coldness in the air—sudden and biting. The pointer moved swiftly over the board, as if with a life of its own.

I put my hand to my mouth, shivering.

Suddenly the sliding door on the other side of the room slammed open. Ted stood there, red-faced with fury and more than a little drunk.

"What the hell is going on here?" he said.

The girls looked up, jerking their hands from the pointer, as if it had burned them.

"Didn't I tell you to leave that ridiculous game alone?" He lurched toward the table.

Alison got off her chair and ran around to Carolyn.

Ted grabbed the Ouija board and hurled it toward the fireplace. "Well? Didn't I tell you?"

"Daddy . . ." Carolyn was clutching Alison's arm. "Daddy, we had to!"

"Had to!" He hurled the pointer after the board.

"The ghosts—"

"I've had enough of your damned ghosts!"

"But we had to find out about the fire!"

That stopped him. "The fire?"

"Elizabeth kept mentioning a fire, but every time she did, Nathan made her be quiet. We had to find out."

"And I suppose they told you all about it."

His sarcastic tone made Carolyn flinch. She stood and stepped back against the sideboard. I started toward her, but a glare from Ted stopped me.

Alison moved in front of her and stared defiantly up at Ted, looking strangely like Lydia did when she stood up to her husband.

"They did tell us," she said. "They told us about the fire in this very room. Paul came back to get Elizabeth to run away with him. He was afraid for her. Nathan had gone crazy."

The room was very quiet, except for her clear child's voice. Quiet and very cold.

"Elizabeth and Paul were here in the dining room. She wanted to leave with him, but at the same time she wanted to stay. Nathan came in. He was furious when he saw them. He fought with Paul, and they knocked over a kerosene lamp. The draperies caught on fire. Everything caught fire."

I was aware of Ted's heavy breathing and a faint whining sound from Carolyn.

"Nathan died in the fire," Alison said. "Elizabeth too. Paul tried to save them, and he died of his burns two days later."

Ted started around the table, fists clenched. "You think I'm going to believe this crap?"

I stepped in front of him, but he pushed me back into the wall.

"It's true." Alison stood there, ramrod straight. "The ghosts have been here ever since the fire, trying to get free. They're trapped in the house. They started to talk to us because—"

"This is ridiculous!" Ted towered over the girls.

Alison stepped back, closer to Carolyn, and then Carolyn spoke—slowly, almost as if she were in a trance. "They started to talk to us because it was happening again."

The words brought me out of my own frozen state, and I pushed away from the wall, knocking Ted to one side. I took each child by the arm and dragged them around the table, out of his reach.

He turned, features contorted. "Happening *again?*"

"No, Ted—" I began.

Carolyn said, "It's all happening again."

Ted reached forward and swept one of the candelabra from the table. It crashed to the floor. He picked up the other, and then turned toward the dark pane of glass at the right side of the fireplace. We were all reflected there, against the blackness of the night.

Somehow, I knew we were not what he saw.

He raised his arm and hurled the candle holder at the window. The glass shattered, and the girls shrank back against me. One of the candles rolled toward the fireplace, still lit.

Too late, I remembered the leaky gas heater.

The explosion was deafening. Wood, metal, and fireplace tiles flew. A blast of flame shot toward the ceiling. Ted staggered back.

Alison screamed and pulled from my grasp, running into the parlor. Carolyn stood still. Flames enveloped the draperies and the table, their heat scorching my skin. Black smoke billowed toward us.

I grabbed Carolyn's shoulder, spun her around, pushed her through the door.

The smoke was thick and choking. My eyes streaming, I looked back over my shoulder. I couldn't see Ted. More flames flashed toward us.

Old dry wood, I thought, dragging Carolyn toward the front door. It reaches its kindling point fast . . . the whole house will go . . .

Alison was outside the door. She grabbed Carolyn's hand and pulled her down the front steps. I followed, coughing and gasping for air.

Someone must have heard the explosion and phoned the fire department. Already I could hear the wail of sirens. I had an insane thought of going back inside to help Ted. But the entire front of the house was ablaze now, and smoke poured from the blown-out windows. There was no way . . .

In minutes the engines were pulling up and men were jumping off them. I grabbed the arm of the nearest fireman and said,

"My husband's in there! For God's sake—"

Another man forced me back.

"Please help him—"

"We'll do what we can."

The girls clung to me on either side, Carolyn crying softly. Someone called my name. Dazed, I turned and found myself looking at Lydia. Her red hair flowed free to her shoulders, her eyes were wild. They must have just gotten home—

"Alison? Where's Alison?"

"I'm here, Mommy."

Lydia knelt and hugged the child, but her eyes were on the flaming house. She looked up at me, horror spreading over her face. "Ted? He isn't . . . ?"

I nodded.

She shoved her daughter away and jumped up. "I've got to help him!"

Uncomprehending, I stared at her.

"I meant to end it, but . . . oh, dear God!" And then she was running toward the burning house, calling for Ted. A fireman grabbed her, and she struggled against him, then went limp.

I tried to suck in my breath, but Lydia's words had struck me like a blow to the stomach. I was thinking of Ted in the tower room, staring at the houses across the street—Lydia's house. I was remembering his unexplained absences during the day—when Lydia was home alone.

It's all happening again.

Oh, God, I thought, it wasn't me. It was Ted. *He* was the one who made it all happen again . . . he and Lydia had brought us to our own kindling point. . . .

The Bingo Master

JOYCE CAROL OATES

There are worse horrors than those caused by things that go bump in the night—horrors of the human mind. These have become a trademark of the fiction of Joyce Carol Oates, whose excellent novels and short stories deal with a full range of extraordinary human emotion. The recipient of a National Book Award for the novel Them, *as well as several O. Henry Prizes for short stories and a Guggenheim Fellowship, Ms. Oates is adept at depicting the dark side of human nature. And, as* "The Bingo Master" *shows, it often takes very little to plunge one into that darkness . . .*

SUDDENLY there appears Joe Pye the Bingo Master, dramatically late by some ten or fifteen minutes, and everyone in the bingo hall except Rose Mallow Odom calls out an ecstatic greeting or at least smiles broadly to show how welcome he is, how forgiven he is for being late—"Just look what he's wearing tonight!" the plump young mother seated across from Rose exclaims, her pretty face dimpling like a child's. "*Isn't* he something," the woman murmurs, catching Rose's reluctant eye.

Joe Pye the Bingo Master. Joe Pye the talk of Tophet—or *some parts* of Tophet—who bought the old Harlequin Amusements Arcade down on Purslane Street by the Gayfeather Hotel (which Rose had been thinking of as boarded up or even razed, but there it is, still in operation) and has made such a success with his bingo hall, even Rose's father's staid old friends at church or at the club are talking about him. The Tophet City Council had tried to shut Joe Pye down last spring, first because too many people crowded into the hall and there was a fire hazard, second because he hadn't paid some fine or other (or was it, Rose Mallow wondered maliciously, a bribe) to the Board of Health and Sanitation, whose inspector had professed to be "astonished and sickened" by the conditions of the rest rooms, and the quality of the foot-longs and cheese-and-sausage pizzas sold at the refreshment stand: and two or three of the churches, jealous of Joe Pye's profits, which might very well eat into *theirs* (for Thursday-evening bingo was a main source of revenue for certain Tophet churches, though not, thank God, Saint Matthias Episcopal Church, where the Odoms worshipped) were agitating that Joe Pye be forced to move outside the city limits, at least, just as those "adult" bookstores and X-rated film outfits had been forced to move. There had been editorials in the paper, and letters pro and con, and though Rose Mallow had only contempt for local politics and hardly knew most of what was going on in her own hometown—her mind, as her father and aunt said, being elsewhere—she had followed the "Joe Pye Controversy" with amusement. It had pleased her when the bingo hall was allowed to remain open, mainly because it upset people in her part of town, by the golf course and the park and along Van Dusen Boulevard; if anyone had suggested that she would be visiting the hall, and even sitting, as she is tonight, at one of the dismayingly long oilcoth-covered tables beneath these ugly bright lights, amid noisily cheerful people who all seem to know one another, and who are happily devouring "refreshments" though it is only seven-thirty and surely they've eaten their dinners beforehand, and *why* are they so goggle-eyed about idiotic Joe Pye!—Rose Mallow would have snorted with laughter, waving her hand in that gesture of dismissal her aunt said was "unbecoming."

Well, Rose Mallow Odom *is* at Joe Pye's Bingo Hall, in fact she has arrived early, and is staring, her arms folded beneath her breasts, at the fabled Bingo Master himself. Of course, there are other workers—attendants—high-school–aged girls with piles of bleached hair and pierced earrings and artfully made-up faces, and even one or two older women, dressed in bright-pink smocks with *Joe Pye* in a spidery green arabesque on their collars, and out front there is a courteous milk-chocolate–skinned young man in a three-piece suit whose function, Rose gathered, was simply to welcome the bingo players and maybe to keep out riffraff, white or black, since the hall *is* in a fairly disreputable part of town. But Joe Pye is the center of attention. Joe Pye is everything. His high rapid chummy chatter at the microphone is as silly, and halfway unintelligible, as any local disc jockey's frantic monologue, picked up by chance as Rose spins the dial looking for something to divert her; yet everyone listens eagerly, and begins giggling even before his jokes are entirely completed.

The Bingo Master is a very handsome man. Rose sees that at once, and concedes the point: no matter that his goatee looks as if it were dyed with ink from the five-and-ten, and his stark-black eyebrows as well, and his skin, smooth as stone, somehow unreal as stone, is as darkly tanned as the skin of one of those men pictured on billboards, squinting into the sun with cigarettes smoking in their fingers; no matter that his lips are too rosy, the upper lip so deeply indented that it looks as if he is pouting, and his getup (what kinder expression?—the poor man is wearing a dazzling white turban, and a tunic threaded with silver and salmon pink, and wide-legged pajama-like trousers made of a material almost as clingy as silk, jet black) makes Rose want to roll her eyes heavenward and walk away. He *is* attractive. Even beautiful, if you are in the habit—Rose isn't—of calling men beautiful. His deep-set eyes shine with an enthusiasm that can't be feigned; or at any rate can't be entirely feigned. His outfit, absurd as it is, hangs well on him, emphasizing his well-proportioned shoulders and his lean waist and hips. His teeth, which he bares often, far too often, in smiles clearly meant to be dazzling, are perfectly white and straight and even: just as Rose Mallow's had been promised to be, though she knew, even as a child of twelve or so, that the ugly painful braces and the uglier "bite" that made her gag wouldn't leave her teeth any more attractive than they already were—which wasn't very attractive at all. Teeth impress her, inspire her to envy, make her resentful. And it's all the more exasperating that Joe Pye smiles so often, rubbing his hands zestfully and gazing out at his adoring giggling audience.

Naturally his voice is mellifluous and intimate, when it isn't busy being "enthusiastic," and Rose thinks that if he were speaking another language—if she didn't have to endure his claptrap about "lovely ladies" and "jackpot prizes" and "mystery cards" and "ten-games-for-the-price-of-seven" (under certain complicated conditions she couldn't follow)—she might find it very attractive indeed. Might find, if she tried, *him* attractive. But his drivel interferes with his seductive power, or powers, and Rose finds herself distracted, handing over money to one of the pink-smocked girls in exchange for a shockingly grimy bingo card, her face flushing with irritation. Of course the evening is an experiment, and not an entirely serious experiment: she has come downtown, by bus, unescorted, wearing stockings and fairly high heels, lipsticked, perfumed, less ostentatiously homely than usual, in order to lose, as the expression goes, her virginity. Or perhaps it would be more accurate, less narcissistic, to say that she has come downtown to acquire a lover? . . .

But no. Rose Mallow Odom doesn't want a lover. She doesn't want a man at all, not in any way, but she supposes one is necessary for the ritual she intends to complete.

"And now, ladies, ladies and gentlemen, if you're all ready, if you're all ready to begin." Joe Pye sings out, as a girl with carrot-colored frizzed hair and an enormous magenta smile turns the handle of the wire basket, in which white balls the size and apparent weight of Ping-Pong balls tumble merrily together, "*I* am ready to begin, and I wish you each and all the very, very best of luck from the bottom of my heart, and remember there's more than one winner each game, and dozens of winners each night, and in fact Joe Pye's iron-clad law is that *nobody's* going to go away empty-handed—Ah, now, let's see, now: the first number is—"

Despite herself Rose Mallow is crouched over the filthy cardboard square, a kernel of corn between her fingers, her lower lip caught in her teeth. *The first number is—*

It was on the eve of her thirty-ninth birthday, almost two months ago, that Rose Mallow Odom conceived of the notion of going out and "losing" her virginity.

Perhaps the notion wasn't her own, not entirely. It sprang into her head as she was writing one of her dashed-off swashbuckling letters (for which, she knew, her friends cherished her—*isn't Rose hilarious,* they liked to say, *isn't she brave),* this time to Georgene Wescott, who was back in New York City, her second divorce behind her, some sort of complicated, flattering, but not (Rose suspected) very high-paying job at Columbia just begun, and a new book, a collection of essays on contemporary women artists, just contracted for at a prestigious New York publishing house. *Dear Georgene,* Rose wrote, *Life in Tophet is droll as usual what with Papa's & Aunt Olivia's & my own criss-crossing trips to our high-priced $peciali$t pals at that awful clinic I told you about. & it seems there was a scandal of epic proportions at the Tophet Women's Club on acc't of the fact that some sister club which rents the building (I guess they're leftwingdogooder types, you & Ham & Carolyn wld belong if you were misfortunate enough to dwell here-about) includes on its membership rolls some two or three or more Black Persons. Which, tho' it doesn't violate the letter of the Club's charter certainly violates its spirit. & then again,* Rose wrote, very late one night after her Aunt Olivia had retired, and even her father, famously insomniac like Rose herself, had gone to bed, *then again did I tell you about the NSWPP convention here . . . at the Holiday Inn . . . (which wasn't built yet I guess when you & Jack visited) . . . by the interstate expressway? . . . Anyway: (& I fear I did tell you, or was it Carolyn, or maybe both of you) the conference was all set, the rooms & banquet hall booked, & some enterprising muckraking young reporter at the Tophet Globe-Times (who has since gone "up north" to Norfolk, to a better-paying job) discovered that the NSWPP stood for National Socialist White People's Party which is (& I do not exaggerate, Georgene, tho' I can see you crinkling up your nose at another of Rose Mallow's silly flights of fancy, "Why doesn't she scramble all that into a story or a Symboliste poem as she once did, so she'd have something to show for her exile & her silence & cunning as well," I can hear you mumbling & you are 100% correct) none other than the (are you PREPARED???) American Nazi Party! Yes. Indeed. There is such a party & it overlaps Papa says sourly with the Klan & certain civic-minded organizations hereabouts, tho' he declined to be specific, possibly because his spinster daughter was looking too rapt & incredulous. Anyway, the Nazis were denied the use of the Tophet Holiday Inn & you'd have been impressed by the spirit of the newspaper editorials denouncing them roundly. I hear tell—but maybe it is surreal rumor—that the Nazis not only wear their swastika armbands in* *secret but have tiny lapel pins on the insides of their lapels, swastikas natcherlly. . . .* And then she'd changed the subject, relaying news of friends, friends' husbands and wives, and former husbands and wives, and acquaintances' latest doings, scandalous and otherwise (for of the lively, gregarious, genius-ridden group that had assembled itself informally in Cambridge, Mass., almost twenty years ago, Rose Mallow Odom was the only really dedicated letter writer—the one who held everyone together through the mails—the one who would continue to write cheerful letter after letter even when she wasn't answered for a year or two), and as a perky little postscript she added that her thirty-ninth birthday was fast approaching and she meant to divest herself of her damned virginity as a kind of present to herself. *As my famous ironing-board figure is flatter than ever, & my breasts the size of Dixie cups after last spring's ritual flu & a rerun of that wretched bronchitis, it will be, as you can imagine, quite a challenge.*

Of course it was nothing more than a joke, one of Rose's whimsical self-mocking jokes, a postscript scribbled when her eyelids had begun to droop with fatigue. And yet . . . And yet when she actually wrote *I intend to divest myself of my damned virginity*, and sealed the letter, she saw that the project was inevitable. She would go through with it. She *would* go through with it, just as in the old days, years ago, when she was the most promising young writer in her circle, and grants and fellowships and prizes had tumbled into her lap, she had forced herself to complete innumerable projects simply because they were challenging, and would give her pain. (Though Rose was scornful of the Odoms' puritanical disdain of pleasure, on intellectual grounds, she nevertheless believed that painful experiences, and even pain itself, had a generally salubrious effect.)

And so she went out, the very next evening, a Thursday, telling her father and her aunt Olivia that she was going to the downtown library. When they asked in alarm, as she knew they would, why on earth she was going at such a time, Rose said with a schoolgirlish scowl that that was her business. But was the library even open at such a strange time, Aunt Olivia wanted to know. Open till nine on Thursdays, Rose said.

That first Thursday Rose had intended to go to a singles bar she had heard about, in the ground floor of a new high-rise office building; but at first she had difficulty finding the place, and circled about the enormous glass-and-concrete tower in her ill-fitting high heels, muttering to herself that no experience would be worth so much effort, even if it was a painful one. (She was of course a chaste young woman, whose general feeling about sex was not much different than it had been in elementary school, when the cruder, more reckless, more knowing children had had the power, by chanting certain words, to make poor Rose Mallow Odom press her hands over her ears.) Then she discovered the bar—discovered, rather, a long line of young people snaking up some dark concrete steps to the sidewalk, and along the sidewalk for hundreds of feet, evidently waiting to get into the Chanticleer. She was appalled not only by the crowd but by the exuberant youth of the crowd: no one older than twenty-five, no one dressed as she was. (*She* looked dressed for church, which she hated. But however else did people dress?) So she retreated, and went to the downtown library after all, where the librarians all knew her, and asked respectfully after her "work" (though she had made it clear years ago that she was no longer "working"—the demands her mother made upon her during the long years of her illness, and then Rose's father's precarious health, and of course her own history of respiratory illnesses and anemia and easily broken bones had made concentration impossible). Once she shook off the solicitous cackling old ladies she spent what remained of her evening quite profitably—she read *The Oresteia* in a translation new to her, and scribbled notes as she always did, excited by stray thoughts for articles or stories or poems, though in the end she always crumpled the notes up and threw them away. But the evening had not been an entire loss.

The second Thursday, she went to the Park Avenue Hotel, Tophet's only good hotel, fully intending to sit in the dim cocktail lounge until something happened—but she had no more than stepped into the lobby when Barbara Pursley called out to her; and she ended by going to dinner with Barbara and her husband, who were visiting Tophet for a few days, and Barbara's parents, whom she had always liked. Though she hadn't seen Barbara for fifteen years, and in truth hadn't thought of her once during those fifteen years (except to remember that a close friend of Barbara's had been the one, in sixth grade, to think up the cruel but probably fairly accurate nickname The Ostrich for Rose), she did have an enjoyable time. Anyone who had observed their table in the vaulted oak-paneled dining room of the Park Avenue, taking note in particular of the tall, lean, nervously eager woman who laughed frequently, showing her gums, and who seemed unable to keep her hand from patting at her hair (which was baby-fine, a pale brown, in no style at all but not unbecoming), and adjusting her collar or earrings, would have been quite astonished to learn that that woman (of indeterminate age: her "gentle" expressive chocolate-brown eyes might have belonged to a gawky girl of sixteen or to a woman in her fifties) had intended to spend the evening prowling about for a man.

And then the third Thursday (for the Thursdays had become, now, a ritual: her aunt protested only feebly, her father gave her a library book to return) she went to the movies, to the very theater where, at thirteen or fourteen, with her friend Janet Brome, she had met . . . or almost met . . . what were thought to be, then, "older boys" of seventeen or eighteen. (Big boys, farm boys, spending the day in Tophet, prowling about for girls. But even in the darkened Rialto neither Rose nor Janet resembled the kind of girls these boys sought.) And nothing at all happened. Nothing. Rose walked out of the theater when the film—a cloying self-conscious comedy about adultery in Manhattan—was only half over, and took a bus back home, in time to join her father and her aunt for ice cream and Peek Freans biscuits. "You look as if you're coming down with a cold," Rose's father said. "Your eyes are watery." Rose denied it; but came down with a cold the very next day.

She skipped a Thursday, but on the following week ventured out again, eyeing herself cynically and without a trace of affection in her bedroom mirror (which looked wispy and washed-out—but do mirrors actually age, Rose wondered), judging that, yes, she might be called pretty, with her big ostrich eyes and her ostrich height and gawky dignity, by a man who squinted in her direction in just the right degree of dimness. By now she knew the project was doomed but it gave her a kind of angry satisfaction to return to the Park Avenue Hotel, just, as she said in a more recent letter (this to the girl, the woman, with whom she had roomed as a graduate student at Radcliffe, then as virginal as Rose, and possibly even more intimidated by men than Rose—and now Pauline was divorced, with two children, living with an Irish poet in a tower north of Sligo, a tower not unlike Yeats's, with *his* several children) for the brute hell of it.

And the evening had been an initially promising one. Quite by accident Rose wandered into the Second Annual Conference of the Friends of Evolution, and sat at the rear of a crowded ballroom, to hear a paper read by a portly, distinguished gentleman with pince-nez and a red carnation in his buttonhole, and to join in the enthusiastic applause afterward. (The paper had been, Rose imperfectly gathered, about the need for extraterrestrial communication—or was such communication already a fact, and the FBI and "university professors" were united in suppressing it?) A second paper by a woman Rose's age who walked with a cane seemed to be arguing that Christ was in space—"out there in space"—as a close reading of the Book of Saint John the Divine would demonstrate. The applause was even more enthusiastic after this paper, though Rose contributed only politely, for she'd had, over the years, many thoughts about Jesus of Nazareth—and thoughts about those thoughts—and in the end, one fine day, she had taken herself in secret to a psychiatrist at the Mount Yarrow Hospital, confessing in tears, in shame, that she knew very well the whole thing—*the whole thing*—was nonsense, and insipid nonsense at that, but—still—she sometimes caught herself wistfully "believing"; and was she clinically insane? Some inflection in her voice, some droll upward motion of her eyes, must have alerted the man to the fact that Rose Mallow Odom was someone like himself—she'd gone to school in the North, hadn't she?—and so he brushed aside her worries, and told her that of course it was nonsense, but one felt a nagging family loyalty, yes one did quarrel with one's family, and say terrible things, but still the loyalty was there, he would give her a prescription for barbiturates if she was suffering from insomnia, and hadn't she better have a physical examination?—because she was looking (he meant to be kindly, he didn't know how he was breaking her heart) worn out. Rose did not tell him that she had just *had* her six months' checkup and that, for her, she was in excellent health: no chest problems, the anemia under control. By the end of the conversation the psychiatrist remembered who Rose was—"Why, you're famous around here, didn't you publish a novel that shocked everyone?"—and Rose had recovered her composure enough to say stiffly that no one was famous in this part of Alabama; and the original topic had been completely forgotten. And now Jesus of Nazareth was floating about in space . . . or orbiting some moon . . . or was He actually in a spacecraft (the term "spacecraft" was used frequently by the conferees), awaiting His first visitors from planet earth? Rose was befriended by a white-haired gentleman in his seventies who slid across two or three folding chairs to sit beside her, and there was even a somewhat younger man, in his fifties perhaps, with greasy quill-like hair and a mild stammer, whose badge proclaimed him as H. Speedwell of Sion, Florida, who offered to buy her a cup of coffee after the session was over. Rose felt a flicker of—of what?—amusement, interest, despair? She had to put her finger to her lips in a schoolmarmish gesture, since the elderly gentleman on her right and H. Speedwell on her left were both talking rather emphatically, as if trying to impress her, about *their* experiences sighting UFO's, and the third speaker was about to begin.

The topic was "The Next and Final Stage of Evolution," given by the Reverend Jake Gromwell of the New Holland Institute of

Religious Studies in Stoneseed, Kentucky. Rose sat very straight, her hands folded on her lap, her knees primly together (for, it must have been by accident, Mr. Speedwell's right knee was pressing against her), and pretended to listen. Her mind was all a flurry, like a chicken coop invaded by a dog, and she couldn't even know what she felt until the fluttering thoughts settled down. Somehow she was in the Regency Ballroom of the Park Avenue Hotel on a Thursday evening in September, listening to a paper given by a porkish-looking man in a tight-fitting gray-and-red plaid suit with a bright-red tie. She had been noticing that many of the conferees were disabled—on canes, on crutches, even in wheelchairs (one of the wheelchairs, operated by a hawk-faced youngish man who might have been Rose's age but looked no more than twelve, was a wonderfully classy affair, with a panel of push-buttons that would evidently do nearly anything for him he wished; Rose had rented a wheelchair some years ago, for herself, when a pinched nerve in her back had crippled her, and *hers* had been a very ordinary model)—and most of them were elderly. There *were* men her own age but they were not promising. And Mr. Speedwell, who smelled of something blandly odd, like tapioca, was not promising. Rose sat for a few more minutes, conscious of being polite, being good, allowing herself to be lulled by the Reverend Gromwell's monotonous voice and by the ballroom's decorations (fluorescent-orange and green and violet snakes undulated in the carpet, voluptuous forty-foot velvet drapes stirred in the tepid air from invisible vents, there was even a garishly inappropriate but mesmerizing mirrored ceiling with "stardust" lighting which gave to the conferees a rakish, faintly lurid air despite their bald heads and trembling necks and crutches) before making her apologetic escape.

Now Rose Mallow Odom sits at one of the long tables in Joe Pye's Bingo Hall, her stomach somewhat uneasy after the Tru-Orange she has just drunk, a promising—a highly promising—card before her. She is wondering if the mounting excitement she feels is legitimate, or whether it has anything to do with the orange soda: or whether it's simple intelligent dread, for of course she doesn't want to win. She can't even imagine herself calling out *Bingo!* in a voice loud enough to be heard. It is after 10:30 p.m. and there have been a number of winners and runners-up, many shrieking, ecstatic *Bingos* and some bellowing *Bingos* and one or two incredulous gasps, and really she should have gone home by now, Joe Pye is the only halfway attractive man in the place (there are no more than a dozen men there) and it isn't likely that Joe Pye in his dashing costume, with his glaring white turban held together by a gold pin, and his graceful shoulders, and his syrupy voice, would pay much attention to *her.* But inertia or curiosity has kept her here. What the hell, Rose thought, pushing kernels of corn about on much-used squares of thick cardboard, becoming acquainted with fellow Tophetians, surely there are worse ways to spend Thursday night? . . . She would dash off letters to Hamilton Frye and Carolyn Sears this weekend, though they owed her letters, describing in detail her newly made friends of the evening (the plump, perspiring, good-natured young woman seated across from her is named Lobelia, and it's ironic that Rose is doing so well this game, because just before it started Lobelia asked to exchange cards, on an impulse—"You give me mine and I'll give you yours, Rose!" she had said, with charming inaccuracy and a big smile, and of course Rose had immediately obliged) and the depressingly bright-lit hall with its disproportionately large American flag up front by Joe Pye's platform, and all the odd, strange, sad, eager, *intent* players, some of them extremely old, their faces wizened, their hands palsied, a few crippled or undersized or in some dim incontestable way not altogether *right,* a number very young (in fact it is something of a scandal, the children up this late, playing bingo beside their mamas, frequently with two or three cards while their mamas greedily work at four cards, which is the limit), and the dreadful taped music that uncoils relentlessly behind Joe Pye's tireless voice, and of course Joe Pye the Bingo Master himself, who has such a warm, toothed smile for everyone in the hall, and who had—unless Rose, her weak eyes unfocused by the lighting, imagined it—actually directed a special smile and a wink in her direction earlier in the evening, apparently sighting her as a new customer. She will make one of her droll charming anecdotes out of the experience. She will be quite characteristically harsh on herself, and will speculate on the phenomenon of suspense, its psychological meaning (isn't there a sense in which all suspense, and not just bingo hall suspense, is asinine?), and life's losers who, even if they win, remain losers (for what possible difference could a home hair dryer, or $100 cash, or an outdoor barbecue grill, or an electric train complete with track, or a huge copy of the Bible, illustrated, bound in simulated white leather, make to any of these people?). She will record the groans of disappointment and dismay when someone screams *Bingo!* and the mutterings when the winner's numbers, read off by one of the bored-looking girl attendants, prove to be legitimate. The winners' frequent tears, the hearty handshaking and cheek-kissing Joe Pye indulges in, as if each winner were specially dear to him, an old friend hurrying forth to be greeted; and the bright-yellow mustard splashed on the foot-longs and their doughy buns; and the several infants whose diapers were changed on a bench unfortunately close by; and Lobelia's superstitious fingering of a tiny gold cross she wears on a chain around her neck; and the worn-out little girl sleeping on the floor, her head on a pink teddy bear someone in her family must have won hours ago; and—

"You won! Here. Hey! She won! Right here! This card, here! Here! Joe Pye, *right here!*"

The grandmotherly woman to Rose's left, with whom she'd exchanged a few pleasant words earlier in the evening (it turns out her name is Cornelia Teasel; she once cleaned house for the Odoms' neighbors the Filarees), is suddenly screaming, and has seized Rose's hand, in her excitement jarring all the kernels off the cards; but no matter, no matter, Rose *does* have a winning card, she has scored bingo, and there will be no avoiding it.

There are the usual groans, half-sobs, mutterings of angry disappointment, but the game comes to an end, and a gum-chewing girl with a brass helmet of hair reads off Rose's numbers to Joe Pye, who punctuates each number not only with a *Yes, right* but *Keep going, honey* and *You're getting there,* and a dazzling wide smile as if he'd never witnessed anything more wonderful in his life. A $100 winner! A first-time customer (unless his eyes deceive him) and a $100 winner!

Rose, her face burning and pulsing with embarrassment, must go to Joe Pye's raised platform to receive her check, and Joe Pye's heartiest warmest congratulations, and a noisy moist kiss that falls uncomfortably near her mouth (she must resist stepping violently back—the man is so physically vivid, so real, so *there*). "*Now* you're smiling, honey, aren't you?" he says happily. Up close he is just as handsome, but the whites of his eyes are perhaps too white. The gold pin in his turban is a crowing cock. His skin is *very* tanned, and the goatee even blacker than Rose had thought. "I been watching you all night, hon, and you'd be a whole lot prettier if you eased up and smiled more," Joe Pye murmurs in her ear. He smells sweetish, like candied fruit or wine.

Rose steps back, offended, but before she can escape Joe Pye reaches out for her hand again, her cold thin hand, which he rubs briskly between his own. "You *are* new here, aren't you? New tonight?" he asks.

"Yes," Rose says, so softly he has to stoop to hear.

"And are you a Tophet girl? Folks live in town?"

"Yes."

"But you never been to Joe Pye's Bingo Hall before tonight?"

"No."

"And here you're walking away a hundred-dollar cash winner! How does that make you feel?"

"Oh, just fine—"

"What?"

"Just fine—I never expected—"

"Are you a bingo player? I mean, y'know, at these churches in town, or anywheres else."

"No."

"Not a player? Just here for the fun of it? A $100 winner, your first night, ain't that excellent luck!—You know, hon, you *are* a real attractive gal, with the color all up in your face, I wonder if you'd like to hang around, oh say another half hour while I wind things up, there's a cozy bar right next door, I noted you are here tonight alone, eh?—might-be we could have a nightcap, just the two of us?"

"Oh I don't think so, Mr. Pye—"

"Joe Pye! Joe Pye's the name," he says, grinning, leaning toward her, "and what might your name be? Something to do with a flower, isn't it?—some kind of a, a flower—"

Rose, very confused, wants only to escape. But he has her hand tightly in his own.

"Too shy to tell Joe Pye your name?" he says.

"It's—it's Olivia," Rose stammers.

"Oh. Olivia. Olivia, is it," Joe Pye says slowly, his smile arrested. "*Olivia,* is it. . . . Well, sometimes I misread, you know; I get a wire crossed or something and I misread; I never claimed to be 100% accurate. Olivia, then. Okay, fine. Olivia. Why are you so skittish, Olivia? The microphone won't pick up a bit of what we say. Are you free for a nightcap around eleven? Yes? Just next door at the Gayfeather where I'm staying, the lounge is a cozy homey place, nice and private, the two of us, no strings attached or nothing. . . ."

"My father is waiting up for me, and—"

"Come *on* now, Olivia, you're a Tophet gal, don't you want to make an out-of-towner feel welcome?"

"It's just that—"

"All right, then? Yes? It's a date? Soon as we close up shop here? Right next door at the Gayfeather?"

Rose stares at the man, at his bright glittering eyes and the glittering heraldic rooster in his turban, and hears herself murmur a weak assent; and only then does Joe Pye release her hand.

And so it has come about, improbably, ludicrously, that Rose Mallow Odom finds herself in the sepulchral Gayfeather Lounge as midnight nears, in the company of Joe Pye the Bingo Master (whose white turban is dazzling even here, in the drifting smoke and the lurid flickering colors from a television set perched high above the bar), and two or three other shadowy figures, derelict and subdued, solitary drinkers who clearly want nothing to do with one another. (One of them, a fairly well-dressed old gentleman with a swollen pug nose, reminds Rose obliquely of her father—except for the alcoholic's nose, of course.) She is sipping nervously at an "orange blossom"—a girlish sweet-acetous concoction she hasn't had since 1962, and has ordered tonight, or has had her escort order for her, only because she could think of nothing else. Joe Pye is telling Rose about his travels to distant lands—Venezuela, Ethiopia, Tibet, Iceland—and Rose makes an effort to appear to believe him, to appear to be naïve enough to believe him, for she has decided to go through with it, to take this outlandish fraud as her lover, for a single night only, or part of a night, however long the transaction will take. "Another drink?" Joe Pye murmurs, laying his hand on her unresisting wrist.

Above the bar the sharply tilted television set crackles with machine-gun fire, and indistinct silhouettes, probably human, race across bright sand, below a bright turquoise sky. Joe Pye, annoyed, turns and signals with a brisk counterclockwise motion of his fingers to the bartender, who lowers the sound almost immediately; the bartender's deference to Joe Pye impresses Rose. But then she is easily impressed. But then she is *not*, ordinarily, easily impressed. But the fizzing stinging orange drink has gone to her head.

"From going north and south on this globe, and east and west, travelling by freighter, by train, sometimes on foot, on foot through the mountains, spending a year here, six months there, two years somewhere else, I made my way finally back home, to the States, and wandered till things, you know, felt right: the way things sometimes feel right about a town or a landscape or another person, and you know it's your destiny," Joe Pye says softly. "If you know what I mean, Olivia."

With two dark fingers he strokes the back of her hand. She shivers, though the sensation is really ticklish.

". . . destiny," Rose says. "Yes. I think I know."

She wants to ask Joe Pye if she won honestly; if, maybe, he hadn't thrown the game her way. Because he'd noticed her earlier. All evening. A stranger, a scowling disbelieving stranger, fixing him with her intelligent skeptical stare, the most conservatively and tastefully dressed player in the hall. But he doesn't seem eager to talk about his business, he wants instead to talk about his life as a "soldier of fortune"—whatever he means by that—and Rose wonders if such a question might be naïve, or insulting, for it would suggest that *he* was dishonest, that the bingo games were rigged. But then perhaps everyone knows they are rigged?—like the horse races?

She wants to ask but cannot. Joe Pye is sitting so close to her in the booth, his skin is so ruddy, his lips so dark, his teeth so white, his goatee Mephistophelian and his manner—now that he is "offstage," now that he can "be himself"—so ingratiatingly intimate that she feels disoriented. She is willing to see her position as comic, even as ludicrous (she, Rose Mallow Odom, disdainful of men and of physical things in general, is going to allow this charlatan to imagine that *he* is seducing *her*—but at the same time she is quite nervous, she isn't even very articulate); she must see it, and interpret it, as *something*. But Joe Pye keeps on talking. As if he were halfway enjoying himself. As if this were a normal conversation. Did she have any hobbies? Pets? Did she grow up in Tophet and go to school here? Were her parents living? What sort of business was her father in?—or was he a professional man? Had *she* travelled much? No? Was she ever married? Did she have a "career"? Had she ever been in love? Did she ever expect to be in love?

Rose blushes, hears herself giggle in embarrassment, her words trip over one another, Joe Pye is leaning close, tickling her forearm, a clown in black silk pajama bottoms and a turban, smelling of something overripe. His dark eyebrows are peaked, the whites of his eyes are luminous, his fleshy lips pout becomingly; he is irresistible. His nostrils even flare with the pretense of passion. . . . Rose begins to giggle and cannot stop.

"You are a highly attractive girl, especially when you let yourself go like right now," Joe Pye says softly. "You know—we could go up to my room where we'd be more private. Would you like that?"

"I am not," Rose says, drawing in a full, shaky breath, to clear her head, "I am not a *girl*. Hardly a girl at the age of thirty-nine."

"We could be more private in my room. No one would interrupt us."

"My father isn't well, he's waiting up for me," Rose says quickly.

"By now he's asleep, most likely!"

"Oh no, no—he suffers from insomnia, like me."

"Like you! Is that so? I suffer from insomnia too," Joe Pye says, squeezing her hand in excitement. "Ever since a bad experience I had in the desert . . . in another part of the world. . . . But I'll tell you about that later, when we're closer acquainted. If we both have insomnia, Olivia, we should keep each other company. The nights in Tophet are so long."

"The nights *are* long," Rose says, blushing.

"But your mother, now: *she* isn't waiting up for you."

"Mother has been dead for years. I won't say what her sickness was but you can guess, it went on forever, and after she died I took all my things—I had this funny career going, I won't bore you with details—all my papers—stories and notes and such—and burnt them in the trash, and I've been at home every day and every night since, and I felt good when I burnt the things and good when I remember it, and—and I feel good right now," Rose says defiantly finishing her drink. "So I know what I did was a sin."

"Do you believe in sin, a sophisticated girl like yourself?" Joe Pye says, smiling broadly.

The alcohol is a warm golden-glowing breath that fills her lungs and overflows and spreads to every part of her body, to the very tips of her toes, the tips of her ears. Yet her hand is fishlike: let Joe Pye fondle it as he will. So she is being seduced, and it is exactly as silly, as clumsy, as she had imagined it would be, as she imagined such things would be even as a young girl. So. As Descartes saw, I am I, up in my head, and my body is my body, extended in space, *out there,* it will be interesting to observe what happens, Rose thinks calmly. But she is not calm. She has begun to tremble. But she *must* be calm, it is all so absurd.

On their way up to Room 302 (the elevator is out of commission or perhaps there is no elevator, they must take the fire stairs, Rose is fetchingly dizzy and her escort must loop his arm around her) she tells Joe Pye that she didn't deserve to win at bingo and really should give the $100 back or perhaps to Lobelia (but she doesn't know Lobelia's last name!—what a pity) because it was really Lobelia's card that won, not hers. Joe Pye nods though he doesn't appear to understand. As he unlocks his door Rose begins an incoherent story, or is it a confession, about something she did when she was eleven years old and never told anyone about, and Joe Pye leads her into the room, and switches on the lights with a theatrical flourish, and even the television set, though the next moment he switches the set off. Rose is blinking at the complex undulating stripes in the carpet, which are very like snakes, and in a blurry voice she concludes her confession: ". . . she was so popular and so pretty and I hated her, I used to leave for school ahead of her and slow down so she'd catch up, and sometimes that worked, and sometimes it didn't, I just hated her, I bought a valentine, one of those joke valentines, it was about a foot high and glossy and showed some kind of an idiot on the cover, *Mother loved me,* it said, and when you opened it, *but she died,* so I sent it to Sandra, because her mother had died . . . when we were in fifth grade . . . and . . . and . . ."

Joe Pye unclips the golden cock, and undoes his turban, which is impressively long. Rose, her lips grinning, fumbles with the first button of her dress. It is a small button, cloth-covered, and resists her efforts to push it through the hole. But then she gets it through, and stands there panting.

She will think of it, *I must think of it,* as an impersonal event, bodily but not spiritual, *like a gynecological examination.* But then Rose hates those gynecological examinations. Hates and dreads them, and puts them off, canceling appointments at the last minute. *It will serve me right,* she often thinks, *if . . .* But her mother's cancer was elsewhere. Elsewhere in her body, and then everywhere. Perhaps there is no connection.

Joe Pye's skull is covered by mossy, obviously very thick, but close-clipped dark hair; he must have shaved his head a while back and now it is growing unevenly out. The ruddy tan ends at his hairline, where his skin is paste-white as Rose's. He smiles at Rose, fondly and inquisitively and with an abrupt unflinching gesture he rips off the goatee. Rose draws in her breath, shocked.

"But what are *you* doing, Olivia?" he asks.

The floor tilts suddenly so that there is the danger she will fall, stumble into his arms. She takes a step backward. Her weight forces the floor down, keeps it in place. Nervously, angrily, she tears at the prim little ugly buttons on her dress. "I—I'm—I'm hurrying the best I can," she mutters.

Joe Pye rubs at his chin, which is pinkened and somewhat raw-looking, and stares at Rose Mallow Odom. Even without his majestic turban and his goatee he is a striking picture of a man; he holds himself well, his shoulders somewhat raised. He stares at Rose as if he cannot believe what he is seeing.

"Olivia?" he says.

She yanks at the front of her dress and a button pops off, it is hilarious but there's no time to consider it, something is wrong, the dress won't come off, she sees that the belt is still tightly buckled and of course the dress won't come off, if only that idiot wouldn't stare at her, sobbing with frustration she pulls her straps off her skinny shoulders and bares her chest, her tiny breasts, Rose Mallow Odom, who had for years cowered in the girls' locker room at the public school, burning with shame, for the very thought of her body filled her with shame, and now she is contemptuously stripping before a stranger who gapes at her as if he has never seen anything like her before.

"But Olivia what are you *doing*? . . ." he says.

His question is both alarmed and formal. Rose wipes tears out of her eyes and looks at him, baffled.

"But Olivia people don't *do* like this, not this way, not so fast and angry," Joe Pye says. His eyebrows arch, his eyes narrow with disapproval; his stance radiates great dignity. "I think you must have misunderstood the nature of my proposal."

"What do you mean, people don't *do*. . . . What people . . ." Rose whimpers. She must blink rapidly to keep him in focus but the tears keep springing into her eyes and running down her cheeks, they will leave rivulets in her matte makeup which she lavishly if contemptuously applied many hours ago, something has gone wrong, something has gone terribly wrong, why is that idiot staring at her with such pity?

"Decent people," Joe Pye says slowly.

"But I—I—"

"*Decent* people," he says, his voice lowered, one corner of his mouth lifted in a tiny ironic dimple.

Rose has begun to shiver despite the golden-glowing burn in her throat. Her breasts are bluish-white, the pale-brown nipples have gone hard with fear. Fear and cold and clarity. She tries to shield herself from Joe Pye's glittering gaze with her arms, but she cannot: he sees everything. The floor is tilting again, with maddening slowness. She will topple forward if it doesn't stop. She will fall into his arms no matter how she resists, leaning her weight back on her shaky heels.

"But I thought—Don't you—Don't you want—?" she whispers.

Joe Pye draws himself up to his fullest height. He is really a giant of a man: the Bingo Master in his silver tunic and black wide-legged trousers, the rashlike shadow of the goatee framing his small angry smile, his eyes narrowed with disgust. Rose begins to cry as he shakes his head No. And again No. No.

She weeps, she pleads with him, she is stumbling dizzily forward. Something has gone wrong and she cannot comprehend it. In her head things ran their inevitable way, she had already chosen the cold clever words that would most winningly describe them, but Joe Pye knows nothing of her plans, knows nothing of her words, cares nothing for *her*.

"No!" he says sharply, striking out at her.

She must have fallen toward him, her knees must have buckled, for suddenly he has grasped her by her naked shoulders and, his face darkened with blood, he is shaking her violently. Her head whips back and forth. Against the bureau, against the wall, so sudden, so hard, the back of her head striking the wall, her teeth rattling, her eyes wide and blind in their sockets.

"No no no no *no*."

Suddenly she is on the floor, something has struck the right side of her mouth, she is staring up through layers of agitated air to a bullet-headed man with wet mad eyes whom she has never seen before. The naked lightbulb screwed into the ceiling socket, so far away, burns with the power of a bright blank blinding sun behind his skull.

"But I—I thought—" she whispers.

"Prancing into Joe Pye's Bingo Hall and defiling it, prancing up *here* and defiling my room, what have you got to say for yourself, miss!" Joe Pye says, hauling her to her feet. He tugs her dress up and walks her roughly to the door, grasping her by the shoulders again and squeezing her hard, hard, without the slightest ounce of affection or courtesy, why he doesn't care for her at all!—and then she is out in the corridor, her patent-leather purse tossed after her, and the door to 302 is slammed shut.

It has all happened so quickly, Rose cannot comprehend. She stares at the door as if expecting it to be opened. But it remains closed. Far down the hall someone opens a door and pokes his head out and, seeing her in her disarray, quickly closes *that* door as well. So Rose is left completely alone.

She is too numb to feel much pain: only the pin-prickish sensation in her jaw, and the throbbing in her shoulders where Joe

Pye's ghost-fingers still squeeze with such strength. Why, he didn't care for her at all. . . .

Weaving down the corridor like a drunken woman, one hand holding her ripped dress shut, one hand pressing the purse clumsily against her side. Weaving and staggering and muttering to herself like a drunken woman. She *is* a drunken woman. "What do you mean, people—*What* people—"

If only he had cradled her in his arm! If only he had loved her!

On the first landing of the fire stairs she grows very dizzy suddenly, and thinks it wisest to sit down. To sit down at once. Her head is drumming with a pulsebeat she can't control, she believes it is maybe the Bingo Master's pulsebeat, and his angry voice too scrambles about in her head, mixed up with her own thoughts. A puddle grows at the back of her mouth—she spits out blood, gagging—and discovers that one of her front teeth has come loose: one of her front teeth has come loose and the adjacent incisor also rocks back and forth in its socket.

"Oh Joe Pye," she whispers, "oh dear Christ what have you *done*—"

Weeping, sniffing, she fumbles with the fake-gold clasp of her purse and manages to get the purse open and paws inside, whimpering, to see if—but it's gone—she can't find it—ah, but there it *is:* there it is after all, folded small and somewhat crumpled (for she'd felt such embarrassment, she had stuck it quickly into her purse): the check for $100. A plain check that should have Joe Pye's large, bold, black signature on it, if only her eyes could focus long enough for her to see.

"Joe Pye, *what* people," she whimpers, blinking. "I never heard of—*What* people, where—?"